"As the rich body of scholarship on multilingualism and English suggests, it is difficult to generalize the equalizing and stratifying, or democratizing and repressive, functions of contemporary globalization processes. The effects are inconsistent, interrelated, and interwoven in diverse localities. It is for this reason that the autoethnographies in this book are much needed in the scholarship on language politics. Scholars from different parts of the world provide situated and embodied narratives of how they have experienced globalization processes in their communicative life. They provide moving renditions of how globalization is instantiated in diverse settings, communities, and identities. More importantly, they open up fresh questions and themes for inquiry on language politics at a time when many countries are struggling to reconfigure their positioning in relation to globalization."

—*Suresh Canagarajah, Penn State University*

"Narratives connect life experiences, emotions, and thoughts to language. Beyond that, narratives construct subjective realities and meanings and connect them to their objective counterparts. Globalization is changing narratives both at the local and global level. Autoethnographies can best capture these changing glocal narratives. This book brings together brilliant autoethnographies that reflect the relationship between language, narrative, and globalization. I highly recommend this outstanding and timely volume to researchers and educators, as well as students."

—*Farzad Sharifian, Monash University*

"In this novel collection, Maryam Borjian offers individual personal responses to the massive change in our environment that we have come to call globalization. The focus is on language, the way in which we organize and express our emotions and thoughts, bringing this abstract force into a human perspective."

—*Bernard Spolsky, Bar-Ilan University*

"By situating language at the heart of globalization and human subjectivity at the heart of how we know, the personal-political stories in this important book contribute diverse and vital insights into our understanding of language in the world."

—*Alastair Pennycook, University of Technology Sydney*

"Maryam Borjian's new book is an important and timely contribution to the analysis of language and globalization. Adopting autoethnographic approaches and written by a diverse group of authors, the chapters reveal the rich interaction of the professional and the personal. How is my human experience as a language user and learner integrated with my professional life as a scholar, teacher, writer, or activist? This profound question, at the heart of these important reflections, is one that everyone interested in language and globalization should ask."

—*James W. Tollefson, University of Washington*

LANGUAGE AND GLOBALIZATION

In this collection of real-life, personal narratives on the theme of language and globalization, scholars from a range of different sub-disciplines of linguistics, time periods, and geographical spaces throughout the world examine the interaction and intersectionality of languages and globalization and the implications of such interactions for world languages and cultures. A feature of the book is the application of autoethnography as its underlying approach/method, in which contributors draw on their own lived experiences (of life, scholarship, and work) to investigate and reflect on linguistic globalization and its issues and challenges against the backdrop of the globalized world of the 21st century.

Maryam Borjian is Language Coordinator and Associate Professor in the Department of African, Middle Eastern, and South Asian Languages and Literatures at Rutgers, The State University of New Jersey, USA.

LANGUAGE AND GLOBALIZATION

An Autoethnographic Approach

Edited by
Maryam Borjian

To prof. Ghil'ad Zuckerman

with gratitude and Admiration

M. Borj

Routledge
Taylor & Francis Group
NEW YORK AND LONDON

First published 2017
by Routledge
711 Third Avenue, New York, NY 10017

and by Routledge
2 Park Square, Milton Park, Abingdon, Oxon, OX14 4RN

Routledge is an imprint of the Taylor & Francis Group, an informa business

Library of Congress Cataloging in Publication Data
A catalog record for this book has been requested

ISBN: 978-1-138-22780-4 (hbk)
ISBN: 978-1-138-22781-1 (pbk)
ISBN: 978-1-315-39462-6 (ebk)

Typeset in Bembo
by diacriTech, Chennai

To my students at Rutgers,
The State University of New Jersey (New Brunswick),
For being inspired by my stories,
For inspiring me through their stories,
And for encouraging me to bring more stories into my classrooms.
If it had not been for them, this book would not have come to life.

Maryam Borjian

CONTENTS

FOREWORD

Why We Care: Language in a Globalized World

Ofelia García

I am '*de dónde crece la palma*.' These are words taken from the verses of the 19th-century Cuban poet and patriot, José Martí, and used in singing the popular Guántamera. Rooted in Cuban soil, royal palm trees grow very tall, looking out beyond the local landscape and swaying in the wind. I have been a New Yorker since I was eleven years old, developing roots along the linden trees that often grow in the cracks of NYC sidewalks. But the shadows of my New York linden trees always reflect *palmas reales* that watch, like sentinels, over my Cuban American life. Despite a political and economic embargo (blockade, Cubans would call it) that has separated my two countries, my life has been made whole through my efforts as a sociolinguist and educator to try to illuminate the shadows that are cast on the lives of language minoritized youth in the United States. In making sense of the experiences of others and caring for them, I make sense of myself. I care because I know what it feels like to be told I am stupid because I didn't speak English, to be placed in remedial language arts classes where language use was solely mechanical, to score low on standardized assessments that did not measure what I knew, to be told that my Spanish was not 'good' because it showed signs of English, to be told to teach in English only when my students spoke Spanish. My sense of language in the world did not come solely from books, but more, from experience. The value of Maryam Borjian's book is precisely that she puts alongside each other the autoethnographies of scholars with different orientations, as they explore the role of language and globalization. By doing so, Borjian's book offers not only deep insights into language and globalization, but also into the reasons why we, as scholars, educators, poets, and citizens, care deeply about the topic.

To help us understand the relationship between language and globalization, Borjian doesn't just produce more theoretical scholarship, or even case studies of globalization around the world. Instead, she journeys inward, into the personal narratives of many—linguists and other language scholars, poets, teachers, students. The many autoethnographies here collected, then, reflect issues of language and globalization from many perspectives. Human subjectivity, as Borjian says, is then placed at the heart of objectivity. Borjian describes the enterprise of this book, saying:

> Imagining themselves in the position of a storyteller and through a personal narrative, they [the contributors to this volume] draw upon their lived experiences (of life, work, and scholarship) to tell the reader a story—the story of language and globalization through their eyes. These stories do not attempt to offer any 'absolute' truth about language and globalization, but rather a 'relative' truth, which is derived from the authors' existential experiences with language, and their temporal and spatial realities.

Thus, in many ways, this book follows the call of many critical poststructuralist and postcolonial scholars to go beyond Western logocentrism and to find a new locus of enunciation.

Borjian's approach in this book attempts to replace the traditional Western logocentrism that identifies the words of a text with the truth the text contains. Through the many personal stories told in this book, globalization is herewith treated in ways that remind us of Derrida's concept of 'différance' (1974). 'Globalization' only means through the multiple experiences and signs that differ from each other in the stories told by many. In this way, meaning is always deferred. The autoethnography approach followed in this book reminds us that there is no absolute truth, but that truth is always relative.

But beyond a poststructuralist ethos, this book, edited by an Iranian-American scholar, also takes a postcolonial lens to question and disrupt how knowledge about globalization has been produced by Europe and North America for their own sake. Borjian has engaged many non-European scholars in this storytelling—Armenian, Australian, Bangladeshi, Ethiopian, Maori, South Korean—alongside Europeans and Americans, but all telling the story of language and globalization from a different locus of enunciation. Many of the authors live and work in contexts other than the ones in which they were born and straddle different languages and worlds. The book, then, not only questions a Eurocentric system of knowledge about globalization, but also produces what Walter Mignolo (2005) calls a 'border gnosis.' By bringing forth the force and creativity of the knowledge of those who have been repressed during colonizing and recent globalizing processes, Western knowledge about language and globalization is displaced and rearranged.

The postcolonial lens taken up by Borjian in this book, then, works against coloniality, that is, the racial and social hierarchical orders that presume certain people's knowledges to be inferior as justification for their domination (Quijano, 2000). By telling these stories, globalization is decolonized and transformed, so as to resist the coloniality of power that has been installed in building a global world system.

Maryam Borjian's approach in this book is not a universal approach to globalization, but a pluriversal one. It overcomes the limitations of territorial and disciplinary thinking. Although the theoretical approach of the many authors is very different—pluriversal—what the book makes obvious is that academic knowledge production has been part of the perpetuation of the ideological state apparatus, to serve the interests of capitalism (Spivak, 1988). Through the storytelling of many, the authority of Western intellectuals is, thus, challenged, as well as the official story on globalization.

Issues of global English, language and identity, and language death and birth are approached in this book through the many lenses the storytellers hold. In these stories, English is a thief, as well as a language of opportunity; an unwanted imposition, as well as a privilege. English teaching is a myopic industry, as well as a well-intentioned activity. Regardless of the lens taken, however, the contributions make evident that 'native speakerism' (Bunce, this volume) and an English-only ideology (Choudhury, this volume) work against the decolonization of language education to which this volume aspires. Despite the different stories told about language and identity in globalization, all the stories told seem to agree that globalization bypasses, or even skirts, many people in the less developed world. Inequalities persist as coloniality endures.

Another important contribution of this book is taking language and globalization out of the academy and into the hands of those who work in museums, libraries, community centers and the media. Stories told in poetry clubs, in PBS documentary films, in libraries, museums, prisons and churches contribute to knowledge-making that goes beyond the narrow and limiting ways in which language is understood and used in schools. All the stories contribute to questioning whose stories are legitimate and what is authentic.

By putting all the different autoethnographies alongside each other, Borjian disrupts the ways in which language and globalization has been narrated within the academy by sociolinguists and other language scholars. The approach followed in this book disrupts the dichotomies that have been constructed in language studies. English, for example, appears not simply as a 'killer language,' or, on the other hand, 'the language of growth and development.' By retelling English through the stories of multilingual authors with multiple experiences, English emerges not as an autonomous language, but as a language practice that is part of a multilingual repertoire controlled by speakers and not by nation-states and global power. By centering the study of language and globalization in personal stories, Borjian takes away the power of named languages as a nation-state construction used for global control. Instead, what emerges is the language practices of people, with tensions and contradictions, as speakers attempt to communicate in different planes and contexts, with different people, at different time scales.

The autoethnographies of this book act as the royal palm trees with which I began this preface. They sway, but remain rooted in a local reality, while looking beyond the local landscape. They give us a vision that goes beyond languages, beyond nation-states, and center on the speakers themselves, as they live their lives in a global context that cannot be ignored. Beyond named languages, beyond nation-states, Borjian gives us a vision of people languaging, languaging in global contexts, using all their linguistic repertoire and resources to mean, to be, to go beyond the constraints with which nation-states privilege some and exclude others. In so doing, this autoethnographic approach dissolves the dichotomies with which we have studied language and globalization, giving us a fresh lens to study the multiple realities in which we speak, live, work, dream and care for each other.

Ofelia García
The Graduate Center, City University of New York, USA

References

Derrida, J. (1974). *Of grammatology*. Baltimore and London: Johns Hopkins University.
Mignolo, W. (2005). *Local histories: Local designs*. Princeton: Princeton University Press.
Quijano, A. (2000). Coloniality of power, eurocentrism and Latin America. *Nepantla: Views from South 1* (3), 533–580.
Spivak, G. (1988). Can the subaltern speak? In C. Nelson & L. Grossberg (eds.), *Marxism and the interpretation of culture* (pp. 66–111). Basingstoke: Macmillan.

PREFACE

This book is a collection of real-life, personal narratives, or stories, on the theme of language and globalization. These stories are written by scholars from a range of different subdisciplines of linguistics, time periods and geographical spaces throughout the world. Drawing on their lived experiences of life, work and scholarship and through a personal narrative, the chapter authors invite the reader into their own personal, professional or scholarly lives in which they tell their stories of language and its issues and challenges against the backdrop of the global world of the 21st century.

The idea for a book of stories on the linguistic dimension of globalization emerged from the Language and Globalization course that I have been teaching over the past several years or so in the Department of African, Middle Eastern and South Asian Languages and Literatures (AMESALL) at Rutgers, The State University of New Jersey. As an Iranian-American (Iranian by birth, American by naturalization), in teaching this course, I tend to draw upon the richness of Persian literature and of those in other non-Western localities of the world (Africa, the Middle East and South Asia) as a springboard to bring in stories that parallel the themes related to globalization that are central to my course. Initially, I used these stories only to add colors, voices and faces, to the otherwise abstract themes of my class. Gradually, however, I began to use them as a means to offer a non-Eurocentric lens to my students—the majority of whom are from the suburbs of New Jersey, some with limited exposure to the world outside the US, others without it; some with proficiency in other languages, others without it. It was there, in my classrooms, and through my interactions with many students, that I realized that when I combine numbers, figures, quantitative or qualitative empirical data, like those in many academic books with stories such as those that I tell in my courses, my audience would be captivated and inspired not just emotionally but also intellectually. Ever since, I have been using stories as a powerful teaching tool in my instruction and have witnessed the enormous power stories have on human minds (not to mention on human hearts). Stories can be used not only as a teaching tool, but also as a learning resource for making sense of the surrounding world, self, others, objects and abstract topics, like globalization and its multiple dimensions.

Language should be placed at the heart of globalization because of the extent that its positive and negative linguistic outcomes impact the lives of many people worldwide: the rich and the poor, the literate and illiterate, the linguistic majorities and minorities, the people of the Global North and those of the Global South. Hence, this is our collective hope, both mine and that of the authors of this volume, that this book with its autoethnographic approach to the linguistic and sociolinguistic dimensions of globalization will be of interest to people inside academia, including language scholars, professors and students. In particular, this book is written for students. As such, the chapters are devoid of overly technical terms and long lists of references and close with discussion questions. We, equally, hope this book will be of interest to those language teachers and practitioners, policy-makers, transnational organizations and donor agencies, who are involved directly or indirectly in language-related projects, and, last but not least, to the citizens of the world, for whom language and globalization is a popular yet vague topic.

ACKNOWLEDGMENTS

This book is the product of many interactions with many gifted individuals, whom I am privileged to call my students at Rutgers, The State University of New Jersey. To them, I am grateful for being inspired by my stories, for inspiring me through their stories (and poems) and for encouraging me to bring more stories into my classrooms. If it had not been for them and their enormous interest in stories, this book would not have come to life.

Although this book bears my name as its sole editor, it is the outcome of a truly collective process, which came to life gradually but gracefully through many interactions with many amazing individuals. First, this book would not have been possible without the chapter authors, many of whom are eminent scholars. I am thankful to each one for accepting to be part of this autoethnographic journey: a journey through which they had to crack wide open their personal, professional and scholarly lives before the eyes of the reader and the wider audience of this book. In addition, I am blessed to be surrounded by many incredible individuals whom I am privileged to call my colleagues and/or friends (both inside and outside Rutgers). My gratitude is due to the following individuals either for offering their invaluable comments and suggestions to strengthen the quality of papers or poems included in this volume or for being there with me behind the scenes to offer me their moral support. These individuals are: Ulrich Ammon (University of Duisburg-Essen, Germany), Sharon Avni (BMCC, The City University of New York), Pauline Bunce (Cyril Jackson Senior Campus, Western Australia), Young-mee Yu Cho (Rutgers University), Jeehyae Chung (Teachers College, Columbia University), Jessie H. Curtis (Rutgers University), Minakshi & Jyoti Datta (Rutgers University), Charles Häberl (Rutgers University), Fakhri Haghani (Rutgers University), Bob Holman (Endangered Language Alliance), Angela F. Howard (Emerita, Rutgers University), Bahar Otcu-Grillman

(Mercy College, New York Campus), Jennifer Manoukian (Rutgers University), Vaughan Rapatahana (Ministry of Education, New Zealand), Becky Schulthies (Rutgers University), Richard VanNess Simmons (Rutgers University), and last but not least, Jaffer Sheyholislami (Carleton University, Canada).

This book was, equally, inspired by the work of other scholars, who believed in the power of stories and had produced their own books of real-life narratives. In particular, I am thankful to Adam Komisarof and Zhu Hua (2016) for producing their own autoethnographic edited volume, for inviting me to be part of their journey and inspiring me through the process; to Alastair Pennycook (2012) for bringing the personal-reflective writing into the academic space and for paving the ground for other scholars, like me, to follow his creative footsteps; and to Vaughan Rapatahana (Rapatahana & Bunce, 2012) for believing in the power of poetry for making the world a better place and for bringing his existential poems (on various aspects of language) to the heart of academic books (for more on these books, please see the list of references in the introduction of this volume).

I am flattered to become an author at Routledge. My special thanks are due to Naomi Silverman, the Commissioning Editor of this book, who was very supportive of this project from the very beginning. Surely, the journey would have not been as blissful and memorable as it turned out to be, had it not been for her patience, efficiency, profound support, and endless kindness. I would like to extend my appreciation to Paul Hindle, Production Editor, and his team (Christina Nyren, Project Manager, and Jennifer Razee, copyeditor and Carol Shields, proofreader) for help with the editing and production of this book.

The last words are always saved for those who have had the most influence in one's work and life. I owe a monumental debt of gratitude to three individuals: Ofelia Garcia (Graduate Center, City University of New York), my mentor and former doctoral advisor at Columbia University; Alamin Mazrui (Rutgers, the State University of New Jersey), my colleague and former Chairperson; and Habib Borjian (Columbia University), my colleague, friend, and the companion of my life over the past two decades or so. Through my interactions with these individuals, I learned not only about linguistic and sociolinguistic topics through the innumerable academic imprints these scholars left on my mind and on the pages of this book, but also, most importantly, about what it means to be a human being. Although their knowledge is abundant, what make them truly exceptional is their boundless humility, modesty, kindness and compassion. They are not just my mentors in academia, but also my role models in life.

Maryam Borjian
New York City, USA

1

INTRODUCTION

Maryam Borjian

The Plea

> *Existentialism [. . .] affirms that every truth and every action imply an environment and a human subjectivity.*
>
> Jean-Paul Sartre (2007: 18)

With these words, the French existentialist philosopher and phenomenologist Jean-Paul Sartre (1905–1980) undermined the foundation of 'scientific truth,' established by the enlightenment ideals of the eighteenth century, positivism and empiricism of the nineteenth century and modernization theories of the twentieth century, all of which perceived human 'reason,' 'rational behavior,' 'logic,' 'accuracy' and 'objectivity' as the basis of knowledge and/or the 'impartial' truth. Since then, the scientific mode of inquiry has been used widely in all academic disciplines, including in the vast realm of humanities and social sciences.

Drawing upon the insights of his existentialist predecessors—Friedrich Wilhelm Nietzsche (1844–1900) and Martin Heidegger (1889–1976)—Sartre argued that science was an abstract entity, aiming to examine variations of abstract factors. Humanity, on the other hand, Sartre argued, was not an abstract object to have solely an abstract existence. Hence, in the view of Sartre, the scientific mode of inquiry was not sufficient enough to examine social issues surrounding human life. It was insufficient because it did not take into account the 'existential' dimension of truth and/or the qualities of 'being' or 'existence' (Heidegger, 1962). These qualities were human subjectivity, his/her belonging to a specific time and space (environment), and his/her existential knowledge and experiences of self, others, objects and the world at large. By emphasizing that human truth had an 'existential' dimension, Sartre called for a research method in the social sciences that would examine things in the flux of everyday life and in pre-reflective activities, which would, in turn, allow the researcher to unravel the holistic web of existential meanings surrounding human life and actions (Sartre, 2007; for more on phenomenologists and their critics of the scientific mode of inquiry, see Peet, 1999).

The Purpose

> *No scientist knows the world merely by holding it at arm's length: if we ever managed to build the objectivist wall between the knower and the known, we could know nothing except the wall itself. Science requires an engagement with the world, a live encounter between the knower and the known. That encounter has moments of distance, but it would not be an encounter without moments of intimacy as well.*
>
> Parker J. Palmer (2007: 55)

Language and Globalization: An Autoethnographic Approach can be considered a response to Sartre's call, a collection of intimate encounters between 'the knower' and 'the known.' By situating language at the heart of globalization, human subjectivity at the heart of objectivity, and the qualities of being (a linguist, language scholar, researcher, poet, teacher or student) and belonging to a specific time and space (environment) at the heart of truth, this book brings together scholarship on the theme of language and globalization.

The questions addressed within this volume are as follows:

- How does language interact with its surrounding social variables (linguistic, educational, social-cultural, political, economic, or ideological) in the backdrop of the increasingly globalized world of the 21st century?
- What are the implications (both positive and negative) of such interactions upon world languages, cultures and peoples around the world?

The evidence provided in this book is not empirical but rather existential. Instead of applying a traditional approach to produce a standard academic book, this book applies autoethnography as its underlying method. Autoethnography, as stated by autoethnographers (Anderson, 2006; Chang, 2008; Ellis, et al., 2011; Komisarof & Zhu, 2016) is ethnographic inquiry that utilizes the autobiographical materials of the researcher as the primary source of data. Hence, the writer examines his/her self and draws on his/her own lived experiences to reflect on an academic topic through a personal narrative. In this book, the contributors take this approach to tell the readers about their views on language and globalization.

Being born at different times and belonging to different geographical spaces from throughout the world, what the chapter authors have in common is their close affinity to the cause of language, to which they have devoted their personal, professional and/or scholarly lives. Imagining themselves in the position of a storyteller and through a personal narrative, they draw upon their lived experiences (of life, work and scholarship) to tell the reader a story—the story of language and globalization through their eyes. These stories do not attempt to offer any 'absolute' truth about language and globalization, but rather a 'relative' truth, which is derived from the authors' existential experiences with language, and their temporal and spatial realities (environment), which have, in turn, shaped and reshaped the authors' personal views on language. Hence, these stories aim to unravel the holistic web of 'existential' meanings, as echoed by Sartre (2007), or the qualities of 'being,' as echoed by Heidegger (1962), which surrounds any social issues, including language and its many challenges in the 21st century.

The Book and Its Features

This book brings together perspectives and contributors through a shared methodology. Each of these important features is discussed individually below.

Perspectives

> *Globalization is, at its best, a process of synergizing multiple viewpoints and, by doing so, creating new energy and perspectives.*
>
> Adam Komisarof & Zhu Hua (2016: 11)

Since the early 1990s, when it became a buzzword both in academia and in popular culture, thousands of books have been written on the theme of globalization. In the realm of linguistics and language studies, the earliest books on the topic (Ammon, 2001; Block & Cameron, 2002; Canagarajah, 1999; Crystal, 1997; de Swaan, 2002; Fishman et al., 1996; Graddol, 1998; Kachru, 1990; Pennycook, 2001; Phillipson, 1992; Skutnabb-Kangas, 2000) were all revolutionary and innovative, for their linguist authors took their unit of analysis, language, way beyond the micro-focus of most linguistic departments at the time and placed it at the heart of the world that was becoming interconnected and interdependent. Through these works, we have learned about the intersection of language with the multiple dimensions of globalization (economic, political, ideological, educational or sociocultural) and the impact of such interactions on world languages, cultures and peoples. Since then, many other books have been written on the same subject (Block et al., 2011; Blommaert, 2010; Coupland, 2013; Erling & Seargeant, 2013; Fairclough, 2006; García, 2009; Kachru & Smith, 2008; Lin & Martin, 2005; Mazrui, 2004; Park, 2009; Pennycook, 2012; Rapatahana & Bunce, 2012; Bunce et al., 2016, to name just a few). Hence, today, we have come a long way from the roaring 1990s, in which we knew very little about globalization. Thanks to the research of these scholars, and many others who are not mentioned here, we know much more about multiple dimensions of globalization and their dynamic interactions with language.

Yet, globalization, as I show in Chapter 2 of this book, has been a contested term, about which there are more disagreements than agreements. This contradiction is partly due to the fact that there are multiple theoretical lenses through which globalization has been examined and reexamined, giving rise to a debate among scholars over the concept of globalization and its intended/unintended and positive/negative outcomes. Instead of taking sides or favoring one view over another, this book brings together scholarship from different perspectives. Hence, the views overlap with one another sometimes, converge with one another at other times, and diverge from one another at some other times. However, instead of using a theoretical lens as a frame of reference, the chapter authors of this volume use their lived experiences as their unit of analysis, through which the reader can learn about the theoretical position of the chapter authors, and how such experiences have contributed to the very position from which they have come to view language and globalization. The multiplicity of views embedded in this volume will, in turn, make this book inclusive, in which different forms of truth (those of the left, the right, and those in between) are brought together and presented to the reader in a single volume.

This multi-perspective approach of the book is rooted partly in existentialism, as discussed above, and partly in postmodern thought, especially as articulated by Michel Foucault (1972), who built upon the insights of his existentialist predecessors and argued that 'reality' was solely 'constructed' and 'truth' was solely 'relative.' Such an approach to truth will, in turn, allow the book to be a 'writerly' text as opposed to a 'readerly' text. Whereas in a readerly text, the author is the sole creator of the text and its underlying truth, in a writerly text the reader is invited to the text to write or assign his/her own meanings to it as a means to construct his/her own truth based on his/her personal engagement with the text, and consequently, to become a coauthor of the text (Barthes, 1967). Hence, this book invites the reader to the book, in whole, and its chapters, in part, to engage with the various forms of truth about language and globalization and to choose the view that most resonates with him/her.

Method

> *Each man is the novelist of himself.*
>
> Ortega y Gasset (cited in Cascardi, 1997: 91)

Autoethnography is the methodological framework on which this book stands. It is "an approach to research and writing that seeks to describe and systematically analyze (graphy) personal experience (auto) in order to understand cultural experience (ethno)" (Ellis et al., 2011: 1). In this book, contributors draw on their own lived experiences of life, work and scholarship (auto) to reflect on their views towards language and globalization (ethno). Although it originally emerged from the field of anthropology in the 1970s, autoethnography is an established research methodology today, used by scholars across academic disciplines. It is valued for its emphasis on "the reflexive relationship between the research and the researcher, objectivity and subjectivity, process and product, self and others, and the individual and society" (Komisarof & Zhu, 2016: 11).

Autoethnographies tell stories. Stories—as far back as mythological and historical accounts can recall—have been an inseparable part of human existence. Long before the invention of writing, our ancestors were storytellers who transmitted their ideas and knowledge from one generation to the next through a rich oral tradition. After the invention of writing, the oral and literary styles of storytelling came together to live side by side, serving multiple functions in human societies: to construct beauty; to spark emotions, sympathies or empathies; to transmit knowledge or words of wisdom or to express human existential issues and challenges, whether certainties or uncertainties, longings or belongings and hopes or fears. Stories have, equally, served as agents of change and transformation both at the personal and societal levels. Due to their enormous influence on the human mind and heart, stories have captivated, moved and inspired humans throughout centuries. They have had an influence not only on the way we think, but also on the way we act, individually or collectively. Whether perceived as a work of art, an agent of transformation or a means of making sense of the surrounding world, stories have long occupied a center-stage position in human life (for more on the power of stories, see Svoboda, 2015).

In this book, the stories or narratives are real-life experiences of linguist scholars. As stories, autoethnographies are powerful, thought-provoking and inspirational. They have the ability to move and inspire readers, allowing them to understand patterns of life of languages, cultures and events in the real world not merely as an academic, empirical exercise, but also as a personal and existential experience, adding the power of a face and a voice to topics that otherwise may seem abstract to some readers. Thus, autoethnographies have the power to reach out to and connect with more people.

In addition, as argued by Pennycook (2012), "[c]ritical resistance also needs critical writing" (p. 29). By using the autoethnography to add the existential dimension to the topic of linguistic globalization, this book can be seen as a form of critical resistance: resistance to academic conformity that separates personal-reflective writing from so-called scientific-empirical research, favoring the latter over the former. By mixing the writing genres, this book brings the 'unexpected,' reflective-personal writing, into the academic space (Pennycook, 2012).

Contributors

Variety is more than the spice of life; it is largely of its essence.

John Dewey (1964: 85)

This book benefits from having contributions from a very diverse group of scholars. Although language is the unit of analysis, the authors of this volume differ in their points of departure. That is partly because they belong to different subdisciplines of linguistics, namely TESOL/applied linguistics, sociolinguistics, theoretical linguistics, field linguistics, language and area studies, language and literature, the sociology of language, and last but not least, language and education. Thus, this book offers a rich array of topics on various aspects of language, unified in a single volume.

The contributors of this book also focus on different time periods. On the one hand, this book has contributions from eminent scholars whose engagement with language covers a time span of a half-century or so. Through their fruitful scholarly and professional track records, they have not only raised awareness about language matters, but also have served as mentors for many established and emerging scholars, whose views are equally presented in this volume. Likewise, scholars who have taken language-related matters outside academia and placed it at the heart of the media, literature and or other public domains (like museums, libraries and poetry clubs) are also part of this book. Yet, scholars are not the only contributors of this volume, for the voice of an undergraduate student poet is also presented in this book.

The contributors of this volume speak different languages as their first or second first language, namely Amharic, Arabic, Armenian, Bengali, English, Esperanto, German, Hebrew, Korean, Māori, Norwegian, Persian, Spanish and Swahili, to name but a few. Thus, this book examines the theme of language and globalization from the perspective of speakers of different languages.

Last but not least, the contributors of this book belong to different parts of the world—not just in terms of their countries of birth, but also in terms of their countries of residence and work. Hence, through the pages of this book, we will travel across the world: from the center nations of the Global North (the United States, the United Kingdom, Germany, Norway, Australia and New Zealand) to the periphery nations of the Global South (Bangladesh, Ethiopia, Mexico, the Philippines, Kenya, Tanzania and South Africa) and to the emerging economic centers of power (like South Korea, Singapore and Hong Kong). We will, equally, travel to the heart of minoritized speech communities in megacities (like New York) or in small localities of the world: from Aotearoa, to Brunei Darussalam, Republic of Nauru, or to various places in Alaska, to be surrounded by the speakers of many minority and endangered languages.

Hence, such diversity on the part of the contributors makes this book a transspatial, transtemporal, transcultural and translinguistic zone of contact.

Foreword and Afterword

The book begins and ends with a Foreword and Afterword written by two eminent scholars: Ofelia García and Alamin Mazrui, respectively. García is known internationally for her pioneering research on various aspects of language, including Bi/Multilingualism, Translanguaging, Language Policy and Planning, Ethno-Linguistic Minorities, the Sociology of Language, and, last but not least, Language and Education. Over the past several decades, she has championed the cause of linguistic equality, diversity and pluralism in society and in education. Alamin Mazrui, whose name equally needs no introduction, is known for his pioneering research in the areas of Political Sociology of Language in Africa and the African Diaspora, African Literature in English and Swahili, Politics of Cultural Production in East Africa, Cultural Discourses on Human Rights in

Africa, and Islam and Identity in Africa and the African Diaspora. Through his prolific scholarly track record, he has raised awareness about the issues of linguistic inequality, social justice and linguistic human rights, especially in colonial and postcolonial contexts. In these two sections, these scholars offer their analytical commentaries on this book.

Between the Foreword and Afterword, there are 14 chapters. Instead of larding the chapters with many technical terms and references, we have decided to slow down the pace and do more with less; and this very less, on which the book stands, is the stories of language and globalization, whose countless threads are the lived experiences of their chapter authors. The chapters are arranged thematically and divided into four parts, namely:

Part I — Theoretical and methodological frameworks: Issues, challenges and changes
Part II — Global English: Views from the classroom
Part III — Language, identity and crossing the boundaries of the expected
Part IV — Language death and birth

The parts each have an introduction; the aim of which is to provide the scope of the section and a summary of the chapters within. The closing part of the book (Part V, Epilogue) includes Marwa Adina's poem, in which she, as a Muslim-American and an undergraduate student, reflects on her border-crossing (from Morocco to the Ivory Coast and then to the United States), her struggles in maintaining her identity (in whole), in remaining loyal to her mother-tongue (Arabic), and her Islamic roots (in part). The book closes with Alamin Mazrui's Afterword, that brings an Africanist lens to the theme of language and globalization.

References

Ammon, U. (ed.) (2001). *The dominance of English as a language of science: Effects on other languages and language communities*. Berlin: Mouton de Gruyter.

Anderson, L. (2006). Analytic autoethnography. *Journal of Contemporary Ethnography, 35* (4), 373–395.

Barthes, R. (1967). The death of the author [translated by Richard Howard]. Retrieved February 10, 2016 from: www.tbook.constantvzw.org/wp-content/death_authorbarthes.

Block, D. & Cameron, D. (eds.) (2002). *Globalization and language teaching*. London: Routledge.

Block, D., Gray, J. & Holborow, M. (2011). *Neoliberalism and applied linguistics*. London: Routledge.

Blommaert, J. (2010). *The sociolinguistic of globalization*. Cambridge: Cambridge University Press.

Bunce, P., Phillipson, R., Rapatahana, V. & Tupas, R. (eds.) (2016). *Why English? Confronting the Hydra*. Bristol: Multilingual Matters.

Canagarajah, S. (1999). *Resisting linguistic imperialism in English teaching*. Oxford: Oxford University Press.

Cascardi, A. (1997). Chronic toward novel: Bernal Diaz history of the conquest of Mexico. In D. W. Foster & D. Altamiranda (eds.), *Spanish American literature: A collection of essays* (pp. 87–102). New York: Garland.
Chang, H. (2008). *Autoethnography as method.* Walnut Creek, CA: Left Coast Press.
Coupland, N. (ed.) (2013). *The handbook of language and globalization.* Malden, MA: Wiley-Blackwell.
Crystal, D. (1997). *English as a global language.* Cambridge: Cambridge University Press.
de Swaan, A. (2002). *Words of the world: The global language system.* Malden, MA: Blackwell.
Dewey, J. (1964). *John Dewey on education: Selected writings.* In R. D. Archambault (ed.). Chicago: University of Chicago Press.
Ellis, C., Adams, T. E. & Bochner, A. P. (2011). Autoethnography: An overview. *Forum: Qualitative Social Research, 12* (1), 1–14.
Erling, E. & Seargeant, P. (2013). *English and development: Policy, pedagogy and globalization.* Bristol: Multilingual Matters.
Fairclough, N. (2006). *Language and globalization.* New York: Routledge.
Fishman, J., Conrad, A. & Rubal-Lopez, A. (eds.) (1996). *Post-imperial English: Status change in former British and American colonies, 1940–1990.* Berlin: Mouton de Gruyter.
Foucault, M. (1972). *The archeology of knowledge and the discourse on language* [translated by M. S. Smith]. New York: Pantheon Books.
García, O. (2009). *Bilingual education in the 21st century: A global perspective.* Malden, MA: Wiley-Blackwell.
Graddol, D. (1998). *The future of English: Guide to forecasting the popularity of the English language in the 21st century.* London: The British Council.
Heidegger, M. (1962). *Being and time* [translated by J. Macquarrie & E. Robinson]. New York: Harper & Row.
Kachru, B. (1990). *The alchemy of English: The spread, functions and models of non-native Englishes.* Champaign, IL: University of Illinois Press.
Kachru, Y. & Smith, L. (2008). *Cultures, contexts and world Englishes.* London: Routledge.
Komisarof, A. & Zhu, H. (eds.) (2016). *Crossing boundaries and weaving intercultural work, life, and scholarship in globalizing universities.* New York: Routledge.
Lin, A. & Martin, P. W. (eds.) (2005). *Decolonization, globalization: Language-in-education policy and practices.* Clevedon: Multilateral Matters.
Mazrui, A. M. (2004). *English in Africa after the Cold War.* Clevedon: Multilingual Matters.
Palmer, P. J. (2007). *The courage to teach: Exploring the inner landscape of a teacher's life.* San Francisco, CA: John Wiley & Sons.
Park, J. (2009). *The local construction of a global language.* Berlin: Mouton de Gruyter.
Peet, R. (1999). *Theories of development.* New York: Guilford Press.
Pennycook, A. (2012). *Language and mobility: Unexpected places.* Bristol: Multilingual Matters.
Pennycook, A. (2001). *Critical applied linguistics: A critical introduction.* Mahwah, NJ: Lawrence Erlbaum.
Phillipson, R. (1992). *Linguistic imperialism.* Oxford: Oxford University Press.
Rapatahana, V. & Bunce, P. (eds.) (2012). *English language as Hydra: Its impacts on non-English language cultures.* Bristol: Multilingual Matters.
Sartre, J. P. (2007). *Existentialism is a humanism* [translated by C. Macomber]. New Haven: Yale University Press.
Skutnabb-Kangas, T. (2000). *Linguistic genocide in education—or worldwide diversity and human rights?* Mahwah, NJ: Lawrence Erlbaum.
Svoboda, E. (2015). The power of story. *Aeon.* Retrieved May 7, 2016 from: https://aeon.co/essays/once-upon-a-time-how-stories-change-hearts-and-brains.

PART I

Theoretical and Methodological Frameworks: Issues, Challenges and Changes

INTRODUCTION

Theoretical and Methodological Frameworks: Issues, Challenges and Changes

Maryam Borjian

> *Globalization [. . .] is a ubiquitous word that travels across the media, academic literatures, and the local bars as something that everyone 'knows' and that seems to need no author. Yet, globalization is an empty signifier whose spaces are filled continually with multiple and differentiated meanings.*
>
> Thomas Popkewitz (2004: vii)

'Globalization' is a contested term, about which there are more disagreements than agreements. It is, in the words of Popkewitz (2004), an 'empty signifier' that has been filled and refilled by various layers of meaning—meanings that are often contradictory and incompatible. This contradiction is partly because those who have examined globalization have come from diverse academic backgrounds, including economics, political sciences, anthropology, cultural studies, education, linguistics and other disciplines. Thus, it is natural for scholars to place their own academic field at the heart of their definition of globalization. The majority of economists, for example, perceive the economic dimension of globalization, especially the free-marketization of the world economy, as the core of globalization. Others, may privilege political, ideological, environmental, socio-cultural, -educational or -linguistic aspects of globalization, and thus, perceive each of these as the 'essence' of globalization (Steger, 2013).

Adding to the confusion is the diversity of the theoretical lenses through which globalization has been examined and reexamined. It is commonly accepted that a globalist lens (of the right) is sharply different from a Marxist, neo-Marxist lens (of the left), and that these two are not identical with a postmodern hermeneutic lens (of the other side of the left). The contradictory nature of the theoretical lenses has led Manfred Steger (2013) to argue that globalization is a 'story,' or a 'narrative,' which has been told and retold, albeit differently, by globalization scholars. To capture the diversity of theoretical lenses, Steger coins three terms to group globalization scholars, namely: 'hyperglobalizer optimists,' 'hyperglobalizer pessimists' and 'globalization skeptics.'

But who are these scholars? How do they define globalization? What are their agreements and disagreements? Using Steger's three-way classification of globalization scholars, on the one hand, and blending scholarship on the theme of globalization from across academic disciplines (economics, political sciences, sociology, cultural studies, linguistics and education), and on the other hand, in Chapter 2 of this volume, I invite the reader to join me on a journey to a resort on the east coast of Mexico, where I tried to capture the diverging images of globalization through the lenses of my camera as a means to show the existence of multiple forms of truth about globalization.

Chapter 3 is written by Ulrich Ammon, a seminal German sociolinguist, known internationally for his pioneering research on various aspects of language, namely sociolinguistics, language policy, the second-ranking international languages, linguistic inequality in scientific research, and, last, but not least, the German language. Ammon does not place himself in any of the three theoretical schools of thought, proposed by Steger (2013) and discussed by me in Chapter 2. His preference is rather to place himself somewhere in between these theoretical lenses. As a 'critical-modernist,' he borrows freely ideas from both Functionalism and Conflict Theory (meaning from the right and the left of the theoretical spectrum). Consequently, he welcomes linguistic globalization with its universalization of the English language, hoping it brings more peace, justice and opportunities worldwide, but he is equally critical of inverse possibilities for speakers of other languages. In particular, Ammon has extensively written about the worldwide standing of the second-ranking international languages (including German) and problems of their speakers in the 21st century, as these languages have become marginalized by English in numerous domains of the global language constellation. Nonetheless, he does not agree that the universalization of English would minimize the world's linguistic diversity in the long run. Methodologically speaking, Ammon is an empiricist, who favors 'mathematical' and 'logical' way of thinking; thus, allowing his empirical data to inform his research rather than subscribing himself to a single theoretical lens (for more on this aspect of Ammon's research, see, for example, Ammon, 2010; 2013). Using such a theoretical and methodological position, he takes the reader to a vertical and horizontal (temporal and spatial) journey through his life to reflect on the evolution of his research over time—a journey from a 'village outlook to a global overview,' using his own terms.

Ammon's chapter provides a much needed historical lens to the transformation of research within the broader field of language studies (including sociolinguistics and language policy) over a period of four decades or so: a move from a local, regional and national outlook (with a 'pluricentric' focus) to a worldwide perspective, in which the local is combined with the global, the regional with the international, and the national with the transnational. Such a shift in research focus is due to many reasons, including the advancement of communication technology, the shrinkage of time and space, the weakening of the borders of the nation-states, the rise of the global market economy, and, last but not least, the flows of peoples, ideas and information across borders (both geographical and virtual), as the consequence of contemporary globalization, which has, in turn, made the world of the 21st century more interconnected and interdependent (for more on these aspects of globalization, see Appadurai, 1996; Ritzer, 2010).

In Ammon's view, we are the product of our time and space. Consequently, our world views (including research questions) are shaped and reshaped by our temporal and spatial realities and our qualities of being or existence. Hence, he hopes that the research endeavors of our global time, including those of his, would fruitfully combine the local with the global, as a means to make the world more rational—and, as a consequence, more peaceful.

References

Ammon, U. (2013). World languages: Trends and futures. In N. Coupland (ed.), *The handbook of language and globalization* (pp. 101–22). Malden, MA: Wiley-Blackwell.

Ammon, U. (2010). Linguistic inequality and its effects on participation in scientific discourse and on global knowledge accumulation—with a closer look at the problems of the second-rank language communities. *Applied Linguistic Review, 3* (2), 333–35.

Appadurai, A. (1996). *Modernity at large: Cultural dimensions of globalization.* Minneapolis: University of Minnesota Press.

Popkewitz, T. (2004). Foreword. In G. Steiner-Khamsi (ed.), *The global politics of educational borrowing and lending.* New York: Teachers College, Columbia University Press.

Ritzer, G. (2010). *Globalization: A basic text.* Malden, MA: Wiley-Blackwell.

Steger, M. (2013). *Globalization: A very short introduction.* Oxford: Oxford University Press.

2

THE DIVERGING IMAGES OF GLOBALIZATION

A Journey in Books and Photos

Maryam Borjian

> *Man is the measure of all things.*
>
> Protagoras, ancient Greek philosopher (490–*c.* 420 BCE)
>
> (Cited in Miller, 1998: 43)

Introduction

What is globalization? That is the question.

In early December, 2016, I stood in silence, on the balcony of my hotel room, in an exotic resort complex, a tourist hub, on the east coast of Mexico. The all-inclusive resort, in which I planned to stay for a week-long vacation, was named Paradise—a man-made Paradise, built for international tourists and travelers to offer them all the earthly comforts and luxuries that they could conceivably desire while staying at the resort.

Filling my lungs with the fresh and pleasantly balmy air of the tropical climate all around, I took in the view from the balcony. I looked up, down, to the right, to the left and straight ahead, to examine the boundaries of the universe that was stretching before my eyes: the eyes of an Iranian-American (Iranian by birth, American by naturalization), a resident of New York City, a first-time visitor to Mexico, with no proficiency in Spanish, nor any familiarity with Mexican culture, except those few fragmented elements of Mexicanness that had long ago been brought by Mexican immigrants to New York City and were now interwoven with the tapestry of the city's metropolitan-cosmopolitan way of life.

As I gazed at the universe that was stretching before my eyes, I saw the azure sky with patches of large white clouds above, a wide and large courtyard below, and, all around, surrounded by glittering turquoise- or lapis-tiled swimming pools, tall palm trees reaching for the sky and rows of little wooden, straw-roofed huts, in which many tourists with happy faces were at rest. Here and there, there were many little flower beds, rimmed by narrow paths and pathways through which the hotel's waiters and waitresses, all elegantly dressed, were walking swiftly, while greeting their foreign guests with a single Spanish word, *'hola,'* and offering them a cold glass of margarita, tequila, orange or mango juice.

Not far in the distance stood the blue ocean in solitude. Along its shore, there were many other cheerful tourists, some of whom were swimming in the blue body of the boundless ocean, while others were sun-tanning, lying still under the pleasant rays of sun, and still others were taking a peaceful walk along the coastline, while dipping their feet in the glittering, wet sand of the beach. The white foam of the breakers was quietly washing the seashore, while I was capturing the beauty of the Mexican horizon thorough the eyes of my camera—an old-fashioned camera, whose many lenses were sitting in my shoulder bag, waiting to be used at some point during my short stay at the resort.

Hyperglobalizer Optimistic Lens

The first lens that I placed on my camera was a 'hyperglobalizer optimistic lens,' a term coined by Steger (2013) to refer to the neoliberal, globalist supporters of globalization, like Francis Fukuyama (1989), Samuel Huntington (1996) and Thomas Friedman (2000; 2005)—the authors of many prize-winning, best-selling books.

It all began with the fall of the Berlin Wall in 1989, followed by the fall of the Soviet Union in 1991, that put an end to the Cold War, which had divided the world into two conflicting zones of interest—the capitalist West and the socialist East—during most of the 20th century. This change in the geopolitical configuration of the world was so sudden that some thought that the world was becoming a new universe, whose boundaries were uncharted. Others associated this change with the formation of a new era in human history, about which they knew nothing. It was within such a climate, during the roaring 1990s, that 'globalization' became a buzzword in both Western academia and popular culture.

Among the earliest scholarly writings on the topic of globalization from a hyperglobalizer optimistic lens, the most notable one was perhaps "The End of History and the Last Man," an essay published in 1989 that turned into a book in 1992. The author was Francis Fukuyama, an American neoconservative political scientist and political economist, who perceived globalization as not just a 'new' phase in human history, but also as the 'last' phase, characterized by the universalization of Western liberal values and ideals, such as democracy, about which he wrote:

> What we may be witnessing is not just the end of the Cold War, or the passing of a particular period of postwar history, but the end of history as such; that is, the end point of mankind's ideological evolution and the universalization of Western liberal democracy. (Fukuyama, 1989: 2)

A few years later, in 1993, Samuel Huntington, an American political scientist, published another essay in an issue of *Foreign Affairs* called "The Clash of Civilizations," which became a book in 1996, attracting enormous attention in the US media. Huntington, too, gave us the impression that globalization was an 'inevitable' process of the universalization of Western civilization, battling the parochial forces of nationalism, localism, tribalism and religious fundamentalism, among the many other -isms that were rooted in non-Western civilizations (Steger, 2013). This image of globalization, this march of liberal democracy throughout the world, combatting triumphantly the 'backward' forces of tribalism and localism, was absolutely pleasing.

Having disappeared into the deep darkness by the turn of the century, socialism, modernism and colonialism were fully forgotten in the minds of these globalist scholars, for they were, now, busy fashioning globalization and imagining its many positive outcomes—thanks to the 'global' media with their 'global' journalists, like Thomas Friedman, the author of *The Lexus and the Olive Tree* (2000). I had just reached the section of Friedman's book in which he reflects on the basic 'truth' about globalization and wondering if truth could ever be absolute; I continued reading his words:

> And the most basic truth about globalization is this: No one is in charge [. . .]. We all want to believe that someone is in charge and responsible. But the global marketplace today is an Electronic Herd of often anonymous stock, bond, and currency traders and multinational investors, connected by screens and networks. (Friedman, 2000: 113)

As Friedman's fame grew bigger, the list of his books grew lengthier. In 2005, he authored *The World Is Flat*, a book that remained on *The New York Times* best-seller list for over a year. In this book, he went one step further not just to praise globalization for its free-marketization of the world economy, or the universalization of corporate capitalism in the 21st century, but also to praise the positive outcome of such free-marketization; that was turning our planet into a 'flat' space; a space with no lofty mountains or deep valleys, which had long divided the world into rich center versus poor periphery nation-states.

Placing such a beautiful and glamorous lens on my camera, I began my first round of sightseeing around the Mexican resort. The scenes my camera captured that day and the day after through this lens were spectacularly beautiful, all depicting an earthly universe (the resort) that challenged the idea of a heavenly paradise: a universe that was 'privatized,' 'decentralized,' 'efficient' and 'market-driven.' These are the very good qualities associated with globalization with its neoliberal face, defined as the unconditional submission of one's national economy, like that of Mexico's, to the 'no'-law, 'no'-regulation policy of the 'free'-market economy. Before its arrival into Mexico, so echoed by Luis

Rubio, the former President of the Mexican Citibank, Mexico was something like this:

> A lack of self-confidence leads a country to keep chewing on the past. [. . .] A lack of self-confidence [in Mexico] means that everyone in the country thinks the U.S. is going to take Mexico to the cleaners. [. . .] Unfortunately, Mexico did not have a strategy for going forward. (Cited in Friedman, 2005: 433)

But, Mexico gained that confidence at last, said Luis Rubio. "What NAFTA [The North American Free Trade Agreement] accomplished was to get Mexicans to think forward and outward instead of inward and backward" (cited in Friedman, 2005: 433).

As I spoke with the managers of the resort, I was told that the 'owners' of the Paradise were not the 'top-down,' 'powerful' forces of Mexico, like Mexican politicians, who were the giant property owners of the world of the 20th century, during most of which the Keynesian (controlled) economy, with its profound support of a large government, was in full bloom. Rather, as I was told, the 'owners' of the Paradise were a body of 'faceless,' 'bottom-up,' 'private' and 'multinational' shareholders and entrepreneurs from all over the world: Spain, Argentina, Brazil, Canada, France, Peru, the United States, India, Mexico, Dubai, Korea and China. It was a strange yet pleasant feeling for me to learn that the 'owners' of such a giant property, the whole Paradise, were just some 'ordinary' citizens of the world, who had come to participate in the world's power-sharing and property-owning only after the rise of globalization with its 'free'-marketization of the world economy—all the very good qualities of free-marketization that were confirmed by Chong and López-de-Silanes (2004), in their lengthy report on Privatization in Mexico, written for Inter-American Development Bank.

With my eyes fixed on the distant horizon, I filled my lungs with the fresh tropical air of the world around and whispered to myself. This is globalization. It is 'real.' It is 'happening.' It is 'inevitable' and 'irreversible.' It is 'multifaceted' and 'dynamic.' It is 'decentralized,' 'privatized' and 'deregulated.' It is 'economically prosperous' and 'socially mobile.' And also, it is an 'agent-free' process, a 'zero-sum game,' in which everyone can win—both the rich folks of the Global North and the poor folks of the Global South.

Hyperglobalizer Pessimistic Lens

Pleased with my mastery of some basic photographic skills, I cast another last glance at the photos of the Paradise that my camera had captured. The more I gazed at the pictures, however, the more I felt that there was something radically odd about them. I had a sense of placelessness, a feeling that I was, and was not, in Mexico. Emerging from the shades of memory, I remembered the few other resorts that I had visited previously (thanks to my American passport) in Florida, the Bahamas, Puerto Rico, Malaysia and Dubai. I had the feeling that I could be in any of these places but in none of them, as they all resembled one another: that was the domination of global consumerism and capitalism. Across all these localities, I saw the triumph of 'Americanization,' 'corporatization,' 'McDonaldization' and 'dot.comization' as described by the 'hyperglobalizer pessimists,' another term coined by Steger (2013) to refer to the critics of globalization; those who apply a Marxist, neo-Marxist critical lens to reflect on the unequal outcomes of globalization (Barber, 2007; Harvey, 2007; Ritzer, 1993; 2010; Stiglitz, 2007).

In all these places I saw more elements that are commonly associated with the 'global' culture, together with those of Yahoo, Google, Apple iPhones, Adidas, and repetitive TV commercials, than the elements of the local cultures. This feeling of 'placelessness,' this profound 'resemblance' and this sense of 'sameness' across all these localities gave me the impression that all these places must have sprung from one source and the very source was now present in all of them. Absorbed in my thoughts, I paused and whispered to myself: Does globalization mean a greater 'homogenization' of the world? Are we moving towards one common point characterized by one dominant global economy, policy, language and culture, which is Anglo-American in origin, taste and color?

While resting in the shade of a tall palm tree, close to a McDonalds, I searched my iPad to learn more about the negative outcomes of globalization and came across the following passage written by Raymond Lotta (2006). Criticizing Friedman (2005) and his notion of the 'flattening world,' Lotta argued that if we could see the planet earth from above, we would see all these:

> [A] landscape marked by staggering high peaks of controlling wealth and power, by vast valleys of exploited and impoverished humanity, by a deep fault-line between rich oppressor and poor oppressed nations, and by cruel geographies of uneven and unequal development. (Lotta, 2006: para. 6)

With these critical insights in mind, I stood up for another round of walking and sightseeing but this time through another lens on my camera: that of the 'hyperglobalizer pessimists' with a Marxist, neo-Marxist critical lens. The images that my camera captured this time, through this lens, depicted another, albeit completely different, universe: a universe that was neither glamorous nor heavenly designed. Nor was it economically prosperous or socially mobile. It was rather an earthly universe, a real place on this planet that was highly 'stratified,' 'class-based,' 'divided,' 'unequal,' 'uneven' and also, safeguarded by the many visible and invisible 'borders' or heavy 'structures' and 'substructures' that exist in the world (Ritzer, 2010).

Contrary to my initial assumption, I learned rather gradually that the owners of the Paradise were not just a group of 'ordinary' citizens and shareholders of the world. In fact, many of them were said to be Mexican politicians, who were, now, representing themselves as only private shareholders and entrepreneurs to satisfy the requirements of the transnational loan-lending institutions, like those of the International Monetary Fund (IMF), The North American Free Trade Agreement (NAFTA), the World Trade Organization (WTO) and the World Bank. These institutions, as argued by Stiglitz (2007), were the ones that had brought neoliberalism to Mexico and other places through their structural adjustment policy. Mexico, on the other hand, had to accept this policy because of its reliance on financial assistance of these organizations. The other owners of the Paradise were said to be the 'global elites' from all over the world (Bourdieu, 2001; Harvey, 2007; Phillipson, 2008). Regardless of their different nationalities, religions, languages or colors of skin, these elites were said to have one thing in common: belonging to the 'privileged social class' of the world, and thus, eligible to benefit from the 'all-inclusive' benefits of globalization.

The images I had captured on my camera this time did not depict the resort as a 'borderless' space. Although it was built close to the adjacent town, it was sharply separated from it. The separation was not made by a tall concrete grey wall, or 'borders,' so echoed by Ritzer (2010), but rather by short, beautiful blue fences, placed all around the resort. What was invisible to tourists was the fact that these little fences were safeguarded by the Mexican armed and secret police forces 24 hours a day, 7 days a week. They were everywhere, even in the ocean in their boats. Their presence was meant to give the tourists a sense of safety and security against the ongoing war between the local drug cartel and the Mexican government.

My initial assumption of being in a 'flat' space faded slowly away, when I paid much closer attention to the resort's employees. Among them, those who were visible were many foreigners with charming accents: Canadians, Spanish (from Spain), French, together with those few Mexicans who were highly fluent in the global language of power, English. The invisible employees—those who worked in the kitchen, washed the dishes or cleaned the rooms—were all Mexicans by nationality and Mexican-Spanish by language, with little proficiency in English. Through the fading memory of one such employee, an old lady, with whom I spoke quite by chance, albeit with the help of a translator, in the resort's courtyard, I was able to trace back the implantation of the Paradise on the east coast of Mexico. This is what she said, with a look of deep nostalgia on her face:

> Just a few years ago, prior to the inauguration of this resort, the Paradise, this land was richly forested. Acres and acres of stands of trees were reaching for the sky. Only fishermen would live here. They would live just along the coast, in their little huts, with their little boats, you know. They would go fishing in the mornings and mend their nets in the evenings. But then one day the construction began and with it all these many resorts slowly came to life. Today there are many of them. They have grown like wild mushrooms all over the east coast of Mexico. I no longer feel that the land is ours. It rather belongs to the foreigners; the majority of them are Americans, who act as if they are in their own backyard. They come whenever they like and they come in hundreds of thousands. And they are rich, you know.

> We are told that their presence is good for our economy, as it creates jobs for Mexicans, and so, we are happy because we have a job. But at the same time, we are sad too that the fishermen are now gone and the trees are being cut [. . .]. (Personal communication, December 2015)

The story of the fishermen and the green rainforest soon took my thoughts to another place, to the jungles of Chiapas in the southeast province of Mexico, the place of the Insurgent Subcommander Marcos, known as Robin Hood of the Lacandon rain forest, the mystery man behind the mask, who has led the Zapatista, an anti-globalization resistant movement in the jungles of Chiapas in Mexico since the early 1990s—coinciding with the very arrival of neoliberalism in Mexico. Represented as a 'rebel' by the Mexican government and the global media, Marcos has been a 'hero' in the eyes of many Mexican Native-Americans, who see Marcos as the symbol of resistance of the local against the harmonizing, top-down forces of the global (Marcos, 1992).

In search of the past and history of Mexico, those of its Native Americans, in part, as they were symbolized in Marcos's resistant movement, I went to the little stores in the neighboring town. There, I noticed that the past and history of Mexico (and its Native Americans) was treated as a commodity, sold to tourists through innumerable objects: from small art crafts, to large sculptures, expensive illustrated books and to cheap and affordable postcards. It was, in the words of Richard Price (1998), a 'romanticized,' 'folklorized,' 'fictionized' and 'postcardalized' past, fostering in the local people the illusion, or a 'false-consciousness,' of representing themselves in the global culture, while at the same time obscuring the penetrating forces of the almighty global.

This sharp contradiction, this 'inequality,' this 'class division,' this 'unevenness' and this march of 'harmonization' and 'sameness' on our planet made me pause and wonder: Is globalization really a radical break away from modernity and colonialism, or is it just a continuation of what had existed before? Was it not modernity or colonialism with a new face, characterized by global capitalism and consumerism? The structure and the patterns of haves and have-nots of the world seem to be more or less like before, albeit the only difference is the fact that today the world is no longer neatly divided into the old center versus the peripheral nation-states. Today, the 'global elites,' regardless of the boundaries of space, are the ones who rule the planet.

Lens of Globalization Skeptics

To walk into the Mexican restaurant of the resort meant, albeit the way I thought at the time, to have some Mexican food and listen to some Mexican music, to both of which I was an outsider. I went inside and sat down at a small table, close to a window that opened into the deep darkness of the night. The twinkling stars above were sprinkling light on the sleepy earth below. As I was looking at the menu, a band was on the stage before me, tuning their musical instruments.

There was a banner on the wall, on which these words were written: The Mexican Hip Hop Band! 'Hip hop!' I whispered to myself: 'But is hip hop not American music?' Then, I remembered Alastair Pennycook's (2013) essay on the localization of popular cultures, especially hip hop music, about which he wrote:

> Unlike the argument of those who insist that globalization implies '*the homogenization of the world culture* [. . .] spearheaded by films, pop culture, CNN and fast-food chains' [. . .], we need to deal with globalization beyond this dystopic, neo-Marxist critique, which is based only on political economy. [. . .] [T]he flows of popular culture are not simply from center to periphery, but rather operate in more dynamic circuits of influence [. . .]. Once we take seriously the vernacular voices of the popular and their modes of self-fashioning, we are obliged to rethink the ways language and culture work within globalization. (Pennycook, 2013: 593, 605)

Elsewhere, Jan Blommaert (2010) articulated similar insights:

> We have the feeling that we perceive something very similar, something that taps from the same sources and results in the same outcomes. It is in this feeling that makes globalization such a real experience for many people: the layer of similarity creates its own intertextuality and, hence, familiarity. But we should look somewhat deeper and beyond this superficial similarity. (Blommaert, 2010: 142–3)

The hip hop music in the background was loud—in fact, too loud to my ears. As I was eating my Mexican food, which tasted too continental to me and listening to the sound of the Mexican hip hop music, I remembered Pennycook's notion of hip hop, calling it the voice of marginalized musicians, which had transcended cultural, linguistic and geographical barriers to become a universal language among hip hoppers worldwide. Since I was foreign to this music, I could not use it as a yardstick to measure the 'localization' of the global in the local. Yet, compelled by the above skeptical insights, the day after, I took my camera for another round of sightseeing around the resort. This time I wanted to reexamine the boundaries of the Paradise to be able to capture its other side: that of the 'globalization skeptics,' another term coined by Steger (2013) to refer to scholars who apply a postmodern hermeneutic lens to offer an alternative view toward globalization.

The images my camera captured this time, through its skeptical lens, were all depicting another universe: a universe that was 'intertextual,' 'fragmented,' 'flexible,' 'deterritorialized,' and thus, 'ungrounded,' and everything on it was 'on the move' or 'in motion.' Thanks to the postmodern notions of 'conditions' and 'stimulations'—the terms first coined by Jean Baudrillard in 1983 (Butler, 2002) — I first learned that we live, or are enclosed, in a world of image, sign and information that is constructed, fashioned or manipulated by the giant corporations. Such constructed images and signs are disseminated throughout the world by the media and the

Internet through endless repetitive advertisements and TV commercials. Thus, from this point of view, both the glamorous and the unglamorous images of the Paradise that my camera had captured through its hyperglobalizer optimistic and pessimistic lenses, respectively, were not real, but rather 'imagined' and 'constructed' in a way to resemble something real (Anderson, 1983). In other words, the whole Paradise was a giant 'construct,' meant to give the observer the 'illusion' of being in a 'global' space, characterized by 'homogenization,' 'sameness' or the universalization of Anglo-American norms. Yet, none of these were real because these were just an instance of what Baudrillard called the 'hyper-realization' of reality, concealing the fact that the real is not real (Butler, 2002).

Other postmodern concepts that enriched my understanding were the notions of 'flows,' 'fluidity' or 'escapes' (Appadurai, 1996). From these concepts, I learned that we live in a world in which traditional values and perspectives are fractured. The old boundaries, or 'borders,' of the nation-states have been slowly losing ground to the multifaceted forces of globalization, leading to the compression of 'time' and 'space' and increasing the 'flow' of information, peoples, values, capital, among many others, across geographical borders. Hence, we are, now, living in a highly complex world, in which the speed of time supersedes the speed of space, so said Paul Virilio, French postmodern philosopher, whose view on time (or light) and space is reflected below.

> [T]he speed of light does not merely transfer the world. It becomes the world. Globalisation is the speed of light [. . .]. Consequently, history no longer resides in the extension of territories [. . .]. Today, everything is about speed and real time. We are no longer concerned with real space. (Virilio, 2010: para. 12)

Hybridity is another notable postmodern concept. Alamin Mazrui (2007) found, for example, 'hybridity' at the heart of the Swahili language; a language, which in his view, has always gone beyond the borders of the East African nation-states to relate to its speakers. About this hybridity, he wrote:

> [H]ybridity is a configuration that is not at all new to the human condition. It has existed in many guises in previous historical moments. If its relevance has become more salient in recent years, it is only because of the realization that it has the potential to counter certain historical claims [. . .], especially of the colonial kind. Because of colonial fixation with simple binaries and the place of naturalized myths of racial and ethnic origins in imperial ideology, however the fact of hybridity was often held against the Swahili people and their culture. (Mazrui, 2007: 1)

Mazrui's plea there, and also elsewhere (Mazrui, 2016), was, thus, to go beyond 'colonial' and 'imperial fixations' of space, searching not for 'place' as origin but rather for those mixtures that have been part of the languages, cultures and peoples around us. This was precisely Walter Mignolo's (2000) plea, who examined the 'coloniality of power' in the genealogy of thoughts of South/Central America, the Caribbean and Latinos in the US. He also traced the emergence of a new form of knowledge, the subaltern knowledge, as a consequence of going beyond 'border thinking.'

A search for such mixtures took Ofelia García (2014) to the heart of Global Spanish, in which she found a mixture of many language varieties. Like Blommaert (2010) and Pennycook (2012), she, too, argued that in the global world of today, linguistic resources are no longer territorialized because people are on the move, and thus, linguistic resources are on the move, too. As a result of this mobility, many language varieties are born and reborn, evolved and revolved, just like the US Latinos' variety of Spanish: a subaltern variety that is now the most powerful variety of Spanish.

Back at the resort, putting all these insights together, I whispered to myself that the global world is a zone of 'trans'-national, 'trans'-racial, 'trans'-cultural and 'trans'-linguistic contacts. As I walked along the beach, sat at the various exotic restaurants of the resort or spoke with different people around me, I felt that I was in a hybrid, fluid, 'trans-' zone of contacts. The resort's employees were undeniably transnational, belonging to various continents and subcontinents of the world. The transnationality of the foreign visitors and travelers were equally apparent; all bringing their languages and cultures with them, creating a 'hybrid' tapestry, whose countless threads belonged to different parts of the world. The languages of the resort were transnational, too. There, I heard many tongues: some belonged to different continents, others to different language families; some were known to conventional ears, others unknown. The 'global' tongue, English, was there, too, flavored by many varieties: American English, British English, Canadian English, Mexican English, Indian English, African English, global English, English with an accent, English with no accent—all 'world Englishes' and all alike but at the same time different and unique. Even if these varieties of English are not equal in terms of power, they all exist and their existence should be acknowledged.

This 'interconnectedness,' this 'fragmentation' and this march of sociocultural and linguistic 'hybridity' in the world seemed absolutely pleasing to me. I felt that I was a witness to a phase in human history in which modernity, with its rigid and highly territorialized nation-state boundaries, was already behind us, giving way to a postmodern era of 'glocality,' characterized by the shrinkage of time and space and countless interactions between the forces of the global and those of the local.

Gazing at the blue ocean, capped with the white foam in the far distance, I whispered to myself: This is globalization. It is not real but rather it is 'imagined' and 'constructed.' What is real is 'glocalization,' or the interaction between the local and the global; an interaction that is 'fluid,' 'hybrid' and more, 'interconnected' and 'intertextual.' As argued by Suresh Canagarajah (2005), "the global is simply applied, translated, or contextualized to the local" (p. xiv). Thus, there was no need to mourn the death of the local as the local was alive. With my eyes fixed on the distant horizon, I shouted with joy that the 'local' is not dead! It is still around. It exists. It is not only resisting the forces of the global, but it is also influencing it. However, as Canagarajah reminds us, "[a] local grounding should become the primary and critical force in the construction of contextually relevant knowledge if we are to develop more plural discourses" (2005: xiv).

Pleased with my new discovery, I was about to put all my books back into my suitcase, when I came across the following lines in a book, whose authors offered a counterargument to the localization thesis in this way:

> Those who embrace glocalisation have a tendency to stack the odds too much in favour of the local. Indeed, it has become almost canonical to eulogise the authenticity of the local in contrast to the illegitimacy of the global. This stance often seems to be more one of wishful thinking, based on an idealisation of the indigenous acting against outside forces which threaten to destroy it. And who is not against this happening? However, just because we desire resistance to certain globalising forces does not mean that we must see as fact that the local shapes the global more than the global shapes the local. (Block et al., 2012: 60)

After reading these words, I could not help but to pause and wonder: Do imperial/global forces still manifestly rule the planet, despite all our best hopes? Or should we, as suggested by postmodern scholars, apply a rather different approach—putting aside all binary opposing terms and stepping outside a neo-Marxist framework to be open to new possibilities that are emerging as the consequences of globalization?

Conclusion

The taxi to Cancun airport was fast. Locked in my suitcase in the trunk of the car, all my books were, now, away from my reach. The journey to the airport was long—a good hour, during which I amused myself by looking at the photos that my camera had captured over a week of staying at the resort. I wanted to use these photos both to define globalization for myself and to choose the right set of pictures to represent the 'true' image of Mexico in these global times, the Global Mexico, to send them back home to my family, who, unlike me, were the citizens and residents of Iran, living along the shore of the once glamorous, but now unglamorous, Caspian Sea: a geographical space that cannot offer its residents the 'all-inclusive' benefits of globalization.

Yet, as I cast a last glance at my photos, I felt more bewildered and confused than before. The divergent images of the resort that had been captured by my camera, coupled with the ongoing academic debate among globalization scholars, their contradictory views and their sharp agreements or disagreements made me pause and wonder: Which image of globalization is real and which one is not?

Which one is telling the 'truth' and which one is not? Which is the one to believe, and which is the one to doubt?

Cancun airport appeared in the near distance. It was time for me to place all my photos back in my shoulder bag, next to my camera and its many lenses, and bid my farewell to Mexico.

Questions for Discussion

1. This chapter began with a quotation from Protagoras, the pre-Socrates Greek philosopher, who said "Man is the measure of all things." How does this quotation relate to the overall aim and scope of this chapter?
2. After reading this chapter, what can be said about the nature of 'truth,' especially the truth of globalization? Whose truth do you believe? Is there ever a truth? Why/why not?

Author Profile

Maryam Borjian is Associate Teaching Professor and Director of African, Middle Eastern and South Asian Language Program at Rutgers University's Department of African, Middle Eastern and South Asian Languages and Literatures. Her work studies the politics, economics and sociology of language. She is best known for writing *English in Post-Revolutionary Iran: From Indigenization to Internationalization* (Multilingual Matters, 2013), which is a pioneering book on the history and status of English in Iran. "Middle Eastern Languages in Diasporic USA Community," is a special issue that she has co-edited (with Charles Häberl) for the *International Journal of the Sociology of Language* (Mouton de Gruyter, 2016).

References

Anderson, B. (1983). *Imagined communities: Reflections on the origin and spread of nationalism.* London: Verso.

Appadurai, A. (1996). *Modernity at large: Cultural dimensions of globalization.* Minneapolis: University of Minnesota Press.

Barber, B. (2007). *Consumed: How markets corrupt children, infantilize adults, and swallow citizens whole.* New York: W. W. Norton.

Block, D., Gray, J. & Holborow, M. (2012). *Neoliberalism and applied linguistics.* London: Routledge.

Blommaert, J. (2010). *The sociolinguistics of globalization.* Cambridge: Cambridge University Press.

Bourdieu, P. (2001). *Pour un movement social européen.* Paris: Raisons D'agir.

Butler, C. (2002). *Postmodernism: A very short introduction.* Oxford: Oxford University Press.

Canagarajah, A. S. (ed.) (2005). *Reclaiming the local in language policy and practice.* Mahwah, NJ: Lawrence Erlbaum.

Chong, A. & López-de-Silanes, F. (2004). *Privatization in Mexico*. Research Department Working Paper. Inter-American Development Bank. Retrieved January 15, 2015 from: http://idbdocs.iadb.org/wsdocs/getdocument.aspx?docnum=788330.

Friedman, T. (2005). *The world is flat: A brief history of the twenty-first century*. New York: Farrar, Straus and Giroux.

Friedman, T. (2000). *The Lexus and the olive tree: Understanding globalization*. New York: Farrar, Straus and Giroux.

Fukuyama, F. (1989). The end of history and the last man. *The National Interest*. Retrieved April 23, 2016 from: www.wesjones.com/eoh.htm.

García, O. (2014). US Spanish and education: Global and local intersection. *Review of Research in Education*, 38, 58–80.

Harvey, D. (2007). *A brief history of neoliberalism*. Oxford: Oxford University Press.

Huntington, S. (1996). *The clash of civilization and the remaking of world order*. New York: Touchstone.

Lotta, R. (2006). A jagged, unjust, and obsolete world: A critique of Thomas Friedman's *The world is flat*. Retrieved, April 23, 2016 from: http://revcom.us/a/060/flatworld-en.html.

Marcos, S. (1992). Chiapas: The southeast in two winds. Retrieved June 8, 2016 from: http://lanic.utexas.edu/project/Zapatistas/chiapas.html.

Mazrui, A. M. (2016). *Cultural politics of translation: East Africa in a global context*. New York: Routledge.

Mazrui, A. M. (2007). *Swahili beyond the boundaries: Literature, language and identity*. Ohio: Ohio University Press.

Mignolo, W. (2000). *Local histories/global designs: Coloniality, subaltern knowledges and border thinking*. Princeton: Princeton University Press.

Miller, E. (1998). *Questions that matter: An investigation to philosophy*. Boston: Overture Books.

Pennycook, A. (2013). Popular cultures, popular languages, and global identities. In N. Coupland (ed.), *The handbook of language and globalization* (pp. 292–607). Malden, MA: Wiley-Blackwell.

Pennycook, A. (2012). *Language and mobility: Unexpected places*. Bristol: Multilingual Matters.

Phillipson, R. (2008). *Linguistic imperialism continued*. London: Routledge.

Price, R. (1998). *The convict and the colonel*. Boston: Beacon Press.

Ritzer, G. (2010). *Globalization: A basic text*. Malden, MA: Wiley-Blackwell.

Ritzer, G. (1993). *The McDonaldization of society: An investigation into the changing character of contemporary social life*. Thousand Oaks, CA: Pine Forge Press.

Steger, M. (2013). *Globalization: A very short introduction*. Oxford: Oxford University Press.

Stiglitz, J. (2007). *Making globalization work*. New York: Norton.

Virilio, P. (2010). The Kosovo war took place in orbital space: Paulo Virilio in conversation with John Armitage. Retrieved April 26, 2016 from: www.ctheory.net/articles.aspx?id=132.

3

FROM A VILLAGE OUTLOOK TO A GLOBAL OVERVIEW

An Autoethnographic Report of Change in Sociolinguistic Research Questions

Ulrich Ammon

Introduction

This chapter shows how my view of the world and my linguistic research interests have developed in the course of my life through my personal experience, and with the profound changes of the world in recent times, which can perhaps best be condensed into the comprehensive concept 'globalization.'

Trivial as this introductory remark may appear to be to the experts, it might be useful for those less familiar with autoethnography, to avoid misunderstanding. Typical features of this text could be highlighted by calling it a 'narrative' or even a 'story,' instead of a report. It is based on the experience of a single individual, myself, and on the subjective selection of relevant data, which I report from memory, supported by a variety of intersubjectively confirmed or objective data. It remains, therefore, unclear to what extent this 'report,' as I call it, to stress my attempt to be truthful, might be typical of a particular kind of people and societal circumstances.

As an answer to the editor's suggestion, that the authors of this volume also reveal the basic views that guide their scientific work, it may suffice to point out that mine is—roughly speaking—in line with a Darwinist view of the natural history of life and mankind's place in the world. In addition, it follows a structural-functional or conflict theory or, in more important respects, also a Marxist theory of society, though without the latter's 'revolutionary' conclusions. Epistemologically and methodologically, I could characterize my views as a critical rationalist, taking logical-mathematical thinking as reliable (or 'true' methodologically, as long as the postulated meanings and rules are being observed), but empirical knowledge, relying, if only indirectly, on sensual perception, as being generally hypothetical, no matter how strongly corroborated—and, is thus, fundamentally different from dogmatic ideological or religious beliefs, which I principally do call into question.

Local and National Frame: Standard Variety Versus Regional Dialect

I grew up in a village in Southwest Germany (Oppenweiler, 35 km east of Stuttgart) during the end of WWII and the Nazi period (born in July 1943) and the re-establishment of civilization thereafter. In this location, everyone spoke a more or less broad Swabian dialect—with the exception of a few newcomers from Eastern or Northern Germany, who arrived towards the end of and after the war. It was conspicuous that they did not speak a dialect, at least not a Swabian one. A prominent figure among them was an old dentist, who took the place of his colleague killed during the war, and who was sometimes mocked for his unsuccessful attempts at speaking the Swabian dialect, especially to his patients. I had my own experience with such an attempt, when he proved to be absolutely unable, in spite of my careful oral presentation, to pronounce correctly the word *unangenehm* ('unpleasant') ['õã, gne:m] in Swabian, which was a popular schibboleth (a term I learned only later) for being a genuine dialect speaker.

At that time, I became aware, though dimly, that nonstandard dialects also have language norms, notwithstanding their rich variation of forms, some that are sharply observed and controlled. However, everyone in the village also noticed, enviously, that the same dentist was one of the wealthiest inhabitants, with a particularly attractive wife, in spite of his age, and that these privileges were related to him not speaking the dialect but, instead, standard German. In fact, he spoke it flawlessly, in contrast to the indigenous population, most of whom had serious difficulty with the 'correct' version of their own German language. It was also generally known, or rather dimly felt but hardly mentioned, that a full command of standard German was typical of quite a small section of the educated and economically privileged population—something of which I became fully aware only during and from my university studies. However, this topic will be covered more extensively in what follows.

I had a related though slightly different experience late in my time at Gymnasium, a type of selective German high school, where dialect speakers, to whom I belonged myself, could easily be distinguished from speakers of standard German. This was so, in spite of the fact that they had learned not to speak a broad dialect in class, but rather a 'refined' (German *vornehmere*) version, which was typical of the more educated people. However, they still had to make endeavors to speak this standard-close variety fluently, and to avoid the broad dialect forms which kept cropping up. Some teachers used to mock the occasional usage of such forms by echoing them in front of the entire class and thus shaming the culprits.

My own problems with dialect arose from my accent, which was typical of all the native dialect speakers and that was generally accepted, also in class, where only lexical and idiomatic or grammatical deviations from standard German were sanctioned. My problems occurred when I—being an eager participant in class discussions—became one of the few students who were chosen for the public recital of poems at the annual school celebrations involving parents, teachers and pupils. The dialect speakers chosen for such a task received intensive training in 'pure' standard pronunciation (German *Hochlautung*) by an expert teacher. The few students not in need of it had moved from Northern Germany to the economically and technologically more flourishing South. Even those few native dialect speakers, whose parents had ambitiously practiced speaking standard German at home, were stricken with the accent.

I only found out much later—through my own studies rather than from what I had read about the German language—why Northern German pronunciation was void of the dialect accent typical of the South. To summarize roughly, the reason was that the Northern German-speaking regions had based their pronunciation on the written high and middle German texts that they had imported in the wake of the Lutheran Reformation they followed. This newly developed pronunciation was more in line with the written standard than the traditional Southern pronunciation—one of the reasons why the codification of the standard pronunciation at the end of the 19th century was based on Northern German. Another reason for its preference was the political dominance of Prussia, located in the North of the German-speaking area, in the process of building the German nation-state. It was the impact of this politico-linguistic history that forced me to absorb the 'pure' pronunciation of German for reciting poems—which the immigrants from Northern Germany had acquired entirely natural through their families. I knew, of course, nothing of this historical background at that time, and it was never taught at school. It is, by the way, still hardly taught today and perhaps tabooed politically, in order not to incite South–North jealousy, and is a remarkable example of the dearth of sociolinguistic knowledge in German school curricula. No wonder, therefore, that the situation has stayed, basically, unchanged. It was not sociolinguistically explained in the great times of German historical linguistics (epitomized by names like Jacob Grimm or Hermann Paul) and is hardly explained, even among experts today, but rather only occasionally bewailed as the unfortunate linguistic disadvantage of Southern Germans, and seems, in fact, gradually to be mitigated by intensified regional mobility and transregional communication.

I hit on the topic as a field of research, mainly due to two impulses, both intertwined with the educational and geographic expansion of my perception. One was my choice of *Volkskunde* as a subject of study, among others, at the University of Tübingen (in Southern Germany), whose open-minded professor, Hermann Bausinger, was known for his international perspective and new ideas. The subject whose chair he had taken, mostly labeled 'folklore,' in English, was stricken by a conservative or chauvinistic history from which he wanted to free himself of. It was symptomatic of his endeavors that he insisted on the university renaming the subject, finally creating *Empirische Kulturwissenschaft* (literally, 'empirical science of culture') —a struggle at the edge of which I myself was engaged with in the rejected proposal *Subkulturforschung* ('research of subculture'). Bausinger's interests extended into and partially comprised fields that had mainly been developed, or at least enriched, in the Anglo-Saxon world. These fields had been given various labels and overlapped, regarding questions and methods, such as *ethnography*, *ethnology* or *cultural* and *social anthropology*. It was sensational at these times that in Bausinger's seminars, especially for his PhD students, the seminal texts of the various subjects of interest (whose protagonists can now be found in Wikipedia articles, like Franz Boas, Bronislaw Małinowski, James G. Frazer, et al.) were read in English—in times when German was still widely seen, at least within Germany, as a global language of science.

This was in the middle and late 1960s, at which time sociolinguistics also received a significant boost—again, mainly from the Anglo-Saxon world, although exaggerated claims of an Anglo-Saxon or even American research monopoly, which are supported by today's dominance of English as the global scientific lingua franca, are in need of modification. It was Basil Bernstein's theory of the 'restricted' and 'elaborated codes' of the lower or the middle and upper social classes (e.g., Bernstein 1959; 1964) that initially had the strongest impact on sociolinguistics in Germany, especially in West Germany in the late 1960s. This theory seemed to support the anti-capitalism of the student movement, which was fueled by Anti-Americanism arising from the Vietnam War: global perspectives impacting sociolinguistics in Germany—and, of course, elsewhere. Bernstein's 'lower class' was then equalized, more or less, with Marx's 'proletariat,' and Bernstein's 'restricted code' was seen as one of the proletariat's major handicaps, in their aspiration towards greater social equality or even, finally, the socialist revolution.

I found myself on the sociolinguistic front line when I added regional dialect to restricted code as another linguistic handicap of the lower class, as I had experienced it, tentatively, in my village and in school. However, I made a clear distinction between dialect and restricted code from the beginning, by defining the former as a regional nonstandard variety, in contrast to the latter as an insufficiently explicit habit or style of language use, not easily understood by outsiders of one's own social group. The former resulted from the speakers' regional limitation of communication, for which the dialect sufficed and skills of the standard variety were not required, while the latter evolved from tight family structures with few outside contacts that made explicit communication superfluous, i.e., the use of an 'elaborate code.' Both dialect and restricted code then converged, it seemed, to form a severe handicap for effective verbal communication, especially for public speech, which hampered the proletariat's articulation of their own interests and expansion of their political rights. This picture, painted in broad brushstrokes, will have to suffice here as an outline of the basic ideas and concerns.

I carried out detailed socio-historical and sociological studies on the social distribution of regional dialects and standard German, and on prejudices against dialect speakers (who were, as a rule, judged as generally less intelligent than standard-variety speakers) and analyzed numerous previous studies and samples of elicited speech which had been carried out or collected for purposes other than sociolinguistics. The dissertation I wrote on the basis of these studies was published in two volumes, under the respective titles, "Dialect, Social Inequality and School" (Ammon, 1972) and "The Social Distribution of Dialects and the Standard Variety" (Ammon, 1973; cf., for a summary of some aspects in English, Ammon, 1977). The former was especially received widely and discussed. It earned me a generous grant from the German Research Foundation (*Deutsche Forschungsgemeinschaft*) on the one hand, and had, together with other related studies, a considerable impact on a remarkable language teaching project, on the other hand—both were energetically supported by Hermann Bausinger. The latter part of the project had the goal to diminish the difficulties of dialect speakers and improve their acquisition of good skills in standard German in school, and, extended, overall, to dialect areas in West Germany. The project overall was organized and directed by Werner Besch and Heinrich Löffler (cf. Besch & Löffler, 1973) with motivational input by Bausinger (1973). As its basis, teaching materials were constructed in the form of contrastive grammars of dialects and standard varieties that contained detailed proposals for application, in class, for various school levels. Together, with the schoolteacher Uwe Löwer, I wrote the materials for the Swabian dialect area (Ammon & Löwer, 1977).

The additional research I did on the basis of my grant was a refined and statistically representative study of school difficulties faced by dialect speakers. I found these to exist on different school levels and in various kinds and degrees—in oral participation in class, acquisition of reading skills, spelling, written composition—and to be aggravated by teachers' prejudices (as to dialect speakers' assumed lack of intelligence or other deficits), which altogether resulted in bad marks or discouragement from attending selective high schools. One important modification of dialect effects on school results was found by controlling 'nonverbal IQ' (measured by *Raven's Progressive Matrices Test*). It revealed that it was mainly the dialect speakers with a lower IQ who suffered in school, as compared to standard speakers of the same IQ. Those with a higher IQ, however, did not, or were even more successful than standard speakers of the same IQ. These findings could be clues for the conditions under which multilingualism (dialect + standard) can have negative or positive effects on school success. The study was based on the comparison of students of the same habitual dialect broadness in informal speech (controlling Labov's *observer's paradox*). From this, it followed that students who had a hard time in school anyway (with a lower IQ), particularly suffered from being brought up in the regional dialect as the sole or prevalent form of family communication (details in Ammon, 1978).

The dialect-standard question was discussed more or less all over Europe in the following years (cf., e.g., Cheshire, Edwards, Münstermann & Weltens, 1989; Ammon & Cheshire 1989). Its educational and social challenges were, however, eventually dwarfed by those of the immigrants from abroad, who started to pour into the economically more advanced European countries from the 1960s onwards and whose 'language barriers' were far more severe. In addition, a new linguistic challenge arose, even for the most refined speakers of standard German, namely—as international communication became ever more important—to cope with the growing, urgent requirement of at least occasionally, using English.

Global Frame: English Versus Any Other Language

These transnational developments helped to extend my view beyond the national German horizon with its standard variety, which had already been a substantial extension beyond the village and its dialect. My perspective broadened to a truly international, or even global scale, when I had the good fortune to win a Fulbright scholarship for a board-and-tuition-free year of studies at Wesleyan University in Middletown, Connecticut, in the mid 1960s. The eye-opening effect was deepened by a follow-up opportunity a couple of years later to teach at Wesleyan as an instructor of German language and literature for a year. It was typical of those days, and reminds us of the breathtaking speed of globalization, that I considered it entirely normal to travel to the US by ship both times and to communicate back home only by regular mail, nowadays called 'snail mail,' since transatlantic telephone contacts were still a rare and expensive exception—not to speak of the Internet or office-format computers, both of which were beyond imagination.

The visit to the US was, however, a new linguistic experience that left a deep impression on me and kindled specific sociolinguistic interests, though the flames burst out only decades later. Never before had I experienced such an intense linguistic handicap as when I was forced to communicate nearly exclusively in English. I, of course, knew before then, that I could not use German, or at best, use occasionally, but had not expected the grave limitations of a foreign language—that I had learned in school more from reading Shakespeare than for comprehensive oral and written academic purposes and that I now also needed for everyday practical communication.

It seems worth pointing out that I saw my linguistic handicap at that time, naively, as the situation in which foreign students or teachers would find themselves anywhere, analogously in Germany, France, Japan or elsewhere (having to struggle with the local language being a foreign language to them), and therefore, accepted it as absolutely natural and in no way unfair. Only later did I notice that English was a special case or was about to become one, different from any other language, as it is nowadays, illustrating what is meant by calling it 'the global lingua franca.' It was only when I became aware of that status (or standing or function) that I started to perceive the relationship between English and any other language somewhat analogously to the relationship of a standard variety to its regional dialects—notwithstanding, of course, some essential differences. The commonality of this relationship could be, and has been, labeled 'roofing,' if one translates Heinz Kloss's terminological proposal *Überdachung* from German into English (probably first used in Kloss, 1952: 21, footnote 3) in which he referred to a standard variety's (*Kultursprache*, in his terminology) typical relationship to its dialects (which he called *Mundarten*), though the terminology was later used less by himself than by others. The global lingua franca or the standard variety can be seen as roofing the non–lingua francas (more precisely, the non-global lingua francas) or the dialects, respectively, with their 'being roofed' by the global lingua franca, to express the relationship's asymmetry (Ammon, 1989a: 38–40). Using the same terminology entails, however, the danger of equalizing both relationships, which can be avoided by limiting the term 'roofing' to standard varieties and their dialects and to use a different term, e.g., 'dominance' ('being dominant' or 'being dominated') for the global lingua franca, or for other prestigious lingua francas and the languages subordinated to them.

The dominance of the global lingua franca had, and was, felt to have, grave consequences, especially for those other languages, like French, German or Italian, which had previously been international, and still were, to a limited extent, or rather, for their language communities. They could now less and less rely on their own native tongue for international communication, but had to shift to a foreign language, English. The consequences for other communities, whose languages had not had an international standing, were different. They did not feel new, additional pressure, but rather found the growing dominance of English as a relief, for they could now largely rely on a single foreign language, English, instead of having to study and to handle several languages for international communication (cf. some of the contributions to Ammon, 2001). This seems to have been the overriding evaluation, notwithstanding the occasional laments about the loss of multilingualism, especially from linguists, with which they expressed their solidarity with the suffering communities of the erstwhile international languages.

Naturally, I felt the status decline of my own language as a severe loss, as did other native speakers of German—and also the non-native speakers, often Eastern Europeans, who had acquired good German skills, but not English. They, too, could no longer use these skills unimpededly for international communication. Such limitations began to be felt after WWII, or partially even before, but intensified during the 1970s and 1980s, when the generation that had still learned German as a foreign language started to dwindle. The problems, of course, varied for different groups and individuals and in different domains and situations and remained quite unnoticed for a considerable time within German-speaking countries.

However, I became aware of them quite early on, having been sensitized to language barriers by my studies of dialect difficulties and my experiences in the US.

I observed, and also studied, these developments and started publishing my first results in the late 1980s (e.g., Ammon, 1989b; 1990). From the beginning, however, I tried to avoid the one-sided view of the disadvantages of only one's own language community, but instead pointed out parallels with similarly affected language communities (like French or Italian) and even the potentially positive effects on the communities with languages ranking lower in international standing (like Czech, Polish, Lithuanian, etc.). I have always been aware of the tendency that practically everyone is inclined to evaluate language problems and disadvantages from their own background, especially their own language community, and has difficulty developing a more comprehensive perspective including the interests of other language communities. This is a bias from which language policy evaluations and proposals can seriously suffer. It was during the times of the conspicuous spread of English as the global lingua franca, with its disadvantages and advantages for various language communities, that I also became aware of the 'global language constellation,' of which Abram de Swaan was a pioneer, conceiving it comprehensively as a research object and studying it as such (early work, e.g., 1991; comprehensive study 2001).

Based on various studies by myself and others, I published a book on the occasion of the official introduction of English-taught programs to German universities, under the title *Is German Still an International Language of Science? Does English Now also Have This Status for Teaching at German-Speaking Universities?* (Ammon, 1998). I explored the same topic again in various later publications, more thoroughly and enriched with new empirical findings, especially in my recent book, *The Standing of the German Language in the World* (Ammon, 2015), especially in the chapter "German in International Scientific Communication,"

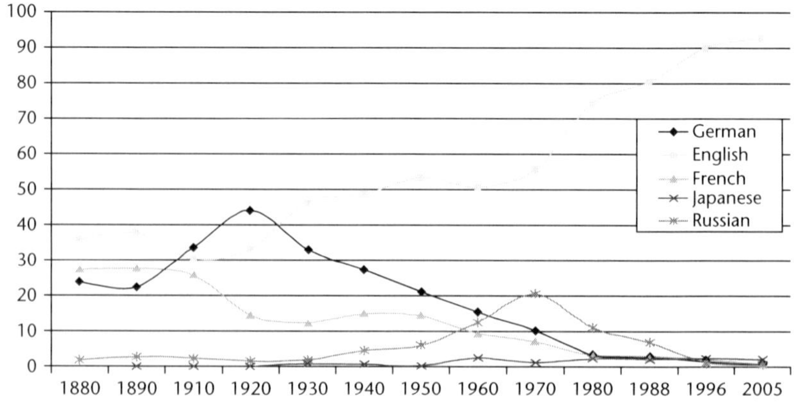

FIGURE 3.1 Proportions of Languages in Publications of the Natural Sciences Worldwide 1880–2005 (Based on Biological Abstracts, Chemical Abstracts, Mathematical Reviews, Index Medicus and Medline, and Physics Abstracts).

(pp. 519–698). One of my findings, which has been published repeatedly, is pictured in Figure 3.1.

It shows the decline of the share of the erstwhile most important languages of science in natural science publications worldwide. The main reasons for the decline of French and German can be guessed easily as the nearly total destruction of both countries by the two world wars and German Nazism, together with the ensuing dearth of resources for scientific research and publication. However, the special conditions of the globalization which followed, especially regarding technical developments such as the Internet and easy access to air travel, had additional indirectly accelerating effects. One of them was the formation of numerous 'invisible colleges,' i.e., intensive worldwide cooperation and formation of groups of scientists from different languages, whose communication functioned best with just one single language, the most well known being English, which mostly serves the purpose better than other languages and thus, has been gaining preference.

The need for Germans and other non-Anglophones to shift to English has varied between domains and situations and has become absolutely necessary for certain diplomatic or economic contact. In academic life, the theoretical natural sciences have leaned most strongly toward English, as they deal mostly with universal questions of interest worldwide and often employ formal language that needs no or little translation. This applies more to publications than oral communication. However, other sciences have followed suit, though less rigorously, like the applied natural sciences and technologies, but also the social sciences and, to a lesser extent, even the humanities.

The alarm was raised beyond academic life when English started to make inroads into other languages' 'motherlands,' such as into German-speaking countries (especially Germany, Austria and Switzerland), where it is even used for university teaching. It became obvious in Germany when English-taught study programs were introduced, with state support, in the winter semester 1997/98. In the year 2016, there were already up to 1,000 English-taught programs at universities in Germany. However, their share should not be overestimated, as German remains the clearly preferred language of teaching at German universities, with less than 5 percent of students involved in English-taught programs and with a solid knowledge of German still generally required for students from abroad (except for short programs or visits). The 'intrusion' of English into German academic life is nevertheless perceived as a cultural threat by those Germans who see their own language as part of their national identity.

The upsides and downsides of today's global language constellation have been the topic of numerous studies, some by the author himself, as the newer titles on my homepage show (www.ulrichammon.de/). However, many details and their consequences are still unknown, leaving those concerned about the disadvantages and possible weakening or strengthening of 'linguistic justice' (Van Parijs, 2011) in limbo. The disadvantages of language communities and their speakers with languages of erstwhile or continued international standing appear grave, as they have not yet adjusted to their losses, comparable to the once rich who feel the pain of poverty more severely than those who have always been poor and are, therefore, familiar with the condition. This new linguistic poverty is noticeable in academic life and beyond. Thus, publishers in Germany, France or elsewhere, who formerly played in the same league as those in Britain or the United States, now suffer from market losses and are forced increasingly to publish in English, which causes additional costs (to pay for the services of native speakers). Similarly, German scientists and scholars have to learn and handle a foreign language, English, and thus, carry an extra linguistic burden compared to their Anglophone colleagues (who can, but don't have to, acquire foreign-language skills). Even after investing in language studies, non-Anglophones need extra time or money to produce flawless texts, and they can appear linguistically clumsy at conferences. Questionnaire studies have disclosed that considerable percentages of German scientists (up to 50%) are dissatisfied with their skills in English and even refrain from publishing or conference participation (up to 20%) if it needs to be done in English (details in Ammon, 2015: 654–70); but, they know, at the same time, that they can reach a global audience only via English. Their distress can even incline them towards the biblical conclusion of the myth of Babel, that the multitude of languages is a curse and should be reduced rather than maintained, or that a single language for the whole of mankind would, ideally, be overall the fairest solution. Linguists are, of course, of exactly the opposite opinion—for their own interests, some would say—but can find it difficult to convincingly disprove the anti-multilingualists' reasoning.

In order, however, to preclude wrong impressions, I want to point out that recent studies do not foreshadow the disappearance of global multilingualism. Though language communities with very few speakers are often inclined to forsake their language and shift to another they find more useful for communicative or economic purposes, some of the larger languages (not only English) have lately even gained speakers. This is also true of German, whose number of native speakers has stabilized and whose number of learners as a foreign language has—on a global scale—even increased. Both tendencies result from the attraction of German-speaking countries for career and study reasons. The latter seems more plausible than the former, which, however, results from massive immigration to German-speaking countries with young immigrants shifting to the new language and eventually adopting it as native. However, the gap in numbers vis-à-vis English remains huge and keeps increasing. I have published a comprehensive overview of the standing of the German language within the global language constellation, showing its relations not only to English, but also to other languages still considered international, and showing the advantages and disadvantages for its speakers as well as discussing ameliorations. This book contains many of my own studies as well as screening a vast number of others (Ammon, 2015). I use the term *Stellung* (of the German language in the world) in the book's title with its meaning comprising 'standing, position, status, prestige, and rank' to indicate the multitude of perspectives (Link to flyer and table of contents: www.ulrichammon.de/resources/Stellung_der_deutschen_Sprache.pdf).

Frame of the Pluricentric Language Community: The Dominant National Variety Versus the Other National Varieties

There is still one other kind of linguistic inequality in which I have become heavily involved for research and teaching; namely, among the various standard varieties within a language or, rather, their speakers. Languages which comprise different standard varieties are called pluricentric, a concept to which Heinz Kloss once again contributed essential thoughts and to whose elaboration Michael Clyne (e.g., 1984), among others, made important contributions (for details of the research history, see Ammon, 1995: 42–60). An obvious example of a pluricentric language is English, with its differences between American Standard English, British Standard English, Australian Standard English and others, and there are numerous other pluricentric languages, such as Spanish, Portuguese and Dutch.

As for German, I became aware of its pluricentricity and especially of conflicts arising from it during my studies of the international standing of the language and of German-speaking countries' endeavors to boost its standing or stop its decline. Through these endeavors, the countries became aware of the differences in prestige of the various standard varieties. Austria was especially dismayed by the noticeable preference for Germany's standard variety in studies of German as a foreign language. Austria not only occasionally complained about this unequal evaluation, but in a few, however unspectacular, cases withdrew from common promotional endeavors. For example, Austria refused to distribute a calendar in German through its national cultural institutes that had been produced in Germany, but had not listed the Austrian standard variants of German. The country also insisted, when it joined the European Union (EU) in 1995, that the standard variants of Austrian German be used in official EU texts together with Germany's variants (attached by a slash in each case), which was readily accepted by Germany as well as the EU (details in Ammon, 1995: 201–213).

In the 1990s, the pluricentricity of German became a somewhat popular topic in certain political and, of course, sociolinguistic circles. Consequently, attention was drawn to the fact that Switzerland also had specific standard German variants, and so did the smaller countries or regions where German had an official status, like Liechtenstein, Luxemburg, South Tyrol in Italy, Eastern Belgium and even some German minorities, especially in Rumania, Namibia and in various Mennonite colonies on the American continent. I decided in the early 1990s to deal with the problem thoroughly, following my studies of the linguistic discrimination of dialects and of languages other than English, and paying attention to potential conflicts, with the focus on attitudes in Germany, even among linguists, that Germany's standard variety was the only correct version of the German language, with anything else being nonstandard or simply regional dialect. This linguistic arrogance attracted my attention and that of other sociolinguists and could negatively affect studies of German as a foreign language.

My first publication on the topic, based on not only quite thorough theoretical studies, but also on pertinent empirical research, was the book *The German Language in Germany, Austria and Switzerland: The Problem of National Varieties* (Ammon, 1995). One of the challenges that appeared essential to me, for further theoretical clarification as well as for practical ameliorations, was a theoretically valid and empirically precise working definition of what should be considered a national or regional language variant or a national variety, with the former relating to a single linguistic form, e.g., a word, and the latter to an entire text or linguistic system. It seemed clear that they had to be specific to some country or region and had to be standard (and, of course, part of the German language). Of the various aspects that had to be considered (see, for details, Ammon, 2015: 107–197), the distinction of standard from nonstandard variants may be worth sketching here, a solution at which I arrived from comprehensive norm-theoretical studies, on the one hand, and the comparison of various languages, on the other, and which can be explained roughly by Figure 3.2 (cf. Ammon, 1995: 73–94; 2003; 2015: 143–46). This solution seems to be valid for numerous languages.

For a general understanding of the concept of a 'standard variety of a language,' it seems helpful to see it as the sum of the forms of the language that can be used without risk of being sanctioned for speaking or writing it in public. Therefore, anyone who regularly speaks and writes in public can, in principle, affect its norm. This is where model speakers and writers come into play with professional speakers and writers, such as prominent authors and actors in the past and journalists and newsreaders in the present, being particularly relevant. Heinz Kloss (1952: 28) rightly pointed out early on that nonfiction has a stronger impact on forming standard norms than fiction, because the latter often intentionally uses clearly nonstandard forms. A variant (or linguistic form) that regularly appears in model texts without being marked there as (a quote from) nonstandard, e.g., orally by an intonational signal or in writing by quotation marks, can, thus, be counted as standard.

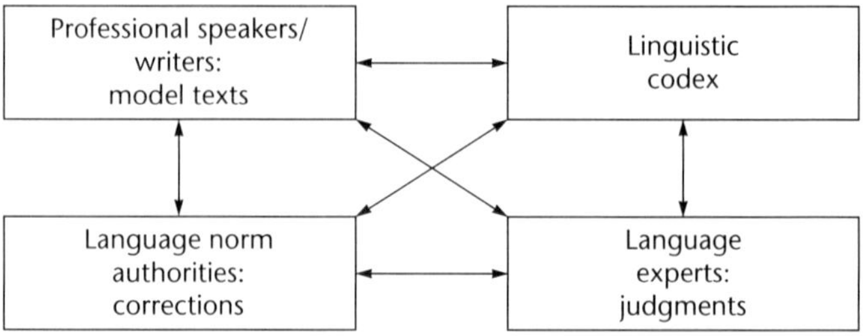

FIGURE 3.2 Model of the Four Social Forces that Primarily Determine in Many Cases What Counts as, or is, Standard in a Language.

A linguistic codex (or language codex) consists, as a rule, of dictionaries, grammars or style sheets. It is, however, more than a mere linguistic description. Linguistic codices are typically made for standard varieties and function as guides for correct language behavior or for correcting it in that direction. They have to be valid so that users or correcting authorities like teachers (see, 'language norm authorities' below) can rely on them, which requires, as a rule, that their respective use or function has been endorsed by superordinate authorities, whose hierarchy can reach up to the sovereign of the state. In unplanned language history, codification usually follows model speakers' or writers' language use. Then, codifiers, e.g., authors of dictionaries, select the variants regularly used by model speakers or writers for inclusion in the codex. The reverse order is, however, also possible, especially in the case of planned languages, e.g., Esperanto.

Language norm authorities are all the people entitled to correct others', their 'norm subjects,' language behavior. Such authorities also exist for nonstandard varieties, e.g., regional dialects, such as parents who correct their children's language behavior. The typical cases for standard varieties are, however, schoolteachers or copy editors or, more generally, individuals or groups for whom correcting language behavior is part of their professional duties. The main function of such authorities is spreading and transmitting standard variety norms; but occasionally, they also help to establish them. Thus, teachers or their organizations became heavily involved in the reform of the standard variety's orthography in Germany in the course of the 1990s.

Finally, the 'language experts' comprise any acknowledged linguists who are taken seriously when they criticize the language codex, or also the language use of model speakers and writers or even the corrective behavior of language-norm authorities. They are a separate group from the codifiers who are, of course, linguists too. Examples of the 'language experts' impact can be observed in Austria. The 35th edition of the 'Austrian Dictionary' (*Österreichisches Wörterbuch*, 1979) incorporated numerous new, typically Austrian words as standard, in the attempt to increase the autonomy of the Austrian national variety of German. Some renowned university linguists raised objections based on a detailed word list—with the effect that many of the incriminated words were excluded from the dictionary's next edition or marked as 'colloquial' or 'dialect,' i.e., nonstandard (cf. Ammon, 1995: 132–136).

The double-headed arrows aiming in all directions symbolize the comprehensive interaction among the four forces, e.g., the model speakers and writers influencing the codification and, in turn, being trained in the language with the codification as a basis; influencing the judgment of the norm authorities and the language experts and being influenced by them, and so forth.

Finally, it should not be forgotten that any codification relates, of course, to the language use of the majority of the population, who, however, have no immediate say in most cases as to what actually counts as standard. In addition, it should be pointed out that the definition of standard is always to some extent fuzzy, if only because the various forces involved in setting it disagree.

Based on these and other, more refined thoughts, I initiated a dictionary of national and regional standard variants of German whose structure was developed with the help of numerous colleagues, also from Switzerland and Austria, especially at the universities of Basel (Hans Bickel and others) and of Innsbruck and Vienna (Jakob Ebner and others for the 1st ed., and Alexandra Lenz and others for the 2nd ed.) (Ammon, Bickel, Ebner et al., 2004; 2nd ed. Ammon, Bickel, Lenz et al., 2016). It was based on the exact definition of model texts, prominently newspapers and valid codices, which were carefully compared between the various nations and regions of the German language, the separate 'centers' (*Zentren*) of the language, as they were called (cf. Ammon, Bickel, Lenz et al., 2016: xii–xiii, xil–lxiii). It is the first dictionary of this kind for any pluricentric language and has been a considerable success being listed on bestseller lists for nonfiction. It contains all national and regional standard variants of German (different from general German variants, standard in all the German-speaking countries and regions). They form separate lemmas, listed in alphabetic order, from each of which references are made to all their synonyms treated in separate articles. That way, any national or regional standard variant can be found easily, with the relevant information.

The dictionary has enhanced cooperation among the various German-speaking countries and regions and helped promote German globally. The fact that a separate edition has appeared for China, with the comprehensive introduction translated into Chinese, indicates the dictionary's global reach. Similar dictionaries, following the tested, fully functional structure of the German version, could or should be produced for other pluricentric languages.

I consider my own pluricentric endeavors as an example of how regional and global research can be fruitfully combined. This thought takes us to my concluding remark, which should be short, to avoid unnecessary repetition. My report shows how my personal life has been entangled with the modern history—of my place of birth, my country and, actually, that of the entire globe. It was from such entanglement that my view of, and interests in, languages has developed, as also has my research as a linguist, especially a sociolinguist. Though serious attempts at explaining the relationship of my own and my surroundings' history appear hopeless, if only because ex post facto explanations are generally treacherous, they may still satisfy our desire to understand our world to some extent. May this desire, gradually at least, make the world more rational—and, as a consequence, more peaceful.

Questions for Discussion

1. Think of languages or varieties of languages of divergent standing and prestige that different people use who interact or live together, drawing from the descriptions in the text above and specify these divergences and their effects on their speakers.

2. Try to gauge the advantages or disadvantages—personally, socially and regarding career perspectives—and think of possibilities of increasing linguistic fairness and justice. Do not forget to examine your proposals carefully for unwelcomed side effects.

Author Profile

Ulrich Ammon has been professor of sociolinguistics at the University Duisburg-Essen and president of GAL, the German branch of AILA. He has published 16 monographs and edited numerous books, among them *The Dominance of English as a Language of Science. Effects on Other Languages and Language Communities.* He has also co-edited the yearbook *Sociolinguistica* (1987 ff.) and the two encyclopedias *Sociolinguistics: An International Handbook* (3 vols., 2nd ed. 2004–6) and *Wieser Encyclopaedia Western European Languages* (2 vols., 2008). Email: ulrich .ammon@uni-due.de.

References

Ammon, U. (1972). *Dialekt, soziale Ungleichheit und Schule.* Weinheim & Basel: Beltz. 2nd, expand. ed. 1973.

Ammon, U. (1973). *Dialekt und Einheitssprache in ihrer sozialen Verflechtung. Eine empirische Untersuchung zu einem vernachlässigten Aspekt von Sprache und sozialer Ungleichheit.* Weinheim & Basel: Beltz.

Ammon, U. (1977). School problems of regional dialect speakers. Methods, results, and ideological implications of empirical investigations in Southern Germany. *Journal of Pragmatics*, 1, 47–68.

Ammon, U. (1978). *Schulschwierigkeiten von Dialektsprechern. Empirische Untersuchungen sprachabhängiger Schulleistungen und des Schüler—und Lehrerbewußtseins—mit sprachdidaktischen Hinweisen.* Weinheim & Basel: Beltz.

Ammon, U. (1989a). Towards a descriptive framework for the status/ function (social position) of a language within a country. In U. Ammon (ed.), *Status and function of languages and language varieties* (pp. 21–106). Berlin: de Gruyter.

Ammon, U. (1989b). Die Schwierigkeiten der deutschen Sprachgemeinschaft aufgrund der Dominanz der englischen Sprache. *Zeitschrift für Sprachwissenschaft*, *8* (2), 257–72.

Ammon, U. (1990). German or English? The problems of language choice experienced by German-Speaking scientists. In P. Nelde (ed.), *Language conflict and minorities* (pp. 33–51). Bonn: Dümmler.

Ammon, U. (1995). *Die deutsche Sprache in Deutschland, Österreich und der Schweiz. Das Problem der nationalen Varietäten.* Berlin & New York: de Gruyter.

Ammon, U. (1998). *Ist Deutsch noch internationale Wissenschaftssprache? Englisch auch für die Hochschullehre in den deutschsprachigen Ländern.* Berlin & New York: de Gruyter.

Ammon, U. (ed.) (2001). *The dominance of English as a language of science: Effects on the non-English languages and language communities.* Berlin & New York: Mouton de Gruyter.

Ammon, U. (2003). On the social forces that determine what is standard in a language and on conditions of successful implementation. *Sociolinguistica*, 17: 1–10. Also in H. Omdal & R. Røsstad (eds.), *Krefter of motkrefter i språknormeringa* (pp. 11–24). Kristiansand: Høyskole Forlaget & Norwegian Academic Press.

Ammon, U. (2015). *Die Stellung der deutschen Sprache in der Welt*. Berlin, München & Boston: de Gruyter.

Ammon, U. & Löwer, U. (1977). *Schwäbisch*. Düsseldorf: Schwann.

Ammon, U. & Cheshire, J. (eds.) (1989). *Dialekt und Schule in den europäischen Ländern/ Dialect and school in the European countries/ Dialecte et école dans les pays européennes*. Tübingen: Niemeyer.

Ammon, U., Bickel, H., Ebner, J. et al. (2004). *Variantenwörterbuch des Deutschen. Die Standardsprache in Österreich, der Schweiz und Deutschland sowie in Liechtenstein, Luxemburg, Ostbelgien und Südtirol*. Berlin & New York: de Gruyter.

Ammon, U., Bickel, H., Lenz, A. et al. (2016). *Variantenwörterbuch des Deutschen. Die Standardsprache in Österreich, der Schweiz, Deutschland, Liechtenstein, Luxemburg, Ostbelgien und Südtirol sowie Rumänien, Namibia und Mennonitensiedlungen*. 2nd, renewed and expand. ed. Berlin & Boston: de Gruyter.

Bausinger, H. (ed.) (1973). *Dialekt als Sprachbarriere?* Tübingen: Tübinger Vereinigung für Volkskunde.

Bernstein, B. (1959). A public language: Some sociological implications of a linguistic form. *British Journal of Sociology*, 10, 311–26.

Bernstein, B. (1964). Elaborated and restricted codes: Their social origins and some consequences. In J. J. Gumperz & D. Hymes (eds.), *The ethnography of communication* (pp. 55– 69). Menasha/ WISC: American Anthropological Association.

Besch, W. & Löffler, H. (1973). Hochsprache/Mundart—kontrastiv. In Bausinger, 89–110.

Cheshire, J., Edwards, V., Münstermann, H. & Weltens, B. (eds.) (1989). *Dialect and education: Some European perspectives*. Clevedon & Philadelphia: Multilingual Matters.

Clyne, Michael (1984). *Language and society in the German-speaking countries*. Cambridge UK: Cambridge University Press.

de Swaan, A. (1991). Notes on the emerging global language system: Regional, national and supranational. *Media, Culture and Society*, 13, 309–23.

de Swaan, A. (2001). *Words of the world. The global language system*. Cambridge: Polity Press.

Kloss, H. (1952). *Die Entwicklung neuer germanischer Kultursprachen von 1800 bis 1950*. München: Pohl.

Österreichisches Wörterbuch. (1979). 35th ed. Wien: Jugend und Volk.

Van Parijs, P. (2011). *Linguistic justice—for Europe and for the world*. New York: Oxford University Press.

PART II

Global English: Views from the Classroom

INTRODUCTION

Global English: Views from the Classroom

Maryam Borjian

> *Indeed, if there is one predictable consequence of a language becoming a global language, it is that nobody owns it any more. Or rather, everyone who has learned it now owns it—'has a share in it' might be more accurate—and has the right to use it in the way they want.*
>
> David Crystal (2003: 2–3)

> *[O]nce Britannia ruled the waves, now it is English which rules them. The British empire has given way to the empire of English.*
>
> Robert Phillipson (1992: 1)

One of the most notable linguistic outcomes of globalization is perhaps the universalization of the English language. Over the past three decades or so, English has enjoyed a center-stage position in many social settings at the international level, such as international commerce, diplomacy, sciences, technology and education. Such dominance on the part of one language has been a subject of both praise and criticism, judging by the many terms and metaphors coined by different scholars to address the English language as: a 'global' language (Crystal, 2003; Graddol, 1998), 'the language of growth and development' (Negash, 2011; also Chapter 4 of this volume), the language of 'imperialism' (Phillipson, 1992), 'the hub of the world language system' (de Swaan, 2013), 'one of the most important world languages' (Ammon, 2013; also Chapter 3 of this volume), a 'killer language' (Skutnabb-Kangas, 2000), a 'lingua Frankensteinia' (Phillipson, 2008), and a 'Hydra' (Rapatahana & Bunce, 2012; Bunce et al., 2016; also, Chapters 5 and 6 of this volume).

Regardless of how English is perceived, there is no doubt that it is the most powerful language of our time; a language that has been 'on the move' (Pennycook, 2012) and tirelessly 'in motion' (Blommaert, 2010). It has been traveling through time, across spaces (geographical and virtual) and around borders (social, political, cultural and linguistic). It has found itself new homes or adopted homes and can be found everywhere and anywhere: both in 'expected' and in 'unexpected' places (Pennycook, 2012). To this end, Part II of this book (Chapters 4–8) is devoted to the theme of English, its position within educational settings worldwide and its positive and negative outcomes.

Chapter 4 is written by Nigussie Negash Yadete—an Ethiopian scholar of TESOL/applied linguistics, a non-native English-speaking educator (NNET, hereafter)—who has devoted most of his professional life to the teaching of English in Ethiopia and elsewhere. Although he does not disregard the unequal distribution of power that exists between the nation-states of the Global North and those of the Global South, and he acknowledges the negative impacts of English on local languages and cultures, he refutes the view that individuals and nation-states (especially those of the postcolonial contexts) should reject English on the pretext of its previous colonial-imperial track records. Applying a 'pragmatic-realistic stance,' using his own term, Negash Yadete perceives English as the language of 'opportunities,' 'development' and 'growth' (at the individual, societal, national and international levels), especially in contexts in which indigenous languages cannot offer such opportunities. He acknowledges the importance of learning indigenous languages, but at the same time, he is an advocate for learning English. In his view, the main challenge of many developing countries, including Ethiopia, in the teaching and learning of English is not 'linguistic imperialism,' but rather a lack of resources, especially of a qualified teaching force familiar with teaching methodologies to teach English in the developing world. Drawing on his own lived experiences, Negash Yadete invites the reader to the journey of his life: from a shepherd boy in rural Ethiopia to a trans-migrant TEFL educator and scholar. He also provides reasons why learning English can be beneficial for all and how it has helped him achieve his goals.

The popularity of English worldwide and in postcolonial contexts has been examined by other scholars, including the late Joshua Fishman (et al., 1996) and Bernard Spolsky (2004), who equally reject the notion of 'linguistic imperialism' as the main force behind the expansion of English. They argue that English has adapted a new role for itself in those settings and elsewhere. This is what I, equally, showed in my research (Borjian, 2013) on English in post-revolutionary Iran: a nation in which English has been localized and indigenized by its post-revolutionary, anti-imperialist government over the past four decades or so, while, by contrast, Standard American and British English have been in vogue amongst Iranian people. This is what Lin and Martin (2005) regard as the 'postcolonial puzzle,' which can no longer be explained by binary opposing terms, like 'linguistic imperialism' or the power of the 'subaltern that strikes back.' For today, many peoples and governments seek to learn and cultivate English locally, without any external coercion.

Chapter 5 is written by Vaughan Rapatahana, a celebrated poet of New Zealand, existential philosopher, speaker of Māori, TESOL/applied linguist scholar, and, last but not least, native English-speaking teacher/educator (hereafter, NET). Rapatahana is known for his critical stance towards the global hegemony of English. In 2012, he and his colleague, Pauline Bunce (the author of Chapter 6 of this book), co-coined the metaphor of 'English language as Hydra,' portraying English as the multi-headed monster of the ancient Greek mythology, which had to be confronted and tamed, for otherwise, it would destroy world languages and cultures. In Chapter 5, he uses the metaphor of 'thief' to describe the English language: a metaphor that emerged from his countless interactions with many students in different parts of the world, to whom he taught English as a foreign language. It was through such interactions that he came to realize that the learning of English was an 'unwanted imposition' on the majority of his students. Likewise, he reflects on the many privileges offered to him as a NET while teaching English overseas. Yet, gradually, he decided to turn his back both to English and to his profession, for he realized that he was emptying the minds of his students of their own local languages, cultures and world views. As a poet, Rapatahana closes his chapter with two of his poems: one on English, and the other on Māori, his mother-tongue; a language that had long been suppressed under the hegemony of English, but has recently been recognized as an official language in New Zealand.

Like Vaughan Rapatahana, Pauline Bunce (Chapter 6) takes a critical stance towards the global English Language Teaching industry (hereafter, ELT). Australian by nationality and a TESOL/applied linguist by profession, she has taught English for many years in different parts of Asia. In her chapter, she invites the reader into her English language classrooms in Hong Kong as a springboard to challenge the dominance of 'native speakerism' that hovers over the global ELT industry. Native speakerism, which has been the subject of criticism by other scholars (Phillipson, 1992; Holliday, 2005), is an ideology that favors the norms and world views of native speakers of English, and uses such norms as the main basis for designing English textbooks, teaching materials, methodologies and standards. Consequently, there is a mismatch between global ELT practices, on the one hand, and the needs of students and the daily reality of classrooms, on the other. Bunce's paper focuses on the needs of students from non-alphabetic-scripted backgrounds, such as her secondary school students in Hong Kong, and how their alphabetic-literacy challenges have been seriously overlooked by a global, yet myopic, ELT industry that presumes its learners have an easy familiarity with the sound-and-letter correspondences of the English alphabet. 'Alphabetism' is only one of many 'blind spots' in global ELT. Bunce is a language activist whose chapter describes her public battles with school, system and professional authorities in order to champion the case for recognizing biscriptal learners of English.

The global ELT industry and its native-speakerism are equally the central themes of Elizabeth Erling's paper (Chapter 7). Yet, unlike Rapatahana and Bunce, Erling offers an alternative image of native speakers: an image, that in her view, is often overlooked in the TESOL/applied linguistic academic research; that is, the 'demonization,' 'villainization,' 'idealization' and even 'othering' of NETs. Her message is that in the context of the market-driven globalized world, we need to remember that the so-called privileges of NETs are riddled with complexity, and are often accompanied by 'essentialization,' 'commodification' and sometimes even 'exploitation.' In her chapter, Erling takes the reader to South Korea in the 1990s, where she began her career as a teacher of English. At the time, she was in her early 20s, living in the US in Atlanta, Georgia, with a bachelor's degree in hand, and with no job, but a soaring student loan whose six-month grace period was coming to an end. It was within such a climate that globalization was roaring and many countries were opening their borders to the global market economy, communication technology, internationalization and the English language: South Korea was one of those nations. Drawing on both her notes and fragments of her memory, Erling reflects on the many issues and challenges that she, as a NET, encountered in Korea (both inside and outside her classrooms). Yet, at the same time, she is equally grateful to Korea for giving her the opportunity to cross national, linguistic and sociocultural borders.

In Chapter 8, Ruhma Choudhury challenges the global ELT industry for its 'English-only ideology,' which favors the use of English only in ESL/EFL classrooms. Being born and raised in Bangladesh, where English came to her as the medium of instruction, she later moved to the US, where she obtained her doctorate in TESOL, taught English and became a scholar of TESOL/applied linguistics. Choudhury unravels her very self to deconstruct the ways in which she had internalized English-only ideology and used it in her own English classrooms for many years. Gradually, however, after coming in contact with critical TESOL/applied linguistic research, she decided not to follow this ideology, allowing students to use their first language in her English classrooms, for, in her view, the former can serve as a resource in learning the latter. Drawing on the postmodern-poststructuralist pedagogy of 'translanguaging' (García, 2009; García & Wei, 2014), Choudhury argues that languages do not sit separately in different compartments in our brains; but rather, they constantly interact with one another. Consequently, such interactions should be taken into account in the teaching and learning of foreign languages, including English. In her view, translanguaging can serve as pedagogy in having bi/multilingual citizens in the 21st century who are proficient in their mother tongue(s) and in the global language of communication.

References

Ammon, U. (2013). World languages: Trends and futures. In N. Coupland (ed.), *The handbook of language and globalization* (pp. 101–122). Malden, MA: Wiley-Blackwell.

Blommaert, J. (2010). *The sociolinguistics of globalization*. Cambridge: Cambridge University Press.

Borjian, M. (2013). *English in post-revolutionary Iran: From indigenization to internationalization*. Bristol: Multilingual Matters.

Bunce, P., Phillipson, R., Rapatahana, V. & Tupas, R. (eds.) (2016). *Why English? Confronting the Hydra*. Bristol: Multilingual Matters.

Crystal, D. (2003). *English as a global language*. Cambridge: Cambridge University Press.

de Swaan, A. (2013). Language systems. In N. Coupland (ed.), *The handbook of language and globalization* (pp. 56–76). Malden, MA: Wiley-Blackwell.

Fishman, J. Conrad, A. & Rubal-Lopez, A. (eds.) (1996). *Post-imperial English: Status change in former British and American colonies*, 1940–1990. Berlin: Mouton de Gruyter.

García, O. (2009). *Bilingual education in the 21st century: A global perspective*. Malden, MA: Wiley-Blackwell.

García, O. & Wei, L. (2014). *Translanguaging: Language, bilingualism and education*. New York: Palgrave Macmillan.

Graddol, D. (1998). *The future of English: Guide to forecasting the popularity of the English language in the 21st century*. London: The British Council.

Holliday, A. (2005). *The struggle to teach English as an international language*. Oxford: Oxford University Press.

Lin, A. & Martin, P.W. (eds.) (2005). *Decolonization, globalization: Language-in-education policy and practices*. Clevedon: Multilateral Matters.

Negash, N. (2011). English language in Africa: An impediment or a contributor to development. In H. Coleman (ed.) *Dreams and realities: Developing countries and the English language* (pp. 161–183). London: The British Council.

Pennycook, A. (2012). *Language and mobility: Unexpected places*. Bristol: Multilingual Matters.

Phillipson, R. (2008). *Linguistic imperialism continued*. London: Routledge.

Phillipson, R. (1992). *Linguistic imperialism*. Oxford: Oxford University Press.

Rapatahana, V. & Bunce, P. (eds.) (2012). *English language as Hydra: Its impacts on non-English language cultures*. Bristol: Multilingual Matters.

Skutnabb-Kangas, T. (2000). *Linguistic genocide in education—or worldwide diversity and human rights?* Mahwah, NJ: Lawrence Erlbaum.

Spolsky, B. (2004). *Language policy*. Cambridge: Cambridge University Press.

4

A JOURNEY WITH ENGLISH

Reexamining the Pragmatic Stance toward the Language of Globalization

Nigussie Negash Yadete

> *The English language is nobody's special property. It is the property of the imagination: it is the property of the language itself.*
>
> Derek Walcott (cited in Edwards, 2008: 37)

Introduction

The dominance of the English language and globalization in the world are inseparably intertwined (Johnson 2009). Unless drastic changes happen that can reverse this trend, the present world is fast globalizing and integrating. The bigger pragmatic reasons of survival within an increasingly competitive and interdependent world would require a global lingua franca for interaction. Due to different historical factors, the English language has assumed its current global status, which has, in turn, led to a contestation, or debate, among scholars, dividing them into the optimistic and pessimistic camps. The optimists (such as Esch, 2009) perceive English as a language of 'empowerment' and 'growth,' both at the individual and societal levels, which is underpinned by the idea that language can be manipulated and used for economic and social gains through a critical awareness of language use, about which Esch says:

> [L]anguage is a symbolic tool for the exercise of power and influence. Through critical language awareness, we can take control of the multiple ways in which we participate in and reproduce dominant discourses in society. (Esch, 2009: 2)

Esch goes on to relate English to two concepts that are dominant in the current development literature: 'Human Capital Approach (HCA)' and the

'Human Capability Development Approach.' The first concept associates learning the English language with the instrumental role it has for individual and societal economic gains, whereas, the second concept refers to its "capacity for personal development and potential for learning further and to access new forms of knowledge which open the mind and benefit society" (Esch, 2009: 4). Thus, Esch's recommendation is to promote the teaching and learning of English for its economic gains, both at the individual, societal and national levels.

On the other side of the theoretical spectrum, there stand pessimist scholars, like the critics of 'linguistic imperialism' (Phillipson, 1992; Salleh, 2012) or 'neonationalism' (Thiong'o, 1988), who perceive English as an instrument of global capitalism, imperialism, dominance, hegemony and exploitation. Their aim is to resist the so-called hegemony of the imperial/colonial languages, which includes English, as a means to empower individuals, especially those from postcolonial contexts, through learning their own languages and cultures.

Some other thinkers, like Ali and Alamin Mazrui, present a balanced view of language. Perceiving any form of 'linguistic determinism,' including 'linguistic imperialism' and 'linguistic neonationalism,' as a radicalized view of Sapir-Whorf's hypothesis of linguistic relativism, they argue that:

> the position of the linguistic neonationalists—who see a cause and effect relationship between African languages and mental decolonization—can find little support in the colonial and post-colonial history of language use and language policies in Africa [. . .]. What the neonationalists have done in fact is make a fetish of a language, endowing it with the power of colonization or liberation in a manner that is ahistorical, static and undialectical. (Mazrui & Mazrui, 1998: 55)

There is no doubt that European colonization of Africa has affected the linguistic dynamics of the colonized countries. However, many writings on the expansion of English as linguistic imperialism seem to present the negative aspects of world history as inherent characteristics of the language itself.

In fact, as historical records show, the English language and its speakers are not the first to invade Africa. With the purpose of empire expansion, many others, namely Arabs, Greeks, Turks and the Portuguese, have come before them. Africa's interaction with all of them has endowed it with more than 'triple heritages' (Mazrui, 1986): indigenous, Islamic, Western, non-Western and Judo-Christian. These heritages permeate our continental, national and individual citizens' stories. For instance, the arrival of Arabic to Africa, which had also impacted the indigenous cultures and languages, has not been criticized as much as English has been for its hegemony on African indigenous languages. Neither has the attempt of other countries—like China (Magaisa, 2009, cited in Negash, 2011)—in exporting their languages and cultures to other nations, been questioned. Africa has experienced its own internal invasions, too, one group subjugating the cultures and languages of other groups. In my home country, Ethiopia, regimes from the north, especially the Amhara ethnic group, employed aggressive empire expansion campaigns that led to the occupation of other self-governing ethnic groups, which were less aggressive. Hence, we cannot escape or undo our complex histories. Instead, we seek methods to heal the pain (if possible) and to move forward.

In Ethiopia, my country of origin on which this chapter is grounded, the English language has assumed prestige, as learning it is perceived to lead to empowerment in the manner discussed above. My aim in this chapter is to reexamine the pragmatic-realistic stance that I (Negash, 2011) and many others (Crystal, 1997; Esch, 2009; Kamal & Norton, 2002; Lee & Norton, 2009) have come to adopt towards English as a global language. Through an autoethnographic method, I will present a retrospective analysis of my journey from a shepherd boy in rural Ethiopia to an expatriate, non-native English-speaking teacher (hereafter, NNET) and an academic. I will also draw on the existing literature and my professional and scholarly experiences to reflect on the opportunities English avails and the challenges it still creates as a global language.

Historical and Political Precedents of English in Ethiopia

My personal story of learning English as a foreign language is situated within national and global historical events. English first arrived in Africa during the slave trade between Europeans and West Africans. It came in the 19th century, during the scramble for Africa, i.e., the invasion, occupation, division, colonization and annexation of African territory by European powers between 1881 and 1914. English in Ethiopia, the only country that withstood European colonization, has a slightly different story. The language came during the World War II and has remained there ever since. On the foot of World War II arose the Cold War (1945–1990), an ideological confrontation that divided the world into two large spheres of interests: the capitalist West and the socialist East (for more on this, see Murphy, 2003). During the long course of the Cold War, the importance of the English language increased or diminished, based on the ideological block a particular country allied with. For the superpowers aggressively promoting their political and economic interests, language was used as the main weapon.

Within such a climate, smaller countries, like Ethiopia, had no other alternative but to side with one or the other ideological block for survival (Findlay, 2011). Haile-Selassie, the Ethiopian emperor at the time, was courting friendships with Great Britain and the United States, both of whom were advancing their own strategic interests in Africa and in other parts of the world, countering the influence of USSR and its allies. It was then that Haile-Selassie, the Ethiopian emperor, introduced English to Ethiopia for pragmatic reasons. He saw its importance as a language of science, technology, diplomacy and commerce. These were functions that no other indigenous languages could fulfill. Because of very favorable policies at the time, the English language also attained a high prestige in the country;

speaking it, especially with an American or British standard accent, became almost a marker of learnedness and high social status (Negash, 2005).

However, in the 1970s the Ethiopian socialist military regime overthrew Haile Selassie's feudalistic imperial system, and established alliance with the socialist block, headed by the USSR, which led to castigating English as the language of imperialism. All Western teachers, especially British and American, were forced to leave the country. At the time, Ethiopia did not have sufficient qualified local teachers. Attempting to give a quick-fix solution to the problem, the new Ethiopian socialist government started assigning students from high school to teach without proper qualification and teacher training. This policy began the ever-spiraling deterioration of the quality of education, in general, and English language teaching, in particular (Tekeste, 2006).

On the other hand, hundreds of Ethiopians were given scholarships in universities in Russia and its allies in the socialist Eastern Europe, with the hope of getting socialist-oriented skilled manpower that would run the socialist government machine. Nonetheless, Russia's cultural and linguistic influences in Ethiopia were minimal, save in the areas of ideology and military (which came in the form of help it gave to Ethiopia during its war with the neighboring Somalia). When I started going to school in 1968, the situation was particularly worse in schools in the rural parts of Ethiopia.

Growing Up Straddling Cultures and Languages

I am not what happened to me, I am what I choose to become.
Carl Gustav Jung (cited in Ferro, 2012: 96)

My positive attitude towards English, a foreign language and my third language, arises from growing up in the culturally and linguistically diverse environments of Ethiopia. I was born and brought up in Arsi, a rural fertile area in today's Oromo Regional State in Ethiopia. My parents were peasants whose ancestors, from Amhara and Oromo ethnic groups, came as soldiers from the central part of Ethiopia during Ethiopian Emperor Menelik's territorial expansion (between 1900 and 1906 to the east, south and west). Menelik's empire-building campaign or 'Ethiopianization' (Zahorik & Tesome, 2009) was a consolidation of his predecessor's, Emperor Tewodros, policy. The 'forced assimilation' policy pursued by subsequent regimes brought all ethnic groups under one unifying supra-ethnic culture and super-language, Amharic.

At one time, the community in which I grew up had resisted the occupying army of Emperor Menelik. By the accounts of some political historians (Ararsa, 2016), the event led to the loss of many lives. Nevertheless, the ruthless social engineering policy of 'Ethiopianization' suppressed and degraded other ethnic identities (Moges, 2010). I was born in Ethiopia many years after these political and social transformations had taken place. I grew up in the community playing and herding cattle and sheep with Christian and Muslim Oromo children. It was not obvious to me that I was a descendant of these 'invading aliens.' I grew up crossing different cultural boundaries, acquiring different cultural and linguistic identities. At home, my mother, a very strong-spirited and intelligent woman, spoke two languages fluently: one, Amharic, her mother tongue, and the other, Oromo, her second language, which she learned after being married to my Oromo father and living in the Oromo-speaking community. My father, too, spoke both languages fluently. These have been the two dominant languages in Ethiopia: Amharic, imposed as an official and *lingua franca* in the country, and Oromo, the language spoken by the largest ethnic group in the country. They were spoken at our home interchangeably, and naturally, we became bilingual. We were, however, oblivious to the power tension and enmity between the two ethnic groups and the contestation between their respective languages. Learning a language, including a foreign language, like English, I naturally perceived as a challenge, which I had to surmount to realize my potential.

Learning English as a Foreign Language in Difficult Circumstances: Primary School

I was the first male child of my parents, who were uneducated farmers, and expected me to become a farmer, too. I recall that I was the most eager of my siblings who wanted to go to school; however, my parents had never talked to us about such a possibility. To quench my insatiable desire for education, one fortunate day in 1968, I literally took myself to school by sneaking away from home. Since there was no preschool system in the village, I started formal school from the first grade of primary school. I was so hungry for learning that I learned fast: the Arabic numerals, basic arithmetic and Amharic letters taught in the primary grades. Amharic language was the medium of instruction in grades 1–6. I remember learning to read and write in Amharic in such a very short period of time that my ability even impressed my parents, who allowed me to continue my education. They said that I was the child whose lot would be education.

Unfortunately, Oromo, one of the two languages I grew up speaking at home and in the community, was excluded from formal education. It was not taught or used as a medium of instruction. Although Oromo was the main language the community used for communication in many social settings, it was not used for written administrative communications. With hindsight, my early education disconnected me from the rich Oromo culture and language: a missed opportunity to build on the experiences and concepts I had learned from childhood. Contrary to what many proponents of 'linguistic imperialism' argue, the diminishing use of the African indigenous languages was not always because of the foreign languages, like English, that had conquered the continent. There is no doubt that the arrival of the European colonial systems and languages was catalytic in ethnic tensions in Africa. Nor is there any doubt that the colonial education systems and language policies did not value the indigenous knowledge and languages. Yet, it would be misleading to blame only colonialism, for the indigenous cultures and languages had, already, been jostling for hegemony before the arrival of the colonial powers and their languages.

My first encounter with English as a foreign language in Ethiopia was in the third grade of school. It was taught as a subject in primary school (grades 1–6). On average, we were taught English four times per week, each time for 45 minutes. Similar to Amharic, we were taught to memorize English letters and the names of pictures from the school textbooks. I heard English spoken only in the classrooms. Therefore, my learning of the language depended solely on what the teacher translated, made us say or do in the classroom; it was an absolutely teacher-dependent learning. As I now recall, the whole teaching and learning setup of the school system in Ethiopia at the time was similar to that of a church and listening to a priest's sermon. In both places, someone stood up on a stage and spoke at length, and the audience listened and watched quietly. The only difference was that in school there were too many exercises and exams, aiming to test our memorization skill. Nonetheless, I loved learning; I loved my teachers and I loved being in the school compound itself. A day in school gave me respite from the hard labor of herding the cattle and sheep in the harsh weather conditions.

The Joy of Learning and the Challenges of Studying in English: Secondary School

From early childhood exposure to working hard in harsh conditions of rural Ethiopia, I had developed endurance. This characteristic helped me to overcome many obstacles I faced in my education. I completed the elementary school faster than my peers, for it took me only four years to finish the standard six years of primary school. I progressed to grade 7, the start of junior secondary level.

Now, the language of instruction changed from Amharic to English. I had to study all subject matters in the language, in which I could hardly converse. To survive the linguistic and conceptual demands, I had to resort to rote learning individually and in groups. The teachers wrote extensive notes on the blackboard, which we copied and memorized and regurgitated in the exams. The exams were, most often, too mechanical, like multiple choice, gap-fill, true/false statements or matching words, with a few short-answer questions.

By the time I started my formal education in 1968, speaking English had become a marker of prestige and learnedness in Ethiopia. Nevertheless, the teaching of English did not improve much in high school. The only time I came across the language was through the textbooks we studied and listening to teachers. There was literally no exposure to the language used by native speakers of English in a natural setting. My English teachers in the secondary school, generally, did not use a teaching methodology that would make learning interesting or would increase communicative competence. They focused on preparing us for grade 12 and the National Secondary School Leaving Examination. Therefore, they spent the majority of time teaching us discrete grammar and vocabulary exercises. At the time, Ethiopia was under a socialist regime with its 'Ethiopianization' of English textbooks, a sort of ELT 'indigenization' and 'localization' process (Borjian, 2013) reported elsewhere in the world. Hence, we did not come across any culturally alien content, for our English textbooks had already been appropriated by our socialist government. My motivation for learning English was driven solely by the hunger for learning and achievement. I wanted to be praised by the teacher, so I competed against my classmates to get the highest marks and the top class rank.

The best memory I have of learning English in the secondary school was in grade 8. The teacher made us practice reading aloud in class and made us compete against one another. This teacher was also my role model in many ways: I liked the way he spoke English, and even the way he dressed and walked. His English sounded nicer than the English other teachers spoke. Luckily, I was the best in my class in reading aloud. Encouraged by my teacher's praise in front of my classmates, I practiced a lot of reading aloud. I did it anywhere, even under the trees. This was how I developed my authentic Ethiopian accent. Further into the high school years, I began to be more comfortable studying through English. However, we had difficulty following lessons taught by Indian teachers, who were brought in from India to fill the trained manpower shortage faced in the country. When the British and Americans left due to the Ethiopian socialist regime, the government had to rely on foreigners who spoke English. As a former colony of Britain, India provided plentiful English teachers for cheaper wages than teachers from other English-speaking countries. My difficulty in the Indian teachers' lessons was to understand their accent. However, after a little while, this eased and I became familiar. We students eventually learned to hear what the Indian teacher said, and we realized they had a lot to offer us. Hence, accents were no longer a barrier to my receptivity of the expatriate teachers. Meeting Indians in my rural secondary school about three decades ago was my first experience of English as a global language. English was the only language connecting me with Indians, who had completely different cultural and linguistic backgrounds.

English at the Tertiary Level: Keeping Up with Students from Private Schools

I completed secondary school and scored good results that enabled me to join university, a setting in which English continued to be the medium of instruction. The university education did not get easier for many students with a low proficiency in English, for we were, after all, from the rural part of Ethiopia. Not only did the language difficulty increase, but also the teaching methodology changed. The teachers did not write extensive notes on the blackboard anymore; instead, they gave long lectures because the students were expected to take notes by themselves. Some studies have indicated that Ethiopian students join universities not only with low English proficiency, but also with a low academic competency (Haile-Michael, 1991; Negash, 2005). To remedy these deficiencies, English-language and academic-skills lessons were taught parallel with other academic subjects in the first year of university. Some teachers still kept emphasizing native-speaker-like accent, rather than the ability to communicate fluently, or intelligibly, in English. In the lessons, students who came from 'posh' private schools in the capital excelled, and we were terrified of saying anything in their presence. The teachers, most of the time, seemed to enjoy the beautiful accents of these elite students. Mostly, they called on them to answer questions. Again, people like me had to resort to sheer hard work and determination to achieve even a marginal pass in the first year of university. In retrospect, I think that it was total ignorance on the part of the teachers for English to be a global language, yet spoken by a greater number of non-native speakers than native speakers. Yet, in the absence of any natural speech community, we were being drilled to acquire a 'native-like' accent. Some teachers resorted to insults when students made mistakes in pronunciation. This made many of us anxious, frustrated and even lose interest in learning the language.

The poor English-language teaching methodology led to many students' failure not only in learning the language, but also in studying other subjects through English-medium instruction. Some education experts (Stoddart, 1986, cited in Haile-Michael, 1991; Tekeste, 2006) have criticized the English-medium policy in Ethiopia, calling it a failed policy and labeling it a medium of obstruction. Yet, these experts overlook the fact that the weakness in teaching methodology is a critical factor, contributing to a low English proficiency on the part of Ethiopian students. One wonders how, in the absence of effective language-teaching methodologies and with scarce resources, there are still many students who achieve a working level of English proficiency. To some extent, the coercive English-medium education policy and the foreign-language immersion model have created some conditions for language acquisition in Ethiopia. Students who engaged positively survived the challenge of the foreign-language barrier, whereas the frustrated ones disengaged and gave up. I believe that is where the battle to educate oneself is won or lost, in resource-constrained countries like Ethiopia.

A Shepherd Boy Becoming an ELT Academic

Although Ethiopia is known for having one of the oldest writing scripts, knowledge transmission has mainly been through oral traditions. While I was in school, books were scarce in Amharic, let alone in other languages. Learning the English language has helped me to overcome this limitation. After I joined Addis Ababa University Institute of Language Studies, in 1987, to major in foreign languages and literature, things started to look bright. The English language helped me to learn from the best minds in Africa and beyond. I began to comprehend and analyze the materials I was reading in English. This showed in my university exam results. What the lecturers failed to give me, I compensated for by reading literary works from Africa and other countries. I have wonderful memories of reading Western literature mostly from Britain and America: the works of Shakespeare, Thomas Hardy, Charles Dickens, Jonathan Swift, Aldus Huxley, George Orwell, Mark Twain, Maya Angelou, J. D. Salinger and many others.

My professors also exposed us to the best literary works of great African writers, such as Chinua Achebe, Wole Soyinka, Al-Tayeb Salih and others who wrote in English. English was the main language that connected African intellectuals, freedom fighters and their students, like me. There were no indigenous languages of the continent that could connect Africans with Africans and Africans with others on shared agendas. It was through English that I learned how the European countries had divided Africa among themselves and imposed cruel rules on the countries they colonized. The Europeans' divide-and-rule policy left 'time bombs,' which have been exploding in the forms of ethnic tensions, from time to time, here and there, throughout Africa. Ethiopia, though it was not officially colonized, experienced more than its fair share of the brutality of European aggression, during two fascist Italian invasions in 1895 and 1935, respectively. The Italians used weapons of mass destruction against the predominantly peasant mass resistance. It was only for the heroic acts of these Ethiopians that the country could stand up as a vanguard of subsequent independence movements elsewhere in the continent. There is no doubt that English was instrumental in spreading the news that galvanized other Africans to fight for independence. The very language that had been used by colonial oppressive systems gradually became a tool to connect African minds and unify them.

From the satirical novels of the African novelists and poets, I also learned about the irony of postcolonial Africa. The departure of the colonizers did not lead to freedom, justice and equality. The African rulers who took over power through resistance movements, that claimed thousands or even millions of citizens, became even more cruel and corrupt than their colonial counterparts (Ushie, 2008). Reading in English helped me to identify with the plight of intellectuals and the masses living under postcolonial African oppressive regimes.

Even today, Africa, unfortunately, needs English to draw attention to the atrocities its people inflict on one another. English, the language of the former colonial rulers, has become an instrument that freedom fighters use against political oppressions. It is a voice for the silenced masses under authoritarian and extremist regimes. It is a tool that the international advocacy groups' use against unfair global trade rules designed by the more powerful nations. It is the language of human rights groups using it to reveal the political incarceration of dissenting voices. It is the language that brings developing countries from different parts of the globe to deliberate on common agendas, such as fighting the economic disadvantages between the Global North and the Global South. It is the same language that all nations can use to address the climatic changes that have threatened the existence of humanity.

Surprisingly, I have no recollection of Ethiopian teachers questioning English or other foreign languages as the languages of colonizers. That is mainly due to the fact that Ethiopia, by its own decision, adopted English as the language of science, education and international communication. Educated Ethiopians do not seem to perceive that their minds have been 'colonized' through a foreign language. It is not apparent in any Ethiopian literary works that adopting English or any foreign language would be a means of allowing 'linguistic imperialism.'

Postgraduate Study in a Foreign Land

My next educational journey took me to the land of the English language itself, the United Kingdom. I spent a total of six and half years there, first, from 1992 to 1994, during which I obtained a master's degree in Teaching English as a Foreign Language (hereafter, TEFL), and then, from 2000 to 2005, during which I obtained my doctorate in language education.

During my graduate studies in the UK, I had the opportunity to meet some wonderful professors, whose guidance helped me to grow intellectually. However, my initial few months in England were not easy. I had difficulty adjusting to the weather, the food, the culture and the English language that was used naturally by its native speakers. I did not find the so-called Queen's English in our classrooms, unlike the way we had been forced to learn it in Ethiopia without even being exposed to it. I recall that I had been so accustomed to the bookish English of our Ethiopian school textbooks that having a conversation with native speakers of English was a formidable task. People spoke in natural accents so diverse that some did not even sound like English to me. Some people spoke unintelligibly and too fast for me to keep up with them. In my MA classes, there were 28 students, more than half of them native speakers, who were, to me, too chatty. The students talked so much, whereas the professors, who I thought had better knowledge, did not. Sometimes these social conversations were not sensible to my ears. I came from a cultural discipline of respecting age, because 'older would be wiser.' My fellow classmates and the English conversation did not fit my established cultural maxims of conversation. In this situation, I was suspicious that I was learning anything important from these chatty sessions. I had a Japanese classmate who also felt the same. My option was to listen. On the other hand, my silence was, at times, perceived as not having anything to say. Fortunately, being quiet did seem to pay off, in my case. I focused on important issues, and from the little that I spoke, my classmates seemed to pick something interesting.

Issues I Have Dealt with as an 'NNET' Academic

The English language has been my second passport and the only common language I have used to interact with non-Ethiopians and people from diverse cultural and linguistic backgrounds. So far, I have had the opportunity to travel to about 14 countries in 4 continents. I have attended and presented at various international conferences as well as trained teachers and teacher trainers from different countries. I am now working as an expatriate English teacher in a different country. Learning and teaching English has broadened my mind and made me an international person from Ethiopia. Nonetheless, proficiency in English has not made me a British, an American or any other native speaker of English, because any of these identities go deeper than proficiency in a language. Contrary to the views of some proponents of linguistic determinism or imperialism (Phillipson, 1992; Saleh, 2012; Thiong'o, 1988), the English language has not colonized my mind either. Nor are my thoughts constrained by it. My feelings and thoughts exist independently of the language. Actually, any language is limited when revealing deep and complex human thoughts. Now, after about forty years or so, I—the shepherd boy from a peasant family in rural Ethiopia—have acquired three languages: Amharic, Oromo, and English. I have these at my disposal to share my feelings and thoughts depending on who my interlocutor is.

I am grateful to my teachers and my students who have given me the joy of learning and teaching English. However, after investing myself in learning and teaching it for forty years or so—when I feel I have finally climbed the mountain and 'made it'—I am reminded that English is not my language. This is only because I am not a 'native speaker.' Then, I ask myself: Is English my language too? Is it really a global language? However qualified or successful, a non-native English-speaking teacher or academic has difficulty to be accepted as an equal to a person who is a 'native speaker.' I observe that this caste system in ELT is still being perpetuated in some contexts. For instance, international ELT jobs may not be open to non-native speakers of English as easily as they may be to native speakers or persons who hold passports of English-speaking countries.

Conclusion

The dominance of the English language in the world invokes much negativity associated with cultural, economic and political power imbalances between the Center and Periphery nations, i.e., native and non-native English-speaking countries, respectively (Phillipson, 1992). Perhaps, similar to millions of other 'non-native' English language speakers, my journey with the English language has been challenging, even at times disturbing and frustrating. It has equally been exciting and has added some unquestionable values to my life. The pragmatic-realistic stance that I have adopted in this chapter may not be in vogue in the Western academic circles, often dominated by the theories of imperialism, neo-imperialism, colonialism and neocolonialism, among others. Yet, in this chapter, I tried to show the reasons why I have such a position. My stance calls for pragmatism—working with the immediate reality, instead of fantasy. Whenever the opportunity has arisen, I have also put forward a case for balance in managing multilingualism in complex contexts like Africa (Batibo, 2007; Negash, 2011). In today's global world, multilingualism is the order of the day. Living in this era compels us to give due value to our indigenous languages, but at the same time, all citizens of the world should have the right and opportunity to become proficient users of English, the de facto global lingua franca. Learning English cannot be a luxury or a privilege given only to the selected few, i.e., the privileged social class. The children in resource-constrained contexts, children of rural areas of developing countries, have as much right as the city children of wealthy families to get the opportunity to learn English.

My own story reveals that absence of equitable allocation of resources can obstruct the learning and advancement of citizens of a country. In spite of not belonging to a well-off family, in my view, determined individuals with some assistance can, indeed, succeed. The education and language planning problems can lead to bad English-language learning experiences. The solution is not castigating a particular language, like English. If properly managed, as suggested by Esch (2009), it can complement the indigenous languages to empower and prepare individuals and nations not only for economic and social gains, but also for the multiculturalism and multilingualism that our time demands. Failing to learn a global language, English (for Africans, for instance), means being disconnected with one another and with the people of the other continents. Being disconnected is no longer affordable in a world that is becoming increasingly globalized and interconnected. Likewise, today's world is currently experiencing an unprecedented rate of human movement. Not knowing a global language inhibits the freedom of movement and disempowers those who, by chance or force of events, move out of the comfort of their cultures and languages.

Questions for Discussion

1. What are the benefits and challenges of learning English in the era of globalization, which demands proficiency in the global language, i.e., English? Should the English language be viewed as a contributor to equitable development or as a tool for maintaining the power gap between the Global North and Global South?
2. How do we resolve the contestation of ownership of the English language and determine what global model and standard we target in ELT education?

Author Profile

Nigussie Negash Yadete is an Ethiopian scholar of TESOL/applied linguistics, a non-native English-speaking teacher/educator (NNET), who has devoted most of his professional life to the teaching of English in Ethiopia and other places in the world (currently in the United Arab Emirates). Nigussie has obtained an MA and PhD from UK universities, and is an associate professor in English-language education. Based on his extensive curriculum and research experience,

Nigussie has coauthored resource books for teachers and teacher trainers in Sub-Saharan Africa and has published academic articles in journals and books. His current research interests include comparative analysis of language ideologies and policies and their impacts on education and development.

References

Ararssa, T. R. (2016). The peoples' ADWA: The imperative of embracing plural interpretation. Retrieved March 21, 2016: from: https://advocacy4oromia.org/2016/05/29/the-peoples-adwa-the-imperative-of-embracing-plural-interpretation/.

Batibo, H. M. (2007). Language use optimization as a strategy for national development. In H. Coleman (ed.), *Language and development: Africa and beyond* (pp. 15–26). Proceedings of the 7th International Language and Development Conference, British Council, Addis Ababa.

Borjian, M. (2013). *English in post-revolutionary Iran: From indigenization to internationalization*. Bristol: Multilingual Matters.

Crystal, D. (1997). *English as a global language*. Cambridge: Cambridge University Press.

Edwards, J. D. (2008). *Post-colonial literature*. New York: Palgrave MacMillan.

Esch, E. (2009). English and empowerment: Potential, issues, way forward. In N. Hussain, A. Ahmed & M. Zafar (eds.), *English and empowerment in the developing world* (pp. 2–26). Tyne: Cambridge Scholars Publishing.

Ferro, L. (2012). Finish line, recovering the self. *Journal of Hope and Healing, 2* (2), 95–98.

Findlay, R. A. (2011). Emperors in America: Haile-Selassie and Hirohito on tour. Dissertations and Theses, Paper 96, Portland State University.

Haile-Michael, A. (1991). Developing a service English syllabus to meet the academic demands and constraints in the Ethiopian university context. Unpublished PhD thesis. AAU.

Johnson, A. (2009). The rise of English: The language of globalization in China and the European Union. *Macalester International, 22* (12), 131–168.

Kamal, F. & Norton, B. (2002). Learner perspectives on the Youth Millennium Project: Critical literacy in action. *Contact, 28* (2), 70–76.

Lee, E. & Norton, B. (2009). The English language, multilingualism, and the politics of location. *International Journal of Bilingual Education and Bilingualism, 12* (3), 277–290.

Mazrui, A. A. (1986). *The Africans: A triple heritage*. Boston: Little, Brown and Company.

Mazrui, A. A. & Mazrui, A. M. (1998). *The power of babel: Language and governance in the African experience*. Chicago: University of Chicago Press.

Moges, Y. (2010). *Language ideologies and challenges of multilingual education in Ethiopia: The case of Harari region*. Oxford: African Books Collective.

Murphy, D. (2003). *The Cold War: 1945–1991. Great Britain: Collins Educational.*

Negash, N. (2005). Exploring adult learning principles in EAP classrooms: An Ethnographic-action research. PhD Thesis Submitted to the University of Exeter, UK.

Negash, N. (2011). English language in Africa: An impediment or a contributor to development. In H. Coleman (ed.), *Dreams and realities: Developing countries and the English language* (pp. 161–183). London, UK: British Council.

Phillipson, R. (1992). *Linguistic imperialism*. Oxford: Oxford University Press.

Salleh, M. H. (2012). Coda: One colonial language: One great tragic epic: English in Malaysia and beyond. In V. Rapatahana and P. Bunce (eds.), *English language as Hydra: Its impacts on non-English language cultures* (pp. 263–72). Bristol, UK: Multilingual Matters.

Tekeste, N. (2006). *Education in Ethiopia: From crisis to brink of collapse*. Uppsala: Nordiska Afrikainstitutet.
Thiong'o, N. (1988). *Decolonising the mind: The politics of language in African literature*. London: James Currey/Heinemann.
Ushie, J. (2008). Two Africans in one: Neo-colonialism and the African writer. *Writer of the Year JAL*, No. 5. Retrieved May 30, 2016 from: www.africaresearch.org/ncol.htm.
Zahorik, J. & Teshome, W. (2009). Debating language policy in Ethiopia. *Asian and African Studies*, *18*, 80–102.

5

ENGLISH LANGUAGE AS THIEF

Vaughan Rapatahana

> *& let's build a new waka, re-write the book, lets english-up/down/all around the world by ignoring English completely. . . . c'mon, it's not that difficult, eh. have a squint below, before you go . . .*
>
> (Rapatahana, 2016: para. 24)

Introduction

Based on my own extensive experience as an English language educator in a variety of traditionally non-English-speaking communities, I want to say this once and for all: that for many people, the English language has been force-fed to them and disseminated as somehow vital to their life-chances as a neutral and value-free panacea for everything, when in fact, it is all too often a thief of their time, their money, their own tongues and thus their cultural identities, their existential well-being.

As Judd (1983) noted about the role of the TESOL (teaching English to speakers of other languages) professional, it:

> is a political act, and those who are engaged in teaching English to non or limited English speakers are directly or indirectly implementing a language policy that promotes a form of language change in students [and] the possible contribution teachers are making to the demise of certain languages or linguistic communities (p. 265).

I wish to have TOEFL professionals critically self-reflect as to their own involvement in the thieving process that I will now explore more fully.

Professionally Lived Experiences

After several stints, over several decades, from the 1970s until this current decade, as a teacher of English as a 'second' language (foreign, surely) in several sites around the globe—including in my own homeland, Aotearoa, New Zealand—I began to feel more and more like a thief. I chose the notion of thief, because I increasingly felt that I was teaching middle-class, *Pākehā* (Caucasian)-derived Western culture and *Pākehā*-obsessed tropes and protocols, via the medium of the English language, to largely non-Caucasian students, whose first languages had never been English. Not only was I party to stealing their dollars, but also their time, their good humor, their own languages, their very *Weltanschauung* or comprehensive world view.

Generally, they expressed no real interest in acquiring the English language, but they had been given no choice by their parents, school administrations or governments—themselves all trapped in the zeitgeist of an increasingly globalized Anglo-American 'Englishism' in a world where there was much more transmission of electronically generated ideas and advertisements, as well as enhanced mobility of people. All around my students there often blared English-language computers, television screens, posters of Hollywood movies, irrelevant song lyrics lambasting local airwaves. English was forever in their face, swirling around them, cleverly placed there by profiteers from the language—whether they be tuition schools proclaiming invincible examination mastery or advertisers for a vast panoply of unnecessary Western products. It still inevitably is, as the various spin doctors of this language continue to push the vital 'requirement' to possess it.

In my role as a fully qualified, 'native-speaking' teacher of English, I have partaken in generously funded long-term stays in the Republic of Nauru (a small, isolated phosphate-producing island in the Central Pacific Ocean), Brunei Darussalam (a small, wealthy, oil-producing Sultanate on the wider island of Borneo), the People's Republic of China, the Hong Kong Special Administrative Region and in the United Arab Emirates. Most of these areas, of course, were formerly British colonies, while even the People's Republic of China suffered under the heinous British-instigated Opium Wars.

I have lived in superior accommodation, generously paid for under the terms of the respective contracts, on ample and above national average (often tax-free) salaries with the attached gratuities, incorporating funded medical insurance schemes, return airfares, interest-free car loans and ample holidays. I was, somehow, ranked as economically more worthy than over 90% of the local indigenous populations—let alone the poor local teachers of the same lingo—only because I was a NET, an apparent native speaker teacher of English. It did not ever seem to matter that I might not actually be a competent classroom teacher at any stage; the tongue itself seemed more important.

But, below the surface-level lip service, many indigenous people were pissed off by the presence of people such as myself. We were re-colonialists and we were ever-diminishing their own indigenous languages, via our well-remunerated preaching from the lectern of English and the concomitant stress on learning it to the detriment of their own tongues: a process which has also been creeping exponentially into primary school classes and kindergartens. We offered no guarantee whatsoever that any of them would ever gain a somehow better employment or could 'keep up' and 'succeed' if they ever 'mastered' the English language either—given that many of them weren't ever interested in so doing—as Zubeida Mustafa (2016), for example, has pointed out with regard to Pakistan, where so many of the younger generation strive unsuccessfully to become proficient in the language.

I can say that I feel some measure of self-disappointment in my own overall career as such an English language mercenary, as I recall sleeping students, heads across their folded arms, in Cantonese medium of instruction school English lessons in Hong Kong, where the tongue remains totally unnecessary for many. Indeed, my own children speak Cantonese as a first language and begrudgingly speak in English only if they have to. Yet, they were compelled to attend several classes in this alien language several times a week, for several years, just like the hundreds of students I taught for over ten years there, who had neither enthusiasm nor use for the tongue.

I remember well, angry young Arab boys in the United Arab Emirates, being forced to speak English arbitrarily, because their own government had insisted that they had to and had gone to huge expense to invite the British-based conglomerates, the Centre for British Teachers and Nord Anglia, among other such corporate dealers, to come to the we-need-English party. For these pupils, suffering mandatory English lessons was an unwelcome imposition, and several reacted with violent disdain to having to partake in such classes.

My recollections include able Bruneian students, who played the game and chanted rote English words in stifling, fan-driven classrooms, who were always picked up by their parents and transported home to a completely Bahasa Melayu or Malay language environment, itself perpetually outlasting the contract lives of their expatriate English mentors. In other words, no one utilized the English language at home or anywhere else, much in a Malay-as-first-language country. And never will.

I well recollect also striving to instill an arbitrarily imposed English-language syllabus on Nauruan students, who had been left to struggle in the incessant dry heat there, while their scholarship-rewarded peers were sent to Victoria, Australia, where they also had to deal with a similar English-language dominant alien curriculum and culture. Those who returned to Nauru Island rarely utilized this foreign tongue there either, for there was no call for them to do so.

I well recall several middle-aged Chinese men and women, sent to the language school where I was a mentor, after work hours, where—dog-tired after an all-day presence in their respective workplaces—they had to face down the demon English, because their employers insisted they do so. They smiled politely, but it must have been a grim experience for them all as they attempted to pronounce the twisted consonant curlicues of the English language.

None of these students needed English in their day-to-day lives, yet they had no choice in the matter. All the while, especially as the language was introduced to younger and younger schoolchildren and the incessant hum of 'Englishism' resounded more and more everywhere, inevitably, the local tongues fell into a process of some attrition, despite what I write above about English not being used at home. Because, by the sheer weight of its imposed omnipresence, agents of the language ensured no one could escape it, as well as ensuring they themselves received profitable emolument for their proffering of it. Some very potent and conniving cabals, then, are making the most from pushing their own self-serving and financially rewarding agendas. It is this minority of first-language speakers of English across the globe—whether they be Anglo-American, or comprador ethnic groupings within their own respective communities—that have the power, want to keep the power, are determined to install and instill their language on a far greater majority of English as a second or foreign language peoples and to ensure that these latter or their governments continue to pay for this wonderful 'gift.'

From my own 35 years plus of experience as a teacher of English as a foreign language, I can without hesitation say, then, that the majority of students I have taught are not so motivated or resourced as to want to accommodate the arrogant visitor: indeed, some are outright hostile to the imposition of this neo-imperialist tongue on their daily lives. They lack the intrinsic motivation, a familial background, a supportive cultural nexus, by which to even begin to garner English language proficiency.

And I also felt the gaze of existentially sullen local English-teaching staff, themselves teaching in a tongue foreign to their very souls, so much so that they preferred to teach English through the gauze of their own first language anyway. Worse, even if they spoke in a localized English, this was forever looked down on as not 'real' or standardized English and was always frowned upon, belittled.

All the time, the lustrous position of the native-speaking English teacher in so many traditionally non-English communities continues unabated, and in fact, all rather worryingly, it continues to exponentially augment itself through a sort of hermaphroditic process, while the image of the white-skinned and, even better, blue-eyed 'native' speaker still prevails in non-Western societies, as Phiona Stanley (2016), for example, has recently written with regard to China and Australia.

Of even more concern to me is the sexual predation by white-skinned native English speaker 'teachers' that all too often takes place in countries in South East Asia—and indubitably elsewhere—which warrants an entire book of its own. There are innumerable references online to such predatory behavior in Asia, as reported as just one example written by Zhou (2014) in the *South China Morning Post*. Such is the perceived 'demand' for the English language: such predators have an all too easily accepted calling card: in other words, they are able to travel and corrupt outside their own homelands precisely because they can speak and write English.

As the 2014 APLE report notes pertaining to Cambodia, "A worrying trend is visible in institutions that aim to benefit children. Fourteen perpetrators [in APLE's database] worked in such an institution before they were arrested. Five perpetrators worked as English teachers . . . the number of cases is increasing and this is alarming. Also, most of these perpetrators have previous convictions . . ." (APLE, 2014: 11).

In fact, such highly privileged native teaching schemes are a complete scandal, thinly wallpapered over by the commercial agents of 'Englishism' and showing few signs of retreat. Take the rampant NET schemes rife throughout Hong Kong as just one example. I have written extensively about this latter scam elsewhere, by the way, most recently in the *South China Morning Post* (Rapatahana, 2014) and earlier in 2012 (Eoyang et al., 2012).

If anything, the industry's tentacular or octopus-like grasp is more so today, as the corporate TOEFL and IELTS language tests grow up worldwide as 'Siamese Twins'—a term so manifestly Orientalist that it makes me wince—while universities scamper toward English-language medium of instruction in an effort to maintain superior Western-generated citation indexes for themselves, so much so that access to academic publishing means English-only journal articles, as Ulrich Ammon (2010), for example, has written about so cogently, with regard especially to the concomitant diminishment of European languages. We also cannot ignore the associated Anglocentric textbook megaindustry, as well as the crepuscular clamp of the English-language International Baccalaureate factories. Nor forget the rapacious dominance of tuition schools promising English-language mastery across Japan, South Korea, and Mainland China, as just some examples—which I witnessed in several locales, whereby tired students completed their long school day and then trudged begrudgingly off to '*twiton*' [sic] classes.

More tragically and worryingly too, is the physical damage the promoters of the well-indoctrinated 'need' for English language inevitably bring about. What about the Korean geese families, where Dad stays home and the family travels to Australia, for example, to enroll in costly English tuition, all paid for by Dad's employment back in Seoul? Or the students in South Korea who have a lingual frenectomy, so as to somehow pronounce English better—a surgical invasion, whereby a muscular striate under the tongue is actually severed so as to, somehow, allow an individual to pronounce English language sounds more 'correctly'! What about the suicides of Korean academics, who feel themselves to be failures because they cannot satisfy some absurd demand for a certain level of English? Ingrid Piller (2010) has written so well about such examples of this—to me, at least—very distressing situation in South Korea.

Such is the unspoken thief that is the English language—more particularly, these profiting agencies of its proliferation worldwide, postulating English language as the great white hope, such as the British Council, the World Bank, IMF, WTO and various US and English examination cabals, among myriad others. However, attainment of it as 'acceptable enough' for first-language speakers of

English is something which millions will never actually attain sufficiently, even if they wish to, as Joseph Park (2012) has so cogently described about his own experiences as an articulate Korean academic. An indication of their glib salesmanship, as reported in the *Guardian* (McVeigh, 2014), whereby the language is presented as a neutral, value-free 'necessity,' is the result of the November 2014, poll sponsored by the British Council as to what are the greatest moments, discoveries and people of the last 80 years—as delineated initially by several so-called experts. The spread of English as 'a global language' ranks 11, above both the Holocaust and the invention of nuclear energy!

Yet, surely there is an aspect of such language dominion which can be categorized as a form of linguistic genocide, as the initiator of the term, Tove Skutnabb-Kangas (2000), to her immense credit, has articulated and anguished over in a series of excellent articles and books over a number of years, describing the horribly detrimental effect exponents of the tongue are enforcing on indigenous languages.

Personal and Linguistic Lived Experiences

Let me be quite clear. I drifted into the teaching of English literature and language because I had a degree in existential philosophy and New Zealand had no openings for such a trade. Except, perhaps, in English as the only language universities in city spaces that were anathema to me.

The further irony is that English is *not* my main language, but because of an accident of birthplace and because *te reo Māori* (the *Māori* language) was not ever taught back when I went to school mid-last century, it has served to privilege me and so many of my peers, most of whom have been monolingual *Pākehā*. They have become richer, with absolutely no guarantee whatsoever that the students they teach will ever attain their level of English language empowerment. I wonder if, in fact, they were ever meant to.

I am compelled to point out that—of course—the *Māori* tongue itself was historically suppressed, almost to the point of extinction, in a deliberate evisceration process by British colonialists, hell-bent on making the dominion of New Zealand a sort of 'Britain of the South Seas,' as Graham Hingangaroa Smith and I (Rapatahana & G. H. Smith, 2012) wrote about the sheer devastation involved in this process. Students who spoke their own tongue at schools, for example, were castigated, shamed and, all too often, physically punished for so doing. Significantly, this thieving process has been going on for centuries across the globe, not merely in my own country of birth. It is by no means a recent phenomenon either.

Indeed, it had been in my own homeland that I had initially turned my back on *Pākehā*-promulgated education in 1983, and had submitted my resignation from that system via a letter quoting Ivan Illich (1971) to the *New Zealand Post-Primary Teachers' Journal*. Illich, of course, espoused the de-schooling of society completely, viewing the institutionalization of education as tantamount to an entrenched continuation of the regnant power nexus. By that time I had already spent some years overseas as a teacher of English.

More, whenever I returned to Aotearoa New Zealand, I had always felt inauthentic unless I was teaching in *Māori*-empowered schooling systems, where the English language was at least parried by the *patu* (club) of *te reo Māori*. This is why, after teaching overseas, I initially taught again only in *Māori* language schools in my homeland, until even that was parried by intrusive *Pākehā* administrations and their subliminal and overt expectations to somehow match up with their English-language examination systems and curricula. I now no longer teach anything in any classroom.

I am always reminded of a *whakataukī*, or pithy saying: *Kāore he whakaute mo ngā reo o māmā tēnei Ingarihi*': This English has no respect for mother tongues. What does this mean? That enforcers of the English language—itself a veritable hybrid creole, after all—have kidnapped and brought up as its own more and more words from other languages, so that the English language is increasingly a mega-carton crammed full of reams and reams of stand-alone words, without the spiritual or even emotive stance and import that they had in their original tongues—a type of juggernaut techne, if you will. This is obviously another arm of the burglar.

But of more concern, these enforcers have also invaded and corrupted these other languages, most especially where the latter have no direct English-language equivalent. The danger for indigenous and mother-tongue languages is their having to incorporate English terminology for items never in their lexical pantheons, or—worse—to replace words already there which had intrinsic ontological weight. Therefore, English increasingly invades and corrupts them with words, terms, phraseology and the concomitant Western cultural biases these all have. A further indication of the encroachment of English language as thief, indeed—perhaps even as a form of Ebola?—Muhammad Haji Salleh (2012), my esteemed poet colleague from Malaysia, articulates this insidious process of existential diminishment, so brilliantly, when he recounts his own experiences of being torn between Malay and English and his later choice to spurn the latter.

And yes, I am also very aware that I am further reinforcing such English-language omnipotence by contributing to this book, published in another ex-English colony, written in excellent, proofread English and reinforcing the ridiculous and restrictive APA referencing strictures and routines as involved. All in uniform font. By contributing to this tome I am in essence supporting the thief, unless I can also deliberately subvert and expose his wily ways.

And yes, once again, I confess to continuing to work as an English-language educator for so long and to reap the mighty fiscal rewards involved, given that of course a small minority of my students did succeed in becoming more literate in the language, even if they rarely utilized it beyond their school days.

However, at the same time, I am endeavoring to expose the villain. Which is why I commenced 'writing out,' in outing this infiltrating tongue, or at least its perpetrators across the Anglo-American power continuum, through my critical articles and books such as *English Language as Hydra* (2012), co-edited by my colleague and friend Dr. Pauline Bunce, who shares with me a massive awareness as to the eroding English-language waves crushing onto the crumbling shores of all-too-many indigenous beaches. Which is also why I write poems—in both my main tongues—exposing the villain for the plunderer he is, or, rather, his agents are. Indeed their actions have compelled me to write critically across a variety of genres in reaction to their pilfering gambits.

I must also say that nowadays I have relinquished my role as a teacher of English language and have returned to a trade in which I had also qualified and which I returned to more recently whenever back in my homeland—that of a specialist advisor in special education, with a special focus on *Māori* students.

Counteracting the Thief

There are counters to the burglary outlined above, that I can suggest. Firstly, at least *te reo Māori* has finally been declared an official language in my own country and that—thankfully —of late I have been able to utilize it far more frequently than ever before. In this small way, then, I offer some solace, for if this trend toward the use of one's indigenous language could only be continued worldwide, there would tread a stalwart policemen on the beat resisting the insidious smash and grab of the English-speaking thief. Indigenous tongues can, indeed, be made to thrive with support, legal backing, indigenous pride and persistence.

More, I urge young people to grab hold of their own languages and to grow them, to de-assimilate themselves from the lingo of Uncle Sam and the Queen, even if they have to live in dominant English-speaking environments. As we also say here in Aotearoa New Zealand, via a well-known traditional saying, *Ko taku reo taku ohooho, ko taku reo taku māpihi maurea*: my language is my awakening, my language is the window to my soul. Learn your language, now, while you have some chance to retain and own your essence.

Another way to challenge the thief is for English language speakers to strive to attain fluency in other languages—so as at the same time to respect them and their cultural nuances and to use them as much as possible. On a personal note, I have a good grasp of both Cantonese and Mandarin, speak Bahasa Melayu fluently, as well as being proficient in Tagalog, the meta-language of Philippines, for my wife comes from that lovely country. I used to listen, appalled, to the smug self-congratulations of many of my English-teaching peers as they mocked their perceived inadequacies of the student bodies they had flown in to 'rescue.' They actually believed that they were 'helping' the students they were flown in to 'teach,' a Mr. Pip mentality that persists today, as Hilary Smith (2016), for one, has noted with regard to her own experiences in Papua New Guinea and the imperious role of the English language there. It behooves English-speaking teachers to learn the languages of the countries they are employed in. Why should it always be the local as imposed upon?

Relatedly, the English-speaking majority should allow for other languages in their own respective communities, where there are exponentially increasing ethnic minorities. Such a case is here, in New Zealand, which is rapidly becoming even more multicultural and where Asians will be the second largest ethnic grouping by 2026 (including my own family). We should attempt to learn other tongues here, and we must accept that these many Asian arrivals, for example, be able to be educated in their own tongues, also. Indeed, there is a vital need in my homeland to have a legal concretization of other languages, if you will—as Stephen May (2015) has so well articulated as sadly and rather worryingly, lacking.

Again—one can also vitiate the thief by stylistically turning the English language on its own ears and thus, reinventing and owning it anew. All the more reason to usurp so-called standardized English with alternatives, different ways of writing, speaking, referencing, admixing with other languages and mixing the metaphors—using it to continue to 'write against the Empire.' As I always strive to do in my own poetry, whereby I am consciously trying to confute and confuse the conqueror, subvert it, bastardize it. As per a 2016 piece articulating exactly that in the Aotearoa New Zealand poetry critique online, *Ka Mate Ka Ora*, entitled "Writing back (to the centre): Practicing My Theory."

Finally and forcefully, only in exposure can there be any progress, any respect for our own first languages and cultures, and for chances of their continued untrammeled survival. Here is a major rationale for such confessions as my own throughout this chapter: to continue to strive for social and cultural justice by challenging this thief and by thus respecting other languages and their speakers. After all, "TESOL teachers are faced with certain moral dilemmas whose solutions, if any, are complex and painful to deal with [such as] the promotion of a language widely used for purposes of political, economic and social power, especially in countries in which the teacher is not a native" (Judd, 1983: 265). As this quotation so clearly articulates, we as English-language mentors, instigators, promulgators, beneficiaries, are beholden to admit to our roles as profiteers, as pushers of an overriding English-language episteme that all too often has no respect for other mother tongues whatsoever. We must be ever honest and vigilant in our roles. For without a mother, what will we all be?

Coda

Yet, this process of countering, of course, does not and should not avoid the English language completely, most obviously in today's boundary-disintegrating world, where an isolation of indigenous cultures and communities would seem virtually impossible, indeed, rather a romantic paean. Instead, perhaps the thief could become a humble invited guest, should the hosts ever decide they do have some need to expose their youth to it. If so, they would ensure to have it taught and learned additively, as just one among a choice of other living tongues. There is absolutely no reason why some English should not be taught, learned, conveyed daily, appreciated—for without question, the language taken in isolation does contain immense literary richness and merit. But, at the same time, it has to be taught to modify its ways, to be seen to behave and to report for duty only if asked.

I'll end with a poem. Or two.

Poem 5.1

railing against

["language . . . first brings man about, brings him into existence" —Heidegger, *Poetry, Language, Thought*, 1971]

I'm railing against **E**
N
its tepid rotes **G**
L
& rotted topos **I**
S
its stupid lexis **H**
& leery syntax
I'm training a **p**
of
stokers,
stirrers
engineers
to derail the caboose
deep i
n
t
o
the coulee it created,

with its *fanfaronade*
its contagion
its wanton w r e c k a g e of ethnic signals
&
the profound
pity
of
this all.

Questions for Discussion

1. Do you feel that your own—or an associate's—indigenous tongue is under threat because the English language is so dominant and domineering? If so, why has this process continued?
2. If you feel that your own—or an associate's—indigenous language is indeed under threat from the agents of English language, what can and should be done about this process?

Author Profile

Vaughan Rapatahana is a New Zealander, with homes also in Philippines and Hong Kong SAR. He is published widely across several genres, both in his own tongue, Māori, and in English. He has worked as an educator in the English language in a number of countries over the years; although, more recently, he has stepped away from doing so. He is the instigator and a co-editor of *English Language as Hydra* (Rapatahana & Bruce, 2012) and *Why English? Confronting the Hydra* (Bruce et al., 2016), both published by Multilingual Matters, United Kingdom. He has a PhD in existential philosophy from the University of Auckland.

References

Ammon, U. (2010). Linguistic inequality and its effects on participation in scientific discourse and on global knowledge accumulation—with a closer look at the problems of the second-rank language communities. *Applied Linguistic Review, 3* (2), 333–335.

APLE Cambodia (2014). Investigating traveling child sex offenders. Retrieved 17 January, 2015 from: www.aplecambodia.org/images/Analytical%20Report%20on%20Investigating%20Traveling%20Child%20Sex%20Offenders%20Web%20Version.pdf

Bunce, P., Rapatahana, V., Phillipson, R. & Tupas, R. (eds.) (2016). *Why English? Confronting the Hydra*. Bristol: Multilingual Matters.

Eoyang, E. C., Bunce, P. & Rapatahana, V. (2012). English language as governess: Expatriate English teaching schemes in Hong Kong. In V. Rapatahana & P. Bunce (2012) (eds.), *English language as Hydra* (pp. 133–157). Bristol: Multilingual Matters.

Illich, I. (1971). *Deschooling society*. New York: Harper and Row.

Judd, E. L. (1983). TESOL as a political act: A moral question. In J. Handscombe et al. (eds.), *The question of control: Selected papers from the annual convention of teachers of English to speakers of other languages* (pp. 265–272). TESOL: Toronto.

May, S. (2015). *New Zealand's increasing 'superdiversity': Auckland leads the way*. Retrieved 13 July, 2016 from: www.cometauckland.org.nz/webfiles/CometNZ/files/Stephen_May_NZs_increasing_Superdiversity.pdf

McVeigh, T. (2014). 80 landmarks in 80 years: the people and events that shaped our world. Retrieved 22 November, 2014 from: *The Guardian*: www.theguardian.com/world/2014/nov/22/80-landmarks-in-80-years-that-shaped-our-world.

Mustafa, Z. (2016). The destruction of Nadia's dream: The English language tyrant in Pakistan's education system. In P. Bunce, R. Phillipson, V. Rapatahana & R. Tupas (eds.) *Why English? Confronting the Hydra*. (pp. 185–196). Bristol: Multilingual Matters.

Park, J. (2102). English language as border-crossing: Longing and belonging in the South Korean experience. In V. Rapatahana & P. Bunce (eds.), *English language as Hydra* (pp. 208–220). Bristol: Multilingual Matters.

Piller, I. (2010). *Warning: Global English may harm your mental health.* Retrieved 15 September, 2014 from: www.languageonthemove.com/recent-posts/warning-global-english-may-harm-your-mental-health.

Rapatahana, V. (2016). Writing back (to the centre): Practicing my theory. Retrieved 19 August, 2016 from *Ka Mate Ka Ora: A New Zealand Journal of Poetry and Poetics*: www.nzepc.auckland.ac.nz/kmko/

Rapatahana, V. (2014). Time to retire the native English teachers scheme. Retrieved 10 June, 2014 from *South China Morning Post*: www.scmp.com/comment/article/1529191/time-retire-native-english-teacher-scheme

Rapatahana, V. & Bunce, P. (2012) (eds.) *English Language as Hydra.* Bristol: Multilingual Matters.

Rapatahana, V. & Smith, G. H. (2012). English Language as Nemesis for Māori. In V. Rapatahana and P. Bunce (2012) (eds.) *English language as Hydra* (pp. 76–103). Bristol: Multilingual Matters.

Salleh, M. H. (2012). Coda: One colonial language: One great tragic epic. In V. Rapatahana & P. Bunce (eds.), *English language as Hydra* (pp. 263–275). Bristol: Multilingual Matters.

Skutnabb-Kangas, T. (2000). *Linguistic genocide in education – or worldwide diversity and human rights?* New Jersey: Laurence Erlbaum.

Smith, H. (2016). Mr. Jones: *Mi Laik Askim Yu Samting.* In P. Bunce, R. Phillipson, V. Rapatahana & R. Tupas (eds.), *Why English? Confronting the Hydra* (pp. 88–92). Bristol: Multilingual Matters.

Stanley, P. (2016). Must the (western) Hydra be blond(e)? Performing cultural 'authenticity' in intercultural education. In P. Bunce, R. Phillipson, V. Rapatahana & R. Tupas (eds.) *Why English? Confronting the Hydra* (pp. 93–105). Bristol: Multilingual Matters.

Zhou, L. (2014). Tougher mainland scrutiny of foreign teachers after child sex scandal fears. Retrieved December 13, 2014 from *South China Morning Post*: www.scmp.com/news/china/article/1593018/tougher-mainland-scrutiny-foreign-teachers-after-child-sex-scandal-fears

And why not another poem, eh? And why not here?

Poem 5.2

before the whiteman came
["on its colonies the sun never sets but the blood never dries," Ernest Jones, 1851.]

at ngatapa
they
stripped the lean māori
bare,
before **they** musketed them,

lined up like lemming
& set them flailing

over the escarpment—
dead or alive—it didn't matter to **them**.

extermination is a plangent thread
seaming through
england's evil empire—

"let's cannonade the sepoy
draw & quarter the carib
decapitate the malay
strychnine some aborigine
& massacre a few hundred māori,
of any gender—
it doesn't matter to **us**."

all the pogrommed
only ever wanted
to be
what they had/have what
they were,

before

the **whiteman** came.

[The Ngatapa Massacre, Aotearoa New Zealand in January 1869: "In all some 130 of the defenders of Ngatapa were captured in the bush and gorges below the pa where they lay asleep, having had neither sleep nor water for two days. They were marched up the hill side again under the outer wall—as it were—of the pa they had defended so long and so heroically, stripped of every vestige of clothing they possessed and SHOT—shot like dogs. There was no mention of a trial . . . That did not matter to us one straw. They were shot and their bodies left to swelter and rot under the summer's sun and bones to bleach to this day. And all this—and very much more—as done under the meteor flag of Mighty England." —J. P. Ward, No. 6 Division, Armed Constabulary, British Forces at Ngatapa]

6

BISCRIPTAL ENGLISH LEARNERS

A Blind Spot in Global English Language Teaching

Pauline Bunce

> *Alphabetism, the belief that alphabetic writing systems are inherently superior to non-alphabetic systems [has], like Anglocentrism, stymied psychologists' and educators' thinking about learning to read across diverse writing systems.*
>
> (Share, 2014: 1)

Introduction

In 2012, Vaughan Rapatahana and I compiled a volume of worldwide accounts and perspectives on the increasingly voracious English Language Teaching (ELT) industry, entitled *English Language as Hydra: Its Impacts on Non-English Cultures*. We likened this burgeoning, global business to the multi-headed monster of Greek mythology, with each of its beguiling heads luring unsuspecting customers into its realm. This is not the usual picture that is painted of this global enterprise, however, as its ascendency is so rarely questioned. In a second Hydra collection (Bunce et al., 2016), we further catalogue its continuing global rampage. How is it that I, a classroom teacher of English as an additional language, have come to the point of deeply questioning the global impact of my own profession? Or should I now say, my 'trade'? Part of the answer will be found here in this autoethnographical account of my English-teaching experiences in Hong Kong, during which I began to see *both* the forest *and* the trees and discovered that my own profession has become so blinded by its partnership with the agencies of globalization that it has lost touch with its classroom core and left itself wide open to being grossly manipulated for profit.

This account will alternate between two perspectives—the personal and the polemic—my classroom experiences while teaching English in Hong Kong secondary schools, and my descriptions of the blinkered, myopic perspectives of the global ELT industry in which I have become embroiled.

My Hong Kong Classroom

When Hong Kong schools commence their academic year in August-September, the annual typhoon season is well under way. It is not uncommon for the first month of school to be punctuated by 'typhoon days' and temporary school closures. All students (and their teachers) look forward to these unexpected 'days off,' despite the dangerous weather conditions. As a typhoon approaches the city, the Hong Kong Observatory issues numerical warning signals regarding the severity of local weather conditions. Whenever a Signal Number Eight is announced, all schools and most businesses will close for the day. In 1999, while working as a 'native English-speaking teacher' (a NET) in a Hong Kong prevocational secondary school, I composed a short, bouncy poem about typhoons for my Form Two[1] students, and asked them to copy it from the board. To my surprise, quite a few of them wrote the poem's title as 'Typhoon Signal Number English,' with the capitalized word 'Eight' transformed into the more familiar (and visually similar) word, 'English.'

I would regularly cringe as I watched some of my students copy even the simplest of words from the board. They looked up really frequently, sometimes letter-by-letter, sometimes stroke-by-stroke. After a while, classroom observations such as these started to suggest a worrying pattern in my Hong Kong Chinese students' problematic encounters with unfamiliar English words.

Global ELT

The global English Language Teaching (ELT) business too readily assumes that first-language literate students, such as my Hong Kong learners, will be able to transfer their established literacy skills to additional languages. Unfortunately, this belief in a *literacy transfer* is an unhelpful and lingering 'blind spot' in current ELT practice. Several luminaries in the field have long preached the adage that 'we only learn to read once'; however, this proposition no longer holds true in the increasingly multi-scripted classrooms of today. The world's written scripts can operate at quite different linguistic levels, have completely different design principles and follow different directionalities. The very idea of a 'word' is problematic for writers of scripts that do not represent word-boundaries at all. Between the horizontal, left-to-right, alphabetic English script and the sometimes columnar, sometimes horizontal, character-based Chinese script, there is an enormous *orthographic distance*.

Despite its current embrace of technological innovation and its ever-expanding global reach, the global ELT industry remains pedagogically trapped in a pre-globalization paradigm in which its learners are thought to still resemble the

European and Latin American learners that filled its classrooms in the twentieth century. This is particularly evident in the pages of its best-selling ELT textbooks. Not only is their *content* overwhelmingly British and American in nature, they still assume that all their learners are alphabet-savvy. Ingrid Gogolin (2006) attributes such assumptions to an ever-lingering 'monolingual habitus' of current language teaching practice in an otherwise multilingual world. Elsewhere, I have termed this blinkered view of English teaching the 'alpha-best alpha-beast' (Bunce, 2016). Whatever one calls it, the English Language Teaching industry is entirely myopic when it comes to the scriptal differences that are now evident in virtually every class of learners. *Biscriptal learners* have yet to be either acknowledged or embraced by the global ELT business.

My Hong Kong Classroom

When I moved to Hong Kong in August 1998, I had joined a new government scheme that was devised to reassure the community that there would be no decline in English standards in the city following its recent reunification with China the previous year. Every secondary school was to be given a Native English-speaking Teacher (NET), over and above its standard staffing formula. As a pioneer in this scheme, I discovered to my surprise that the city's secondary schools were *not* neighborhood-based, 'comprehensive' schools with a wide-ranging local intake. No. Not at all. All the secondary schools in the city had been ranked, or 'banded,' and their intake would match their designation. In 1998, there were five such 'bands,' with Band One schools receiving the top 20% of performers in the primary-school exit examination, Band Two the next 20% and so on. My school was a 'prevocational' Band Five school, and therefore destined to take the lowest 10% of the exam performers. It was a depressing and violent place. Many students (and some parents) were involved in gangland activities and a student from the school had recently been murdered—a fact that I discovered in newspaper coverage of the trial during my first week at the school. Despite the 'banding' system, all students were expected to sit for the same external examinations. Sadly, hardly anyone from the prevocational schools made it through these one-size-fits-all filters to success. For them, there were no praiseworthy accolades in the newspapers, no accomplished alumni giving talks at school assemblies and there was very little sense of purpose among the students.

Like most of Hong Kong's low-banded schools, mine actively avoided any newspaper coverage (Bunce, 2004). However, as one of the co-founders of NESTA, the newly formed Native English-Speaking Teachers' Association, I was sought out by a newspaper reporter who arrived unannounced at my school, seeking some insights into the progress of the newly formed NET scheme. This first encounter with *The South China Morning Post* was fairly innocuous; however, I did mention the recent murder of a student to the reporter and she wanted to do a follow-up article. In the second interview, I commented on the depressing nature of school banding and the pessimistic outlook that pervaded the lowest-banded schools. She invited me to write a feature article on what I saw as widespread *learned helplessness* (Seligman, 1975) in these schools. The subsequent full-page article (Bunce, 1999) catapulted me into city-wide notoriety, and eventually led to a two-page entry in a definitive history of Hong Kong education (Sweeting, 2004: 17–19).

As a direct result of my new public profile, I received a veiled threat to my personal safety from within my school, and it was then that I decided to remain visible in the public arena. If anything should happen to me, it would surely warrant immediate investigation. *The South China Morning Post* was very supportive, and I was given a weekly column entitled 'Staff Room' in which to express my thoughts and observations of school life in the city. At this stage, I had not fully come to terms with my students' English reading difficulties. Eventually, I began to write about them, and my fellow NET teachers concurred—there was something 'not quite right' in our students' English-language reading skills—and this was evident in even the highest banded schools.

Global ELT

What is reading? If you can speak a language, will that give you automatic access to its written script? Is reading a 'natural' skill? Clearly not, or there would be no non-literate people in the world. While speech is as old as humankind, writing (and reading) is a cultural development of the last three or four thousand years of human history. Reading, in any language, cannot be considered to be a natural human activity. Unlike speech, the acquisition of reading and writing skills requires some form of direct tuition. In the absence of literacy instruction, the speakers of scripted languages will remain non-literate.

But what of those learners who will need to become *biscriptal*, or even *triscriptal*, when they embark on English-language learning? Unfortunately, in the ELT literature this particular duality is often subsumed by the related, but substantially different, notions of *bilingualism* and *bilteracy*. What does it mean to be 'biliterate'? What is *literacy*? Is it merely the ability to read and write in a language, or is it something more than that? Literacy is quite a broad notion. It certainly includes the skills of reading and writing in a particular language, but it also involves the possession of cultural knowledge and a positive disposition towards furthering that knowledge (Rayner et al., 2001: 34).

One of the overarching goals of Hong Kong's post-1997 education system is to produce 'trilingual and biliterate' citizens (Bolton, 2002). The aim is to ensure that Hong Kong people will be able to speak three languages (Cantonese, English and Mandarin) and be 'literate' in both Chinese and English. In Hong Kong, such a phrase should probably read, 'trilingual, triliterate and triscriptal' because of the substantial differences between traditionally written Cantonese and the simplified, mainland Mandarin script. Outside the Western world, being able to speak *at least three* languages is commonplace, and multilingualism is downright essential if one is a member of a minority community. In Papua New Guinea, for example, children will grow up speaking one language at home, another in the marketplace, Tok Pisin as a *lingua franca* in the wider society and English at school (Malone & Paraide, 2011). In the hill regions of Tamil Nadu in India, people may speak Badaga at home, Tamil in the town, learn Hindi at school and be expected to know sufficient English 'to get by' when working with overseas fieldworkers (Sawin, 2015). In traditional, pre-colonized Aboriginal society in Australia, it was common for people to know four or five spoken languages, a form of sign language and the 'secret language' of ceremonies (Kendon, 2013). Given the global reality that there are far more multilinguals than monolinguals in the world (Benson, 2013), it is ironic (and telling) that the global ELT industry so often refers to its own practice as teaching 'English as a *Second* Language' (TESL).

In the vast storehouse of ELT literature, there is scarcely a mention of the words, *biscriptal* or *triscriptal*. There are hardly any publications on teaching a new handwriting system to English learners who are already literate in a different script. Rosemary Sassoon's *The Acquisition of a Second Writing System* (1995) stands alone. While there are countless journals and publications on the teaching of reading and writing in English, there are currently only two journals that specialize in studying the world's writing systems: *Written Language and Literacy* which began in 1998, and *Writing Systems Research*, which began in 2009. Neither of these, nor two excellent, but highly academic, volumes in this field (Cook & Bassetti, 2005; Koda & Zehler, 2008) is likely to be found on a busy classroom English teacher's desk.

My Hong Kong Classroom

After several months of puzzlement over my Hong Kong students' worrying problems with English reading, I learned by chance of a three-month, part-time course for 'remedial teachers' entitled 'The Processes of Reading and Its Disorders,' that was to be conducted on weekends at the Chinese University of Hong Kong. It would be led by an ex-Hong Kong, now Canada-based, international authority on dyslexia, Dr. Leong Che Kan. This course, and the research project it required, was a hugely significant turning point for me, both professionally and personally.

My research project for this course involved testing my prevocational students' *phonological awareness* through the use of a set of easily decodable pseudowords—a common testing method that provided a quick assessment of respondents' *sounding-out* abilities. I devised a list of 20 invented words, such as 'pid,' 'feg' and 'blon,' and opportunistically quizzed 70 students from Forms One to Seven.[2] The best performer was, ironically, a 'remedial' Form One student named Billy who had recently arrived from mainland China. He was classed as 'remedial' because he could not speak Cantonese and he had great trouble reading Hong Kong's traditional Chinese characters. Previously, in his mainland school, he had learned *pinyin*, the alphabetic writing system used in the early years of schooling, plus *simplified* Chinese characters. My Hong Kong colleagues derided my 'strange test' and saw

Billy's success as clear evidence of its unsuitability. 'How can you possibly read something that doesn't mean anything?', they chimed. To me, and to Dr. Leong, my informal test had perfectly captured the *phonological deficit* that characterized far too many Hong Kong learners of English—including many of their teachers.

This small-scale research study became the inspiration for an eight-year-long, action-research-based doctoral project that eventually sampled the phonological skills of 778 Hong Kong students—at least half of whom attended the city's most elite Band One schools. Every year, many Band One students eagerly enrolled in a Summer School English Enrichment program that was conducted by an international school, in which I had recently become a teacher. Here, over four summers, I was able to conduct pre- and post-testing of Band One students and run an intensive 'Word Wizards' course with the express aim of improving their knowledge of English phonology, morphology and etymology.

One of the hardest elements of this action-research endeavor was convincing the Summer School's director that local Band One students had any kind of deficit in their reading skills. After all, many of them were reading the Harry Potter series of books and several would, no doubt, grace the front pages of the newspaper when their high-scoring exam results were announced. I made her an offer—I would mark all 135 of the applicants' essays in return for the opportunity to conduct a dictated pseudoword test with the full group. She agreed. When she later examined these students' poor 'spelling test' results, she agreed to my running a daily 'advanced phonics programme'—to which I gave the catchy title of 'Word Wizards.'

Global ELT

Like countless other secondary and tertiary teachers of English as an additional language, I had just *assumed* that my students would be familiar with the operation of an alphabetic script. Yet, worldwide, 'alphabets' are only one type of *writing system*. In an unfortunately titled, but far too rarely cited book entitled, *English L2 Reading: Getting to the Bottom*, Barbara Birch (2002) points out that the world's writing systems can differ on so many levels:

1. Different scripts can represent different linguistic units, such as meaning, syllables, consonants and vowels.
2. Different scripts can be laid out differently on the page: vertically, horizontally and with or without 'word' spacing.
3. Different scripts use different numbers of symbols to represent spoken language in print, e.g., 26 letters, 3,000 characters.
4. The methods that national schools may use to teach children these symbols can vary from country to country, and from script to script.
5. Scripts all differ in their indicators of syntactical elements, e.g., their markers of tense.

6. Even alphabetic writing systems vary in the relative prominence given to consonants and vowels, e.g., Arabic and Hebrew primarily represent consonants.
7. Alphabetic writing systems also vary in their 'transparency', i.e., their predictability in representing the sound system of the spoken language.

Birch (2002: 24)

The world's written scripts do a lot more than simply represent their spoken languages in written formats. Different types of script almost certainly have an effect on the ways in which their users will think about language, and the ways in which they will put their *established knowledge of script* to use in novel situations. All proficient users of a particular script have acquired an *automaticity* in their ease of reading (and writing) that script. Most literate people can hardly remember a time when they could not read. There is a Chinese proverb which succinctly sums up this situation: 'You cannot ask a fish to explain water.' To be 'literate' is to be completely immersed in the script in which your language is written.

Alphabetic *handwriting skills* are also assumed in global ELT practice. English learners who come from different scriptal backgrounds will, no doubt, remember the time and effort that was needed to learn and correctly write their first script. Small errors could indicate a change in meaning and neatness was important. Biscriptal learners of English rarely receive close and regular instruction in the 'mechanics' of pen-holding, letter formation or stroke order. Such learners will experience an initial *haptic dissonance*—a feeling akin to writing with one's non-preferred hand—and will need time to settle into the new, alphabetic writing experience.

Broadly speaking, the world's writing systems can be classified into those in which written symbols connect directly to the *sounds* of the spoken language, and those whose symbols connect directly to *meanings*, as in traditional and simplified Chinese characters and Japanese *kanji*. Sound-based writing systems can be further divided into those in which the symbols (graphemes) represent *syllables* (e.g., Tibetan and Japanese *kana*), and those in which the graphemes represent *phonemes* (individual sounds). Quite a few scripts, such as those of the 'Indosphere' (e.g., Hindi, Thai, Burmese, Khmer and Tamil) represent syllable-units based on a consonant or a final vowel sound. There is no definitive classification of the fascinating worldwide range of written scripts, and the reader is advised to consult Omniglot, the online encyclopedia of writing systems and languages (www.omniglot.com) to gain some idea of the sheer immensity of human ingenuity in this field.

My Hong Kong Classroom

The opportunity to conduct a pseudoword dictation test with Band One students gave me direct access to a qualitatively different set of English learners from my prevocational Band Five students. How would they perform? Out of a total of 2,700 responses to the 20 pseudowords in the 2004 test, only 40% of the responses were correctly spelled, 58% of all responses were deemed incorrect and 2% were merely isolated single letters or blank spaces (Bunce, 2007: 136). The results were dominated by difficulties with short vowels, and even though the test contained some rather 'strange' multisyllabic words, the tiny nonsense word, 'weg' was the worst performer of all. Surprisingly, some 92% of the 135 Band One applicants spelled it incorrectly. Here, indeed, was further evidence of my hypothesis that these students would also demonstrate the same *phonological deficit* that I had previously observed among my Band Five students.

One huge research advantage of working through the 'Word Wizards' course with Band One students was that they were very articulate in English and quite meta-aware of their own learning processes. They told me that, in Hong Kong, it was common for students to describe the English alphabetic script as looking like 'ugly worms' or 'chicken guts.' Their observations of their own learning are priceless. Here is a sample:

> I never looked inside a word before. I knew very little about words. I just recite them many, many times for my memory.
>
> Before I attended this class, I only knew how to memorize English words with hard effort.
>
> I never learn these things in my school before. Words are so interesting and you can play with them too.
>
> Before, I had never looked at the alphabet in such detail, even though I use it every single day.
>
> I've learnt that although I don't know the word, I can still pronounce the word by chop them into different parts or using all the sounds. You can pronounce words that aren't real! But in Chinese cannot.
>
> The formation of a Chinese character stress on the 'meaning' or the 'shape.' It is easy to get the meaning, but you will never get the pronounciation [sic] just by looking at it. An English word is based on the pronounciation [sic], but you might not get the meaning by looking at it.
>
> I thought that words are boring, but now it's fun. I like knowing the story behind them. I didn't know words are made complex with suffixes and prefixes.
>
> Before I can't find the difference between words like 'rod' and 'rode.' Now I can hear it.

Some students were even a little angry that the insights they had gained in this one-month course had never been provided to them in their Band One schools. It was as though every word was a 'one off'; each one needing to be memorized by its visual form and the 'recitation' of its spelling. I was particularly surprised to learn that prefixes, suffixes and roots were rarely identified as common and meaningful word-building units.

Global ELT

The development of efficient reading skills in an alphabetic script depends on the learners' grasp of the *alphabetic principle*—the fundamental encoding and decoding basis of an alphabetic writing system—in which combinations of letters are designed to capture the individual sounds in the spoken language. The alphabetic principle needs to be taught (Byrne, 1998), and it should be an instructional priority for all those learners who have come into English with non-alphabetic reading skills. Visual learners will always struggle with new words. They will probably skip over them, rather than engage with their spelling sequences. Unfortunately, many learners are encouraged to do just this by the followers of *whole-language* approaches to English reading instruction.

Even though the English-language 'reading wars' of the 1990s and early 2000s have now settled down to a working compromise between 'reading for meaning' and phonological skill development (or 'phonics') for English-speaking children, the global ELT industry still marches on with a largely 'whole-language' outlook towards reading and vocabulary development. This hugely commercial enterprise appears to either not be interested in, or to be outright dismissive of, the relevance of phonological skill development for non-alphabetically literate English language learners. In global ELT, it is as though 'literacy' directly equates with alphabetic skills and insights. Here, again, is evidence of the 'monolingual habitus' of this global industry.

Not only have the English 'reading wars' been put to rest by solid, scientific research, we now have brain science working on the side of instruction in phonemic awareness and phonics. Neuroscience can now inform us in detail about the neural processing of different writing systems, even finding different forms of dyslexia in users of different written scripts (Dehaene, 2010; Wolf, 2008). Much of the groundbreaking, cognitive neuroscience research into the absolute basics of reading has been conducted at the University of Hong Kong over the past decade or two. Unfortunately, this vitally important work is almost unknown to the many ELT luminaries who have worked just down the hill at the very same university over the very same time period. Some of these champions of top-down, 'communicative' approaches to ELT have made publishing fortunes in Hong Kong and beyond, with nary a thought for the scriptal challenges faced by their local consumers.

My Hong Kong Classroom

The results of my doctoral research project had confirmed the recurring classroom observations made by many NET teachers in Hong Kong. There was now strong evidence for doing things differently. I was still writing regularly for *The South China Morning Post*, and my columns and feature articles became increasingly focused on the basics of the alphabetic reading process. When it became abundantly clear that the reading difficulties experienced by my Band Five students were also present among the city's high-flying Band One students, some small opportunities for change began to appear in the halls of the Hong Kong government's Education Department. The NET association was invited to run weekend professional development activities for local English teachers, our arguments in favor of a *primary-school* NET scheme were honored, we were given a contract to conduct the annual induction courses for new NET teachers, we developed a *manual* for schools that would help them to make better use of a NET teacher ('*NET-working*', 2000) and we began to be consulted on various aspects of English teaching methodology and the eventual reduction of the number of school 'bands' to three.

The only downside to all this welcomed change of outlook was that 'phonics' had now become a bandwagon onto which all manner of after-school tuition centers, publishing houses, private tutoring services and enterprising individuals had leapt. It had become yet another 'surefire' money-making scheme in an ongoing succession of Hong Kong education 'fads.' Many of the tuition centers' 'phonics programmes' used babyish, first-language learner materials, which were completely inappropriate for *secondary* students with established non-alphabetic literacy skills. The word 'phonics' often became synonymous with the mere 26 letters of the alphabet, rather than the 44 distinct sounds that are present in spoken English. Professional developers from overseas phonics-teaching agencies, newly empowered by their recent success in the 'reading wars,' descended on Hong Kong. All this rush to fulfill a newly identified 'need' occurred without much cognizance being given to the unique strengths and weaknesses of Hong Kong's English learners.

While my 'Word Wizards' course had generated a significant improvement in the students' post-program test results, it has to be said that this had mainly occurred at the level of the *syllable*, the linguistic unit that characterizes Chinese speech: the unit that is represented by a written Chinese character. It had been a stretch too far to establish more than a base level of *phonemic awareness* in my four-week course. I had drilled down into English words from 'above': looking into their etymology, identifying word-building elements, aspects of word meaning (morphology), prefixes and suffixes, counting their syllabic 'beats' and discriminating between 'minimal pairs' such as 'red' and 'rod.' We had played with all 44 phonemes, but there had not been sufficient time to fully establish all the individual sounds. The students were 'comfortable' at the syllable level, as that is the level that they are attuned to. It is hugely challenging for Chinese-speaking learners to hear, for example, the three different sounds that are run together in the word 'man,' or the four different sounds in the five-lettered word, 'school.' *This* is where the alphabetic code really operates. If a learner cannot 'hear' the individual sounds in words, he or she may not be able to reproduce them orally—nor write the likely letter sequences.

Some local English teachers and some NETs, especially those who had completed university courses in psycholinguistics, attempted to introduce the IPA (International Phonetic Alphabet) into their Hong Kong schools. While this had, no doubt, been helpful in their *own* learning, it was yet another 'alphabet' as far as their students were concerned—with even more 'ugly worms' to learn. If the *alphabetic principle* itself was not present, then why introduce another alphabet? I argued strongly against this practice in my columns, but not everyone agreed. Several of my research subjects had mentioned having to learn the phonetic symbols in their schools. For most of them, it did not appear to have provided any new insights. One called them 'phoenix,' two told of having 'dictation tests' on the symbols, and one wrote:

> Before this course ['Word Wizards'], my knowledge about English pronounciation [sic] is extremely insufficient. Although there was a course in Form 1 about all the symbols, I just could not remember those things.

I confess to agreeing with this young learner. The IPA phonetic symbols are of great value in dictionary use, where a pronunciation key is provided, but in my opinion, they turn a biscriptal classroom into a triscriptal one.

Conclusion

I sincerely hope that some kind of *paradigm shift* might have begun in Hong Kong's education system as a result of my writing and research efforts, but the reality is that such a shift very much depends on improving teachers' knowledge and skills in this field. This will require long-term commitment, changes in teacher training and in-service professional development. It cannot just be left on the plates of the solo NET teachers in each of the city's secondary schools. Unfortunately, in Hong Kong, the combination of short-term commercial publishing interests and the equally short 'lifespans' of new ideas in education may see this vitally important educational innovation slowly wither on the vine.

After returning to Australia in 2010, I have continued to promote an awareness of the particular needs of biscriptal learners among the English as an Additional Language fraternity, via a website (www.alphabetheadaches.com) and regular speaking engagements. People are very receptive, and real progress has been made in some quarters. The absolute sticking point, however, is the almost complete lack of age-appropriate teaching resources in alphabetic awareness skills for non-alphabetically literate, biscriptal learners of English—wherever they may be based—in their home countries or in overseas language schools.

While their teachers may sadly lament the yawning gap in suitable resources, the global ELT business seems to have grown increasingly blinkered to the changing nature and needs of its classrooms. The ELT profession has been hijacked by commercial boardrooms that can see no pressing need to change their tried and true formula of 'Oxford-' and 'Cambridge'-labeled texts, courses, teaching and testing materials. Unfortunately, in my opinion, this insincere, myopic and gluttonous industry has completely lost touch with its changing classroom base.

Questions for Discussion

1. In what ways has the writer of this autoethnography experienced both a personal and a professional 'paradigm shift'?
2. Do you think that the global ELT industry will ever properly serve its biscriptal learners? How could this come about?

Author Profile

Pauline Bunce is an Australian teacher of English with extensive international experience. Her doctoral research into the reading challenges posed by the alphabetic English script in Hong Kong secondary-school classrooms has catapulted her into an ongoing professional quest to challenge the mono-scriptal assumptions that are inherent in her global profession. These assumptions are entirely inappropriate, given that most of today's English-learners come from non-alphabetic-scripted backgrounds. Pauline has published widely on the need to systematically introduce biscriptal learners of English to the alphabetic principles that are fundamental to developing efficient reading and writing skills in English.

Notes

1 The second year of high school in Hong Kong (13–14-year-olds).
2 In Hong Kong, there are seven Years/Forms/Grades in high school (from ages 12 to 18).

References

Benson, C. (2013). Towards adopting a multilingual habitus in educational development. In C. Benson & K. Kosonen (eds.), *Language issues in comparative education: Inclusive teaching and learning in non-dominant languages and cultures* (pp. 283–302). Rotterdam: Sense Publishers.

Birch, B. M. (2002). *English L2 reading: Getting to the bottom*. Mahwah, NJ: Lawrence Erlbaum Associates.

Bolton, K. (2002). Introduction. In K. Bolton. (ed.), *Hong Kong English: Autonomy and creativity* (pp. 1–26). Hong Kong: Hong Kong University Press.

Bunce, P. (1999). The dreadful depths of dreary teaching. *The South China Morning Post*, 27 October, 1999.

Bunce, P. (2004). Inside the secretive world of Hong Kong schools. *The South China Morning Post*, 18 February, 2004.

Bunce, P. (2007). *Alphabet headaches: Hong Kong's English literacy challenge*. Unpublished doctoral thesis. Charles Darwin University, Australia.

Bunce, P. (2016). The English alphabet: Alpha-best or Alpha-beast? In P. Bunce et al. (eds.), *Why English? Confronting the Hydra* (pp. 142–53). Bristol: Multilingual Matters.

Bunce, P., Phillipson, R., Rapatahana, V. & Tupas, R. (eds.) (2016). *Why English? Confronting the Hydra*. Bristol: Multilingual Matters.

Byrne, B. (1998). *The foundations of literacy: The child's acquisition of the alphabetic principle*. Hove, UK: Psychology Press.

Cook, V. & Bassetti, B. (eds.) (2005). *Second language writing systems*. Bristol: Multilingual Matters.

Dehaene, S. (2010). *Reading in the brain: The new science of how we read*. New York: Penguin Books.

Gogolin, I. (2006). Linguistic habitus. In J. L. May (ed.), *Concise encyclopedia of pragmatics* (pp. 535–37). Oxford: Elsevier.

Kendon, A. (2013). *Sign languages of Aboriginal Australia: Cultural, semiotic and communicative perspectives*. Cambridge, UK: Cambridge University Press.

Koda, K. & Zehler, A. M. (eds.) (2008). *Learning to read across languages: Cross-linguistic relationships in first- and second-language literacy development*. New York: Routledge.

Malone, S. & Paraide, P. (2011). Mother tongue-based bilingual education in Papua New Guinea. *International Review of Education*, 57, 705–20.

NET-working (2000). A publication of the Education Department of Hong Kong. Hong Kong: Government Printing Department.

Rapatahana, V. & Bunce, P. (eds.) (2012). *English language as Hydra: Its impacts on non-English cultures*. Bristol: Multilingual Matters.

Rayner, K., Foorman, B. R., Perfetti, C. A., Pesetsky, D. & Seidenberg, M. S. (2001). How psychological science informs the teaching of reading. *Psychological Science in the Public Interest*, *2*(2), 31–74.

Sassoon, R. (1995). *The acquisition of a second writing system*. Oxford: Intellect.

Sawin, T. (2015). What 'getting by with English' costs: Fieldworkers' language choices and organizational language policy. *Reconsidering Development*, *4* (1), 66–84.

Seligman, M. E. P. (1975). *Helplessness: On depression, development and death*. San Francisco: W. H. Freeman and Co.

Share, D. (2014). Alphabetism in reading science. *Frontiers in Psychology*, Vol. 5, July 2014, Article 752, 1–4.

Sweeting, A. (2004). *Education in Hong Kong, 1941 to 2001: Visions and revisions*. Hong Kong: Hong Kong University Press.

Wolf, M. (2008). *Proust and the squid: The story and the science of the reading brain*. Cambridge: Icon Books.

7

BEING 'THE VILLAIN'

Globalization and the 'Native-Speaker' English-Language Teacher

Elizabeth J. Erling

Introduction

In this chapter, I will look back at a particular point in my early career as an English-language teacher in the 1990s in Seoul, South Korea. Using autoethnography as a lens, I will consider the role of English-language teachers (ELTs) and the ELT profession in globalization. I will revisit some of the uncomfortable moments that I faced during that time in terms of the global spread of English, the palpable demand for English teaching I sensed and the way in which I was positioned as an English-language teacher. As I transverse through my career as an applied linguist, I continually relate concepts and theories that I encounter to my experience in South Korea—which means that they continue to gain meaning for me. In this chapter, I will attempt to highlight some of these, including linguistic imperialism and the role of the native-speaker English teacher. I will explore how I was affected by the spread of English and the idealization of the native English speaker in the global English-teaching industry. It is my hope in doing so that readers will find ways to relate their own experiences to the discipline of applied linguistics, no matter in which stage in their career they currently find themselves.

The qualitative research method of autoethnography is a particularly suitable lens for this endeavor, as I am attempting to explore my personal experience of English-language teaching and connect it to wider cultural, political and social understandings of globalization and applied linguistic issues (Ellis & Bochner, 2000). The intended goal of sharing these experiences is to sensitize readers to issues of the personal and professional development of native-speaker English teachers: those who have sometimes been framed in the literature as the villain, the egoist, the privileged and the beneficiaries of the spread of English as a result of globalization (de Almeida Mattos, 1997; Barratt & Kontra, 2000;

Holliday, 2005, Holliday et al., 2015). While not wishing to take emphasis away from the privilege accorded to native speakers of English (Piller, 2016), my intention is to show that, in the context of market-driven globalization, this so-called privilege of native speaker English-language teachers is riddled with complexity, and that this privilege is often accompanied by essentialization, commodification and sometimes even exploitation. Using autoethnography provides insight into the complex, and sometimes contradictory, mix of effects of the globalization of English and its impact on the individual level.

So who am I? I consider myself to be an applied linguist and English language teacher and teacher educator. I was born in the United States and am perhaps an idealized native speaker, as I come from a white, English-speaking, monolingual family. I spent my formative years in the Atlanta, Georgia, metropolitan area and attended Georgia State University for my undergraduate studies in English literature and German. I spent two years studying and working in Germany during that time. After graduating, I taught English in Seoul, South Korea, for two years. I then undertook my graduate and doctoral studies in applied linguistics, and have worked in universities in Germany and the UK since 1998. The time I spent in Korea (1995–1997) was a period of my life that has warranted intense reflection throughout my career. During my first few months there, I felt bombarded by new experiences and impressions that I often struggled to understand and was both bewildered and fascinated by them. I also felt relatively isolated. When out and about in Seoul, I was often stopped on the street by people who wanted to try to talk to me or have their photo taken with me. I found it difficult to find people who I felt were genuine about getting to know me. I often felt like they were just trying to get language practice or wanted to be seen with someone blond and white. As I walked through the small streets of my neighborhood, on the way to various schools or houses, people stared and pointed, saying, '*mi-gook saram*'—a word which means 'American' but is regularly applied to any foreigner. Children in my classes asked to look into my blue eyes, and more than once I was asked for a piece of my hair. What helped me to cope with isolation and disorientation was keeping detailed journals, writing letters (this was before the Internet!) and taking lots of photos. As a result, I have a rather vast 'database' of documentation of this period of my life which I have used for reflection and analysis. When reading through these reflections, I have noted the reoccurrence of certain themes that link with theories and topics in applied linguistics, and I draw on some of these themes in this chapter.

Globalization or 세계화: The Increasing Demand for English in Korea

Not recognizing this at the time, I can now see that the situation and context that led me to work as an English-language teacher in South Korea in the 1990s was part of trends implicit in globalization. While there are debates about when globalization began (see Robertson, 2003), it was certainly on the rise in the mid-1990s when I had just finished my Bachelor's studies and was looking for employment. The economic market was increasingly internationalized and, along with this, there was an increase in transnational movements of capital, people, ideas, beliefs, knowledge and news. Travel and digital communication were becoming more accessible and affordable, which led to greater movement of people and ideas (Urry, 2007). Though I had not yet discovered it, the Internet was fast developing, and I opened my first email account at an Internet café in Seoul in 1997. Societies started being seen as part of networks of interaction and interconnectedness (McGrew & Lewis, 1992).

The increased contact between communities that has come about because of globalization involves more people communicating over more language boundaries and therewith increases the need for a common code. For a various set of economic, social, and political reasons (which have been explored by many, e.g., Bailey 1991; Crystal, 1997; Graddol, 1997), English has increasingly been the language fulfilling the need for a global lingua franca. Of course, this increasing demand for English means that there has also been an increase in the need for English-language teachers. With international travel becoming more affordable, and the concurrent dawn of ELT programs like the Japan Exchange and Teaching (JET) Programme in 1987 (see Breckenridge & Erling, 2011), the 1990s saw an increasing number of young people from countries where English is a dominant language setting off to teach English, travel, see the world and gain some teaching/employment experience.

The Republic of South Korea was not exempted from the event of globalization. The country, which had long been labeled the 'Hermit Kingdom' due to its isolationist policies, opened itself to foreign influence as never before with the event of the 1988 Seoul Olympic Games. This also put pressure on the country to apply democratic reforms, which resulted in the election of President Kim Young-sam in 1993. Kim introduced 세계화 (*segyehwa*)—commonly translated as 'globalization'—as the cornerstone of Korea's international trade policy, contributing to the country's rise as one of the four 'Asian Tiger' economies through rapid industrialization. The term *segyehwa*, which implies the internationalization of economic relations, also evokes strong nationalist sentiments, calling on South Koreans to pull together to gain leadership in the international community. Such essentialized notions of national identity intended to secure national unity in the face of international integration, but they also encourage the essentialization of 'the other' (Said, 1978).

Through the opening doors and the policy shift towards internationalization, South Koreans were increasingly exposed to 'other cultures' through the media as well as international visitors. Even in the two years that I was there (1995–1997), I noticed the number of 'foreigners' increasing and other changes in the country's style and character as it was increasingly exposed to 'Western' culture. All of these socio-political shifts resulted in the heightened perceived need for South Koreans to further improve their English communicative skills. English was increasingly demanded for employment and higher education, and offered in schools and private language schools. The national curriculum for English was reformed in the 1990s: the role for English was that expanded attempts were made to implement communicative language teaching (CLT) (Li, 1998). Private language institutes teaching English were growing exponentially, setting into motion what has been called an 'English frenzy' (Park, 2009). 학원, (*hagwon*), or private supplementary tutoring institutes (offering what is often termed 'shadow education'), became increasingly popular in Korea and beyond (Bray & Lykins, 2012). In 2004, it was estimated that Korean households spent about 2.9% of GDP on private tutoring (Kim, 2004), and private investment in English language education in South Korea came to $13 billion in 2009, meaning that South Koreans spend more than $500 per person per year of English-language learning (Piller, 2016: 188).

Though not consciously aware of it at the time, I can now see that I was part of this socio-political moment. In 1995, I was 23, and I had just received my Bachelor's in English. I was living at home, I had no health insurance, my car was breaking down, and there was only a six-month grace period before I had to start paying on the loans I had taken out to afford my university education. While temping as a secretary and data-entry clerk in various companies in Atlanta, every week I looked in the papers for jobs as a teacher, editor, or something suitable for a graduate of English. I had already done a fair bit of traveling and had lived and studied abroad for a year, so the idea of going somewhere else to work and live was not new or unappealing. Every week there was an advertisement in the Education section of the job advertisements in the *Atlanta Journal-Constitution* for English teachers in Korea. Every week I ignored it, having no connection to Korea or any power to imagine myself there. After months of not finding a 'serious job' and becoming increasingly frustrated with my situation, the ad became increasingly interesting. Eventually, I responded and was offered a teaching position in South Korea without much ado.

I remember being both excited and scared to go to Seoul. Although I had always been rather independent, this was the first time that I was doing something completely on my own—without the language skills or the cultural knowledge to make things easier—and I had little security or protection. My situation was probably more precarious than I realized at the time. I later found out that the contract that I had agreed to was basically meaningless, the health insurance and housing promised to me were not forthcoming, and the recruitment agency who had mediated my employment disappeared without a trace soon after my arrival in Seoul. Over time, I realized that contractual issues were quite common among foreign teachers, and I knew people who were imprisoned or deported. Because of issues such as these, the US Embassy had, for some time, an official warning on its website against working in Korea (which has since been removed):

> Due to the growing number and seriousness of problems experienced by American citizens teaching English in Korea, we counsel against taking such

> employment, even at reputable colleges or universities, except upon receipt of a favorable written referral from a current American citizen employee. We receive several complaints daily from Americans who came to Korea to teach English. (Balance, 2002: Para. 9)

The experiences that they report on were similar to my own (and are also echoed further in the Blacklist pieces on Tokyojon's blog):

> Despite contracts promising good salaries, furnished apartments and other amenities, many teachers find they actually receive much less than they were promised; some do not even receive benefits required by Korean law, such as health insurance and severance pay. Teachers' complaints range from simple contract violations through non-payment of salary for months at a time, to dramatic incidents of severe sexual harassment, intimidation, threats of arrest/deportation, and physical assault. (Balance, 2002: Para. 10)

Having no knowledge of where I was going to work beyond what was stated in the contract (which turned out not to be true), I took a job in a *hagwon* that was attempting to expand and increasingly employ 'native-speaker teachers.' My contract was similar to many that were offered at the time: for one year, with a monthly salary, round-trip airfare, and lodging included. My airfare was withheld until the year of employment was complete. The requirements of the job were that I was from an English-speaking country and had a Bachelor's degree (with the subject matter not being important). Since I had studied English and German, I did have extensive knowledge of the English language and experience of studying foreign languages. While I had had no training or experience as a teacher, I was willing to learn and assumed that this experience would allow me some kind of legitimate peripheral participation (Lave & Wenger, 1991) into teaching. I also had a vague notion of eventually returning to higher education to do a Masters in TESOL or applied linguistics.

Being Confronted with the Idea of 'Linguistic Imperialism'

Around the time that I was working in Korea, in the mid-1990s, the fields of applied linguistics and ELT were experiencing significant development—in response to both the growth of varieties of English in various global contexts as well as the increase in English language teaching worldwide. It was when I started my Masters in applied linguistics, directly following those two years, that I was confronted with these ideas. I remember in particular that the work of Robert Phillipson stirred something in me. He put forward his idea of 'linguistic imperialism' (Phillipson, 1992), claiming that industries of ELT were complicit in propelling the hegemony of English. Part of this was a critique of English language teachers in particular, for their role in spreading the language, imposing their values, norms, pedagogies and language on less dominant cultures (see also Holliday, 2005).

As I wrote in my first assignment (Erling, 1997), this idea resonated with some of the moral dilemmas I had in Korea about my role in globalization. Some Koreans were concerned about the traditional national culture and language being eroded due to globalization and the spread of English, and I wondered about how I was contributing to this given that English language teaching was part of the policies intended to further open up and democratize the country. On one hand, I was uncomfortable that my presence in South Korea had potentially played a role in the destabilization of a traditional culture that I had learned to respect and appreciate, but, at the same time, I recognized that the opportunity of living and teaching there had given me possibilities to cross linguistic and cultural boundaries, making connections and friends and this had allowed us all to challenge perceptions, learn and grow. So while engaging with Phillipson's theory of linguistic imperialism did initially cause me some shame and guilt (Rajagopalan, 1999), as I started to think about it more deeply, it also propelled me to follow Pennycook (2001) and strive to find ways to enact a pedagogically and politically engaged applied linguistics that responds to social and cultural issues.

The 'Native Non-Teacher'

It was not only the topic of linguistic imperialism discussed during my post-graduate studies that particularly resounded with my experience in South Korea. Having attended the University of Edinburgh, Alan Davies's book on *The Native Speaker in Applied Linguistics* (1991; 2003) was very influential. Our study program included a demystification of 'the native speaker ideal,' i.e., the assumption that native speakers inherently possess a superior command of the language and intimate knowledge of the culture. I later explored research that legitimizes the contribution of non-native-speaker English teachers and illuminates their struggles to be recognized as language teaching professionals who are on par with their native-English-speaking peers (e.g., Braine, 1999; Medgyes, 1999). Just as new research was recognizing the multitude of identities and motivations that students bring with them to the classroom (e.g., Norton 2000), there were studies that argued for an end to the dichotomization and essentialization of non-native-speaker teachers of English (e.g., Holliday, 2005; Liu, 1999).

I certainly recognized and accepted a need for an end to the dichotomization of native speaker and non-native speakers and for valuing the contribution of non-native-speaker teachers to ELT. Thinking back to my experience in South Korea, I could see that ideologies of the native-speaker teacher were behind the practices at the private language school where I taught. The teaching labor was split between the Korean English teachers, who taught grammar and explained rules in Korean, and the native-speaker teachers, who taught communication. It was also certainly the case that Korean and foreign teachers were treated differentially by our employers. I am quite sure that native speaker teachers got higher pay plus had their accommodation covered. But, they also had less job security and more concern about employment rights, deportation, etc. I could also see some validity in the critique of the native-speaker teacher not being as diligent or well trained as their Korean counterparts. The Korean teachers of English worked longer hours and showed more commitment to the school. My point is not engage in a petty debate about who had it better, as it seems like neither group of teachers had particularly ideal working conditions. I just want to point out that there were very different challenges for these groups of teachers—and that we each had to respond to different expectations coming from the school, the students, and the parents.

Moreover, I could not help but note that while that critique of the native-speaker teacher recognizes the multifaceted identities of non-native-speaker students and teachers, it often does not accord the same value to the identities of native-speaker English teachers. They are often lumped together in the discourse as unskilled, insensitive and crass, regardless of the cultural, ethnic, linguistic and professional diversity that can be found among them. Some scholars have even used pejorative terms to describe them, like the 'professional egotist' (Barratt & Kontra, 2000: 21) and the 'native non-teacher' (de Almeida Mattos, 1997: 38). The villainization of the native speaker teacher is well displayed in an excerpt from Holliday (2005) who describes native speaker English teachers as

> a professional group which, in order to find a status which it cannot find at home, propels itself into the professional domains of other education systems in other countries, while maintaining distance from them; and sees itself as liberally humanist even when it blatantly reduces foreign colleagues and students to a problematic generalized Other. (Holliday, 2005: 29; for further critique, see Erling, 2006)

It has to be admitted that the first part of this description aptly describes some of the narrative that I have related above about the events that led to my teaching in Korea (not able to find the kind of job I wanted 'at home' and thus, seeking employment in another country's education system). However, when I read this I was surprised at how native-speaker teachers are framed in an active position. While it was true that I was distanced from my Korean colleagues, I felt that this was not of my own accord, but that I was not expected (or particularly welcomed) to work or socialize with them. My experience of this felt entirely passive, and I thought that I was adapting to local norms. It seemed that (as I will show below) some of the native-speaker roles that I took on were imposed on me. I also noted that this discussion was told almost entirely from the perspective of the non-native teacher and student of English, while the perspectives of English-language teachers from 'the center' tend to be left out or considered unmarked (but, see Breckenridge & Erling, 2011)—which is why I am telling this story.

Play with Native

It also came as a surprise that the diverse group of native-speaker teachers I knew in Korea—who came from a wide range of backgrounds and levels of experience—were being portrayed as a homogenous group in the applied linguistics literature. So while this description did not map onto my version of reality, it did conform to the constructed and fixed ideal of the native-speaker teacher that was desired and sought after in the context of South Korea. The more one conformed to stereotypical ideals of the native speaker—white, blonde, blue-eyed, young, and preferably not Korean-speaking—the more valuable one was to the employer. My employer, for example, used to hire me out to other schools.

I particularly remember one Saturday when I was asked to work at another school that was having its grand opening. The school, which was brand new and had yet to hire staff, wanted to create the impression that it had a cadre of native-speaker teachers. The school was called "English Camp" and it had a number of themed rooms that were designed to simulate an 'authentic' English-speaking environment (whatever that is), e.g., the school room, play area, kitchen, etc. (for more on the phenomenon of schools like this, see Seargeant, 2005). The sign on the front of the school read: "English Camp is the place we can play with native" (see Figure 7.1). I was asked to 'dress up,' and when I arrived was asked to don a red sash and walk up and down the street in front of the school in order to attract passers-by and new customers into the Grand Opening event. I reflected afterwards in my journal that I felt like an 'English prostitute.'

Although I did not know what to call this at the time, I later encountered the term 'commodification' in work such as Monica Heller's. It has been interesting to follow increasing discussions about the commodification of language as part of globalization, in terms of it being framed as a technical skill resulting in economic gain (see Heller, 2003; 2010). However, I have noted that there has been little discussion about how English-language teachers are commodified as part of processes of globalization. While these teachers are made responsible for the spread of inequality and linguistic imperialism, there has not been much work on how local attitudes and national ideologies work together with global trends to perpetuate their systemic 'utilization.' Native-speaker teachers in South Korea were often presented as the exoticized Other, unessential to the classroom, interchangeable and foreign—regardless of these individuals' personalities, ethnic backgrounds and levels of motivation or experience.

Developing a Professional Identity

Being traded and marketed as a commodity—and positioned as being interchangeable in the classroom—ultimately had an impact on the development of my professional identity as a teacher. I quickly came to see that my experience (or lack thereof) as a teacher—or my desire to do 'a good job'—did not matter as

FIGURE 7.1 English Camp in Seoul, 1995 (Photo by the Author).

much to my employers and students as my white skin, blue eyes, and blond hair (for similar experiences, see Jeon, 2009; Simon-Maeda, 2004). While I was motivated and tried to prepare lessons and think of new ideas when I first got there, I became increasingly frustrated. Instead of being able to work with one group of students over time, I was ushered from classroom to classroom, school to school (in my journal I referred to this as being 'pimped out'). In fact, I was regularly asked to walk into lessons with no previous knowledge of the students or the teaching material and was expected to 'teach.' My coping strategy was to develop a bank of resources that I carried around with me—games, flashcards, songs, etc.—so that I could use them with any group whenever needed. Sometimes I would bring photos from home or things to show-and-tell. Students would ask me about my life, friends, family in the US, and for this we would, of course, have to engage in real communicative activities.

When reviewing my journals, I have noted with interest that I was frustrated by students' lack of interest in their textbooks and by the fact that they always pressured me to play games, sing, or chat (when possible) with them. At the time, I did not recognize these as meaningful learning activities. The 'serious' learning was reserved for the English lessons with the non-native-speaker teachers, who would explain rules and practices and undertake grammar and vocabulary drills. The irony is not lost on me that I now work in international teacher education to support teachers and teacher educators in various countries implementing student-centered communicative language teaching techniques. Part of this is to encourage teachers to move away from the textbook and try out more communicative and creative activities, which are sometimes quite similar to those that I did in South Korea (those that I felt were illegitimate at the time).

Conclusion

My experience in Korea in the mid-1990s, while disorienting and sometimes lonely, gave me an experience of being 'otherized.' I experienced commodification and the feeling of being positioned as an English prostitute. Many teachers in a similar situation experienced exploitation, and I, too, was unjustly treated at times. When I left the country in 1997, with hindsight I can now see that the Asian economic crisis had been lurking around the corner. The last company I worked for disappeared without paying me my final three months' salary.

These experiences meant that in my further studies in applied linguistics, I was sensitive to discussions about linguistic imperialism and the privilege of the native-speaker English teacher. While I do not deny that these debates are interesting and useful to engage in, I have always felt that they convey only part of the story. Privilege can lead to idealization, dehumanization, commodification, utilization and exploitation. And all these, in turn, can cause English language teachers to disengage from the profession. The way that 'native speakers' are portrayed in discussions about globalization and language affects their own motivation, self-perception and professional ambitions and development, as well as those of learners.

I recently came across a blog called "Don't Teach in Korea" started by someone who had taught there. Despite the difficulties I faced while starting out as an English-language teacher in South Korea in the 1990s, this is not a position that I would support. Teaching in Korea marked an important transformation for me, both in terms of my personal and professional identity. Despite the difficulties I faced, I have carried on as an applied linguistics professional and have used that experience as the basis for critical reflection and engagement with many of the ideas and theories that I have come across. I have also maintained ties with Korea, keeping a number of friends that I made at that time and developing other friendships since. While there have always been moments when I have felt a sense of discomfort with my role in globalization, this has not resulted in me abandoning English-language teaching, but has propelled an interest and intrigue and brought me to consider ways of responding to ideologies of English and its role in globalization (see Erling & Seargeant, 2013; Erling, forthcoming).

So while I would recommend that teachers who go out into the world to teach have more teacher training—and more security—than I did then, I also think that the field of applied linguistics has to work harder not to essentialize and villainize teachers entering the profession. There are many such teachers teaching the language globally and we need to recognize their potential to become critical, transcultural, multilingual English-language teaching professionals. Through much of my career, I have been ashamed of my earliest teaching experiences. I have never wanted to admit that I started out as a rogue teacher, a cowboy, a native speaker who got a job based on idealized perceptions of language and ethnicity. Writing these experiences feels in a way like 'coming out.' I hope that laying bare these thoughts and experiences opens a space in which we can better consider how to better create pathways for native-speaker teachers to move from their early, novice experiences in teaching to being critical applied linguistic professionals. Globalization and neo-liberalism are having an impact on us all, turning victims into villains and vice versa, and native-speaker status does not protect teachers from hardship. Applied linguistics and ELT have an important role to play in ensuring the cultivation of empathy and communication across cultures, communities, and careers—for native and non-native speakers alike.

Questions for Discussion

1. What is your role in globalization and the spread of English? Are you comfortable with that role? What might you be able to do to enact a pedagogically and politically engaged applied linguistics that responds to social and cultural issues?
2. Consider an English-language teaching context that you are familiar with. Are there different roles and expectations of and for native- and non-native-speaker English teachers? What ideologies are behind these practices?

Author Profile

Dr. Elizabeth J. Erling started her ELT career teaching in Korea in the mid-1990s and is now a Senior Lecturer in English language teaching at the Open University, UK. She is the editor of *English across the Fracture Lines: The Contribution and Relevance of English to Security, Safety and Stability in the World* (British Council, forthcoming) and *English and Development: Policy, Practice and Globalization* (Multilingual Matters, 2013) and author of several articles published in journals such as *World Englishes* and *Language Policy*.

Acknowledgments

This is something that I have wanted to write for a long time and I thank Maryam for giving me an opportunity to finally do it. I am also grateful to Karen Littleton and Uschi Stickler for their inspiration and support in writing this; to Miriam Meyerhoff, who listened to some of these stories in a pub in Edinburgh back in 2003 and told me to write about them; to Yvonne Breckenridge, who helped me to see some of the larger, critical issues involved in our ELT practice in Asia;

and to Allison Perrett and all the *Sungsandong* crew in Seoul 1995–1997, who shared this transformational experience with me. Finally, I am grateful for the support of the Erling-Gerstenecker family; my love for them is at the heart of everything I do.

References

Bailey, R. W. (1991). *Images of English: A cultural history of the language.* Cambridge: Cambridge University Press.

Balance, J. (2002). Don't teach in Korea. Blog piece by Tokyojon. Retrieved July 5, 2016 from: http://blacklist.tokyojon.com/dont_teach_in_korea.html.

Barratt, L. & Kontra, E. (2000). Native-English-speaking teachers in cultures other than their own. *TESOL Journal, 9* (3), 19–23.

Braine, G. (ed.) (1999). *Non-native educators in English language teaching.* Mahwah, NJ: Lawrence Erlbaum Associates.

Bray, M. & Lykins, C. (2012). Shadow education: Private supplementary tutoring and its implications for policy makers in Asia. Retrieved July 5, 2016 from: http://adb.org/sites/default/files/pub/2012/shadow-education.pdf.

Breckenridge, Y. & Erling, E. J. (2011). The native speaker English teacher and the politics of globalization in Japan. In P. Seargeant (ed.), *English in Japan in the era of globalization* (pp. 80–100). Basingstoke: Palgrave.

Crystal, D (1997). *English as a global language.* Cambridge: Cambridge University Press.

Davies, A. (1991). *The native speaker in applied linguistics.* Edinburgh: Edinburgh University Press.

de Almeida Mattos, A. M. (1997). Native and non-native teacher: A matter to think over. *English Teaching Forum, 35* (1), 38.

Ellis, C. & Bochner, A. P. (2000). Autoethnography, personal narrative, reflexivity. In Norman K. Denzin & Yvonna S. Lincoln (eds.), *Handbook of qualitative research* (2nd ed., pp. 733–768). Thousand Oaks, CA: Sage.

Erling, E. J. (1997). Teaching global English in Korea: An effort to minimise linguistic imperialism. Unpublished Masters essay. The University of Edinburgh.

Erling, E. J. (2006). Review of *The struggle to teach English as an international language* by A. Holliday (2005 Oxford: OUP). In *BAAL News* 83, 29–32.

Erling, E. J. & Seargeant, P. (eds.) (2013). *English and development: Policy, pedagogy and globalization.* Bristol: Multilingual Matters.

Erling, E. J. (ed.) (forthcoming). *English across the fracture lines: The contribution and relevance of English to security, safety and stability in the world.* London: British Council.

Graddol, D. (1997). *The future of English?* London: British Council.

Heller, M. (2003). Globalization, the new economy, and the commodification of language and identity. *Journal of Sociolinguistics*, 7 (4), 473–92.

Heller, M. (2010). The commodification of language. *The Annual Review of Anthropology*, 39, 101–14.

Holliday, A. (2005). *The struggle to teach English as an international language.* Oxford: Oxford University Press.

Holliday, A., Aboshiha, P. & Swan, A. (eds.) (2015). *(En)countering native-speakerism: Global perspectives.* London: Palgrave.

Jeon, M. (2009). Globalization and native English speakers in English programme in Korea (EPIK). *Language, Culture and Curriculum, 22* (3), 231–43.

Kim, T. (2004). Shadow education: School quality and demand for private tutoring in Korea. KDI School of Pub Policy & Management Paper No. 04-21. Retrieved July 5, 2016 from: http://ssrn.com/abstract=635864.

Lave, J. & Wenger, E. (1991). *Situated learning: Legitimate peripheral participation*. Cambridge: Cambridge University Press.

Li, D. F. (1998). "It's always more difficult than you plan and imagine": Teachers' perceived difficulties in introducing the communicative approach in South Korea. *TESOL Quarterly, 32* (4), 677–703.

Liu, J. (1999). From their own perspectives: The impact of non-native ESL professionals on their students in G. Braine (ed.), *Non-native educators in English language teaching* (pp.159–176). Mahwah, NJ: Lawrence Erlbaum Associates.

McGrew. & Lewis, P. G. (eds.) (1992). *Global politics: Globalization and the nation-state*. Cambridge: Polity Press.

Medgyes, P. (1999). *The non-native teacher*. London: Macmillan.

Norton, B. (2000). *Identity and language learning: Gender, ethnicity and educational change*. London: Pearson.

Park, J. S. Y. (2009). *The local construction of a global language: Ideologies of English in South Korea*. Berlin: Mouton de Gruyter.

Pennycook, A. (2001). *Critical applied linguistics: A critical introduction*. London: Lawrence Erlbaum.

Phillipson, R. (1992). *Linguistic imperialism*. Oxford: Oxford University Press.

Piller, I. (2016). *Linguistic diversity and social justice: An introduction to applied sociolinguistics*. Oxford: Oxford University Press.

Rajagopalan, K. (1999). Of EFL teachers, conscience and cowardice. *ELT Journal, 53* (3), 200–06.

Robertson, R. (2003). *The three waves of globalization*. London: Zed Books.

Said, E. (1978). *Orientalism*. New York: Pantheon Books.

Seargeant, P. (2005). "More English than England itself": The simulation of authenticity in foreign language practice in Japan. *International Journal of Applied Linguistics, 15* (3), 326–45.

Simon-Maeda, A. (2004). The complex construction of professional identities: Female EFL educators in Japan speak out. *TESOL Quarterly*, 38, 405–36.

Urry, J. (2007). *Mobilities*. Cambridge: Polity.

8

WHAT MY SCHOOLTEACHERS FAILED TO APPRECIATE ABOUT TRANSLANGUAGING

Ruhma Choudhury

> *Despite the ability of bilinguals to translanguage, monolinguals are often oblivious to the presence of these bilingual practices, or dismissive of their significance, with any differences in language practices often evaluated as a deficiency.*
>
> (García, 2009: 48)

Introduction

From North to South America, Europe to Africa and Asia to Australia, English has made a home for itself in every corner of the world. According to the British Council Report (2013), *The English Effect*, one in every four persons around the globe speaks English as a first, second or foreign language and a substantial increase in English-as-a-second (ESL) or English-as-a-foreign language (EFL) speakers is predicted in the near future, bringing the total number of people using English to close to two billion by 2020. These numbers clearly indicate that English continues to grow in stature as an important international language.

The current spread of English around the world is inexorably tied to economic globalization that has galvanized many countries across the globe to upgrade their workforce's communicative skills in English in order to retain a competitive edge in the global market (British Council, 2013). The British Council Report posits that global workers need to be effective communicators in English in order to communicate their expertise and competencies in the world market, if they are not to be left out of globalization. Given the demand for English over the years, English Language Teaching (ELT) has become a global operation; however, the norms for English teaching and learning flow, primarily, from native English-speaking countries (especially from the UK and the US), which consider

ELT skills to be universally relevant. In a similar vein, the practices that are considered best for teaching English in these countries have received wide support around the world. Two such widely accepted assumptions in ESL and EFL contexts are that English should be taught monolingually because learners' home languages can be an impediment to learning English, and translation from home language (L1) to target language (L2) should be discouraged in language classrooms; otherwise, the standard of English would deteriorate. Such assumptions have, however, been criticized by critical scholars (Canagarajah, 2011; Cummins, 2007; He & Zhang, 2010; Phillipson, 1992, 2008; Tollefson, 1991).

As a Bangladeshi who lives in the US, a teacher/instructor of English for over 20 years and researcher of TESOL/applied linguistics and language policy, I have experienced the deleterious effects and consequences of monolingual instructional approaches on students' language learning. I recall, when I was a schoolgirl in Bangladesh, I was discouraged from using my native tongue, Bengali, in English classes, which had an adverse effect on my language learning, which I describe in detail in the next section.

As an advocate of the postmodern pedagogy of 'translanguaging,' in this autoethnographic essay I will draw on my personal, professional and scholarly lived experiences to demonstrate that a successful learner uses his/her prior knowledge—linguistic as well as general—as a foundation for new learning and new language acquisition. García (2009) defines translanguaging as "*multiple discursive practices in which bilinguals engage in order to make sense of their bilingual worlds*" (p. 45; emphasis original). This is a term she borrowed from Cen Williams (1994, cited in Baker, 2001). Proponents of translanguaging posit that multilingual users do not develop separate competencies for their languages, nor do they use their languages exactly the same way (Canagarajah, 2011; García, 2009; García & Wei, 2014). In actuality, very few mulitilinguals are balanced bilinguals with total mastery over their languages; rather, multilinguals have one linguistic repertoire from which they choose features (e.g., vocabulary, grammar) strategically to facilitate communication. This view is in direct opposition to English-only policy of many ESL and EFL classrooms that dictate that English should be taught monolingually. My purpose here is twofold: (1) to challenge the English-only policy of ELT practices, and (2) to reflect on the benefits of translanguaging as an effective teaching strategy for language instruction in the 21st century for bi/multilingual global citizens. Through this essay, I will take the reader to many places: from my elementary school English classrooms in Bangladesh in the mid-1970s to the early 1980s, to my French classrooms in an English medium school in Cote d'Ivoire in Africa where I spent my teen years (1982–1986), my English classrooms in Bangladesh and in the US since the 1990s, during which I have been teaching English, and, last but not least, to my own research on the subject as a means to draw on my experiences to argue that learners use all their linguistic resources to acquire the target language.

Linguistically speaking, I am a multilingual individual, who is literate in Bengali, English and French, but with unequal mastery: I would rate Bengali as my strongest, followed by English and then, French, in which I have low-intermediate proficiency. In addition to these languages, I also speak Sylheti, a dialect of Bengali, and can follow simple conversations in Hindi, as well. My English teachers, however, showed little interest in my language background. To them, I was a tabula rasa, an empty vessel, which they needed to fill up with English knowledge. They were more focused on what I *did not* know (e.g., English) rather than what I did know (e.g., Bengali, Sylheti). They insisted that each language be kept in a separate container lest the interactions affect the acquisition of English negatively. In fact, banning other languages from English classrooms was the rule of the day.

English-Only Policy

I use the term 'English-only policy' to describe the ideology to which many educators adhere to in ESL and EFL classrooms: English is taught best monolingually (the fallacy of this belief is discussed in detail by Phillipson, 1992). This policy is still prevalent in ESL/EFL classrooms despite evidence from research on cross-linguistic transfer indicating that learner's L1 can act as a bridge to learning a new language and that L1 literacy knowledge transfers to L2 (Choudhury & Garrison-Fletcher, 2017; Collins, 2014; Cummins, 2009). Why is English-only policy popular among some ESL educators? These educators believe that learners' L1 is an impediment to learning English and translation from L1 to L2 is ineffective and, conversely, more exposure to English in the classroom will accelerate English acquisition (Cummins, 2009). In a study designed to discover the attitudes of ESL educators in the US regarding L1 use in the classroom, Auerbach (1993) asked educators in a statewide TESOL conference whether ESL students should be allowed to use their L1 in ESL class; 30% of the ESL educators said no, 20% said yes, while the remaining 50% responded 'sometimes.' Those who responded 'sometimes' explained that L1 should be used only as a last resort, meaning L1 can only be used after several attempts have been made to explain the concept in English. They saw enforcing English-only policy in classrooms as a commonsense practice.

Pivotal in forwarding the English-only policy is the report of the Commonwealth Conference on Teaching of ESL, more commonly referred to as The Makerere Report, as the conference was held at the University College of Makerere, Uganda, in 1961 (Phillipson, 1992). The report discussed the priorities for ELT in the newly independent nation states of the British Commonwealth and outlined beliefs about English teaching that have influenced how English has been taught both in native and non-native English speaking countries. The key beliefs are as follows:

1. English should be used exclusively in classrooms for best results.
2. A native speaker of English is the ideal teacher.
3. The earlier English is introduced, the better the results.

4. More exposure to English will provide better results.
5. If home languages are used, the standard of English will deteriorate.

These beliefs were later criticized by Phillipson (1992: 185–218) as 'fallacies;' nevertheless, they still exert an influence around the world.

My Encounters with English-Only Policy

I experienced the English-only policies firsthand in language classrooms as a student in the 1970s and 1980s and as a teacher in the 1990s in Bangladesh, and later as an ESL instructor in California in the early 2000s.

English has held a prestigious position in Bangladeshi society through tremulous times that led to the independence from the British in 1947 and later from Pakistan in 1971. Bilinguals in English and Bengali have always been perceived to have better educational and professional opportunities than their monolingual Bengali-speaking counterparts. The private Bengali elementary school that I attended in a posh neighborhood of Dhaka, Bangladesh, offered a strong curriculum in English; my parents approved of the rigor, both of the Bengali and English curricula, pleased that their daughter would grow up to become a fluent bilingual speaker of Bengali and English in the same way that they had a generation ago.

In my school, we read stories from the book series *The Radiant Way*, a British-based textbook that depicted the life of English children that I found alien but fascinating. There was a story about a chimney sweeper. I remember this story particularly well because I was punished for asking a friend in class to translate it for me. 'Speak in English,' was a phrase I often heard bellowed out by my teachers as a reminder to adhere to the English-only policy of the classroom and to quell the whispers of Bengali. When caught speaking Bengali, we were often punished, and our punishment ranged from a scold to standing in a corner for the entire class period, depending on the severity of the offense (as deemed by the teacher). That day I spent part of the lesson standing in a corner with my head hung low in shame.

I never questioned why Bengali was ostracized in English classes. Nor did I find it strange that a room full of monolingual Bengali speakers would refrain themselves from using their L1 in order to adhere to the classroom policy of English-only. In fact, getting caught speaking Bengali in class was a constant fear of mine. This fear was sufficiently deep that I would rather use my limited English than Bengali with my classmates and teachers. At the same time, I was also terrified of mispronouncing an English word or using a wrong expression. A safer alternative was to remain quiet when my English failed me. Looking back at those days, I regret the missed opportunities (i.e., using Bengali to develop my English) that my teachers could have capitalized on to assist me in my endeavor to learn English. In their defense, they probably thought that the standard of English would drop if they allowed the use of Bengali in the class.

Despite the consequences the ban of Bengali had on my acquisition of English, I, unconsciously, internalized this policy as a best practice for learning and teaching English. This policy was entrenched so deeply that I imposed the same restrictions on the children when I became an English teacher myself in a private English-medium school (the students and teaching staff were monolingual Bengali speakers) in Dhaka in 1995. Even when the students would come after class, I would refrain from using Bengali with them. In my mind, a teacher should model good behavior and thus, encouraging the students to speak to me in English should be a priority. In fact, I saw my duty as an English teacher to provide my students with the maximum exposure to English.

My views on prohibiting L1 use in English class were reaffirmed several years later when I taught ESL as a graduate student (working towards an MA degree in TESOL) at a community college in California from 2000 to 2002. I encountered the same repression-oriented policy towards L1 use. As an example, my supervisor advised me not to encourage students to use bilingual dictionaries, lest they begin to use them as a crutch. This dependency, she explained, would prevent the students from using monolingual English dictionaries later on in their lives. In other words, even bilingual dictionaries were seen as detrimental to learning English.

Almost a decade later, I encountered the same beliefs regarding English-only ideology when I interviewed English school teachers in rural Bangladesh for my doctoral dissertation (Choudhury, 2010) to discover their views about the Communicative Language Teaching (CLT) approach in 2008. When asked if they used Bengali in the classroom, many denied using it, claiming that instructing in L1 was bad practice, even to provide translations of words; those who admitted to using Bengali justified the use by blaming the low proficiency of the students. The overwhelming sense was that to instruct in Bengali, even for clarifications, reflected poorly on the teachers. They claimed that translation is discouraged under the CLT approach, and as such, they should not adopt it as a teaching strategy.

To sum up, my experiences in English classrooms as both a learner and teacher led me to believe for many years that English had to be taught monolingually. If other languages were allowed, then the standard of English would drop; even worse, the learner's acquisition of English would be hampered due to L1 interference. Years later in my doctoral studies, I was introduced to an alternative view that supports the use of L1 to develop L2 proficiency; this was translanguaging (which I introduce and discuss in depth in the next sections) that made me question my long-held assumptions about English-only ideology.

L1 and L2 Transfer

Contrary to the widespread practice of target-language-only policy (e.g., English-only) in classrooms, language learners themselves use their prior knowledge, including all available linguistic resources, to master a new language (Cummins, 2009; Cummins & Swain, 2014). In other words, a learner's L1 can and *does* facilitate

L2 acquisition. The idea was so revolutionary that when I first encountered it as a doctoral student at Teachers College, Columbia University (2004–2010), it turned my world upside down; I wrestled with this new line of thinking, presented in the course materials and class discussions on language policy and bilingual education. One course in particular, titled 'English and Globalization,' taught by Professor Ofelia García, herself an advocate of translanguaging and linguistic pluralism, threw my neat world into a frenzy as the readings and discussions challenged my long-held beliefs about English teaching and learning. The readings from prominent scholars such as Canagarajah (1999), Mazrui (2004), Phillipson (1992) and Tollefson (1991) critiquing the naïve acceptance of English as a neutral global language challenged the beliefs I had held dear for so long, revealing that these were not set in stone. Furthermore, the monolingual instructional approaches to teaching English that I had heretofore adopted were not corroborated by research on cross-linguistic transfer (e.g., Cummins, 2007).

Hitherto, I never questioned how I *really* learned my languages. What I knew about teaching, primarily, came from observing teachers whose practices I mimicked when I became a teacher myself. As I began to analyze what I read and discussed in class in Teachers College, flashbacks of how I *actually* learned my languages (English, Bengali and French) came flooding back. A case in point is how I understood the differences between *connaître* and *savoir*, the French verbs for 'to know,' in my first French lesson in an English-medium school (French was the second language) in Côte d'Ivoire in 1982. The definition of *connaître* is to know a person or to be familiar with a thing, place or person, while *savoir* refers to knowing information or how to do something.

My French classes were conducted solely in French. We heard the phrase '*s'il vous plaît français*' (French, please) often, to remind us to adhere to French. When my teacher introduced the verbs *connaître* and *savoir* with examples, my English-speaking peers struggled to grasp the differences. The task became even more challenging because they could not talk among themselves in English to figure out the differences. I, on the other hand, had a secret weapon: Bengali; I realized that *connaître* corresponds to the Bengali verb 'cheena' (transliterated) and *savoir* to 'jana' (transliterated). I used my Bengali to guide me to select the correct verb for 'to know,' in a French sentence. Even though there was zero tolerance for other languages in the classroom, I now realize that I used my prior linguistic knowledge to understand new concepts in French. That realization led to another, which was that while language separation is artificially created in the classroom; languages themselves are not compartmentalized in the brain.

According to Cummins (2005), the academic literacy skills in L1 and learning strategies can transfer to L2 so that learners do not need to relearn these skills and strategies in L2. In other words, a strong correlation exists between academic literacy skills in learners' L1 and L2. Therefore, suppressing L1 in new language acquisition is not just unhelpful; it is, rather, harmful, limiting students' ability to make important connections within their expanding linguistic and literacy repertoires.

Translanguaging

Silencing learners' other languages in English classrooms is an ineffective strategy, especially in today's global context where many English language learners are global migrants, living in different parts of the world for economic and educational opportunities. Globalization has intensified language contact due to unprecedented volume of human movement around the world. There are increased interactions among people of different cultures and nations, and this transnational mobility is blurring the lines between languages and nations. While assimilating to the culture of their adopted home, the transnational individuals, like myself, also maintain ties with their country of origin (Choudhury, 2013). Describing the transnational experiences of these bi/multilingual communities, García (2010) explains,

> Bilingual communities often experience transnational lives, shuttling between states, as diasporic communities. But most of the time, bilingual people shuttle between communities that are hybrid themselves, a product of postmodern societies. (García, 2010: 199)

In these hybrid communities that García (2009) mentions above, the multilingual people are not tied to one language/dialect. Instead, their language practices include the mixing of codes and words. These multilingual individuals practice social interactions in which they consider who their interlocutors are and what languages/dialects are to be used in what social contexts. In other words, depending on the modalities and interlocutors, a speaker considers which languages/dialects are needed to engage in successful communication. In doing so, a multilingual person views all her languages as resources for thinking, learning, reading and writing. For instance, she can read information in one language and write about it in another. García refers to this language practice as translanguaging.

Canagarajah (2011) reports that translanguaging as a language practice dates as far back as pre-colonial times in South Asia, South America and Africa. In rural communities of these areas, inhabitants translanguaged to communicate with neighbors with whom they did not share a common tongue. Such translanguaging practices in East Africa are also reported by Alamin Mazrui (2007). Fast-forwarding to modern time, translanguaging occurs naturally in multilingual communities around the world; it is a common phenomenon among multilingual learners who shuttle between their languages and/or dialects to communicate effectively and to make sense of their world. The exclusive use of L2 in language classrooms can, thus, pose challenges to these multilingual learners. If they have difficulty following the medium of instruction, they will not understand the content.

Translanguaging as a strategy in teaching L2, on the other hand, has merits. Cen Williams (1994; as discussed by Baker, 2001) finds four advantages to translanguaging, which are (1) developing a deeper understanding of the content, (2) developing competence in the less proficient language, (3) building better home–school relationships and (4) creating a better learning environment through integration of fluent and less proficient speakers. As a learning strategy, it can help learners understand the subject matter, by allowing their L1 practices to be used alongside the L2 in classrooms, which in turn, facilitates language learning.

My Encounters with Translanguaging

While my teachers' adopted a policy of exclusion to ban L1 from classroom, I, without realizing at that time, used my prior linguistic knowledge as a foundation for new learning. In retrospect, I realized that I translanguaged as far back as elementary school in Dhaka. I recall how easy it was to follow the second grade English lesson on panda and bamboo once I cajoled the translation of 'bamboo' out of a classmate. My ancestors were from Sylhet, a region located north east of Bangladesh, which is famous for its bamboo in the country. Once I knew what bamboo was, the rest of the lesson, with pandas jumping from one bamboo tree to another, began to make sense.

My fondest memory of translanguaging, however, is writing a summary of the then favourite book, *Little House on the Prairie*, in English. I first read this book series in Bengali in my grandmother's house during one summer break. They took up one large shelf of the armoire desk that she kept in her reading area. I would sneak into the room whenever I was bored and cuddle up with a book. When my fourth grade teacher assigned us to write a summary of a book that we had read that summer, I knew exactly which book to write on. Imagine my surprise and glee when I discovered them a few years later in 1982, sitting on a bookshelf in the library of my school in Côte d'Ivoire in Africa. They were all in English!

I began consciously to think about translanguaging and its implications to foreign/target language learning only beyond post-graduate level when, as mentioned previously, I was introduced to the term for the first time in Professor García's course. My ESL pedagogical practices evolved because of what I read, but the change happened slowly. At first, I had to grapple with the idea because I was not sure how I would implement it in class, even though it sounded fascinating and feasible in theory. It was only after 2008 that I finally began to incorporate practices that encouraged L1 in the classroom. It began with small changes. Occasionally, the students were allowed to form groups based on the same language background to work on a task in a linguistically mixed classroom. It took another two years for me to begin designing lessons that incorporated L1 practices of the learners. For instance, they would interview a family member on an issue in their L1 and later write about it in English. In another lesson, students would read about a topic in their L1 and then translate the information for their peers in English.

While I had anecdotal evidence from my ESL classroom that translanguaging can facilitate L2 acquisition, I had no data scientifically gathered to corroborate these observations. In 2014, my colleague Dr. Garrison-Fletcher and I put the theory of cross-linguistic transfer to the test with our ESL students at LaGuardia Community College, City University of New York, by designing a pilot study with monolingual Bengali speakers with low proficiency in English (Choudhury & Garrison-Fletcher, 2017). We posited that developing the participants' academic skills in Bengali would strengthen their academic English language skills because L1 literacy skills and strategies transfer to L2.

Pre-test scores from Bengali assessment determined that the participants' Bengali proficiency was low (eighth grade level), and based on these findings we designed an intervention to provide them with Bengali lessons alongside English instruction that they would receive in their regular ESL course. We also compared their pre-test scores against a Bengali-speaking control groups and found that the average for the experimental group was 75%, while for the control group was 78%. The average scores, thus, were comparable. At the end of the semester, the post-test results revealed that our participants made significant gains in Bengali and the average score spiked to 88%. The participants also outperformed their counterparts in the control group in their ESL exit exams. The pass rate in the control group was 33%, while that of the experimental group was 75%, which was significantly higher than the control groups' average pass rate.

These findings, thus, were in line with research on cross-language transfer that claims that whenever a learner is acquiring a new language, he is building upon his existing knowledge, including linguistic knowledge. Cummins (2009) maintains that the learners are able to link their academic concepts to L2 more effectively when their L1 practices are seen as resources in learning L2. And, he warns, "this linking cannot be done effectively if students' L1 is banished from the classroom" (Cummins, 2009: 319). In a similar vein, Auerbach (1993) claims that using learners' linguistic resources is beneficial at all levels of ESL, particularly with adult ESL learners with limited schooling and literacy skills. For these learners, she maintains that the L1 use in the classroom is not only effective, but necessary.

In our Bengali intervention mentioned earlier, our participants were encouraged to translanguage in order to fulfill the learning goals. For instance, the participants were taught to summarize passages of Bengali texts during lab hours allocated for Bengali instruction and later translate these into English in their regular ESL class. Other times, they would read a passage in Bengali and discuss it in class in English. During their lab hours, they worked together to write a summary of an English text. In this way, they were translanguaging in order to effectively perform a task—summarizing a text. As these participants discussed and wrote about multilingual texts, they developed different perspectives that broadened their understanding of these materials.

Explaining how translanguaging can promote L2 acquisition, García (2009) maintains that translanguaging encourages the use of L1 practices in the classroom, and this systematic use of the L1 eventually leads to the use of appropriate form of the L2. She further explains that translanguaging deepens learners' thinking ability as they work collaboratively with multilingual peers.

Conclusion

Over a span of twenty years, my teaching philosophy concerning L1 use in the ESL classroom has undergone a profound change. It has been a radical departure from banning L1 to embracing pedagogical practices that encourage L1 use in L2 teaching. Today, in my English classrooms, monolingual instructional approaches are out, bilingual dictionaries and translanguaging or bi/multilingual instructional strategies are in. However, some ESL educators and L2 teaching programs are still reluctant to incorporate the home-language practices of their multilingual learners in their L2 pedagogy. In spite of its usefulness in the classroom and its mirroring of linguistic practices among multilinguals out of the classroom, translanguaging as a learning strategy is largely ignored in ESL/EFL classrooms. Dismissing learners' other languages as an 'interference' or 'impediment' to learning English fails to appreciate the reality of how multilinguals learn languages.

Meanwhile, translanguaging occurs even if the instructors follow monolingual instructional approaches in the classroom, as I discovered from my own language-learning experiences. Language learners, like myself, become adept at hiding their other languages so as not to draw attention to themselves, lest the teachers object to violating the monolingual policies of the classroom. In our minds, there is freedom; no one is there policing to keep languages separate. In fact, languages freely interact with one another in the brain, forming one linguistic repertoire. Such interactions should be used as a resource in the teaching and learning of ESL and other foreign languages. The time has come for language educators to reject the reactionary monolingual policy of English-only and embrace translanguaging as a sound pedagogical practice.

Questions for Discussion

1. Did you learn another language in school? If so, describe your second-language learning experiences. Were you allowed to use your first language in your second-language classrooms? Why or why not?
2. How does the author define translanguaging? Why does the author claim that this pedagogy is effective in teaching a second language? Do you agree or disagree with the author?

Author Profile

Dr. Ruhma Choudhury is an Associate Professor in the Department of Education and Language Acquisition at LaGuardia Community College, City University of New York. Her research interests include critical TESOL/applied linguistics, language policy, teacher education and critical approaches to language learning. Her most recent publication "Bengali-Speaking Multilingual Writers in Transition into Community College" (co-authored with L. Garrison-Fletcher) appeared in *Linguistically Diverse Immigrant and Resident Writers: Transitions from High School to College* (Routledge, 2017).

References

Auerbach, E. (1993). Reexamining English only in the ESL classroom. *TESOL Quarterly, 27*, 9–32.

Baker, C. (2001). *Foundations of bilingual education and bilingualism*. Clevedon: Multilingual Matters.

British Council (2013). *The English effect*. Retrieved July 8, 2016 from: www.britishcouncil.org/organisation/policy-insight-research/research/the-english-effect

Canagarajah, A. S. (1999). *Resisting linguistic imperialism in English teaching*. Oxford: Oxford University Press.

Canagarajah, A. S. (2011). Translanguaging in the classroom: Emerging issues for research and pedagogy. *Applied Linguistics Review, 2*, 1–28.

Choudhury, R. (2010). *Appropriateness and relevancy of Communicative Language Teaching (CLT) for Bangladesh: A perspective from Bangladeshi rural secondary school teachers*. (Unpublished doctoral dissertation). New York: Teachers College, Columbia University.

Choudhury, R. (2013). Raising bilingual and bicultural Bangladeshi-American children in New York City: Perspectives from educators and parents in a Bengali community program. In O. García, Z. Zakharia & B. Otcu (eds.), *Bilingual community education and multilingualism: Beyond heritage languages in a global city* (pp. 60–73). Buffalo: Multilingual Matters.

Choudhury, R. & Garrison-Fletcher, L. (2017). Bengali-speaking multilingual writers in transition into community college. In C. Ortmeier-Hooper & T. Ruecker (eds.), *Linguistically diverse immigrant and resident writers: Transitions from high school to college* (pp. 143–56). New York: Routledge.

Collins, B. A. (2014). Dual language development of Latino children: Effect of instructional program type and the home and school language environment. *Early Childhood Research Quarterly, 29*, 389–97.

Cummins, J. (2005). Teaching for cross-language transfer in dual language education: Possibilities and pitfalls. *TESOL Symposium on Dual Language Education: Teaching and Learning in Two Languages in the EFL Setting*. Istanbul, Turkey: Bogazici University.

Cummins, J. (2007). Rethinking monolingual instructional strategies in multilingual classrooms. *Canadian Journal of Applied Linguistics, 10* (2), 221–40.

Cummins, J. (2009). Multilingualism in the English-language classroom: Pedagogical considerations. *TESOL Quarterly, 43*, 317–21.

Cummins, J. & Swain, M. (2014). *Bilingualism in education: Aspects of theory, research and practice*. New York: Routledge.

García, O. (2009). *Bilingual education in the 21st century: A global perspective*. Oxford: Wiley/Blackwell.

García, O. (2010). Latino language practices and literacy education in the U.S. In M. Farr, L. Seloni & J. Song (eds.), *Ethnolinguistic diversity and education: Language, literacy, and culture* (pp. 193–211). New York: Routledge.

García, O. & Wei. L. (2014). *Translanguaging: Language, bilingualism and education*. New York: Palgrave Macmillan.
He, D. & Zhang, Q. (2010). Native speaker norms and China English: From the perspective of learners and teachers in China. *TESOL Quarterly*, *44* (4), 769–89.
Mazrui, A. M. (2004). *English in Africa: After the Cold War*. Clevedon: Multilingual Matters.
Mazrui, A. M. (2007). *Swahili beyond the boundaries: Literature, language and identity*. Athens, OH: Ohio University Press.
Phillipson, R. (1992). *Linguistic imperialism*. Oxford: Oxford University Press.
Phillipson, R. (2008). *Linguistic imperialism continued*. London: Routledge.
Tollefson, J. (1991). *Planning language, planning inequality: Language policy in the community*. London: Longman.
Williams, C. (1994). Arfarniad o ddulliau dysgu ac addysgu yng nghyd-destun addysg uwchradd ddwyieithog [An evaluation of teaching and learning methods in the context of bilingual secondary education] (Unpublished PhD thesis). University of Wales, Bangor, UK.

PART III

Language, Identity and Crossing the Boundaries of the Expected

INTRODUCTION

Language, Identity and Crossing the Boundaries of the Expected

Maryam Borjian

> *The starting-point of critical elaboration is the consciousness of what one really is, and is 'knowing thyself,' as a product of the historical process to date which has deposited in you an infinity of traces, without leaving an inventory. The first thing to do is to make such an inventory.*
>
> Antonio Gramsci (1999: 628)

> *Man is condemned to be free: condemned, because he did not create himself, yet nonetheless free, because once cast into the world, he is responsible for everything he does.*
>
> Jean-Paul Sartre (2007: 29)

'Identity' is an elusive term, and very hard to define. It is partly given, partly made, partly inherited and partly achieved. It has multiple layers (inherited, achieved, attributed, or ascribed) and multiple levels (individual, societal, national, or international) (Blommaert, 2006). It can be something fluid, like the 'seedhead of a dandelion,' which travels across time and space, and thus, being shaped and reshaped while on the move. Or it can be something solid, like 'a centuries-old tree,' having its roots solely in one geographical space (Borjian, 2016). It can grow just in one direction, upward, or in multiple directions: upward, downward, horizontally, or vertically, until it comes upon something solid, just like the South Asian banyan tree (García, 2009; Makoni & Pennycook, 2007). It can be shaped or shattered, constructed or deconstructed, negotiated or contested, depending on the context, the individual, and the many social variables that exist in the social context. And in all these dimensions or processes, 'power' or the 'structure,' as echoed by Gramsci (1999), 'human agency,' as echoed by Sartre (2007), or both (depending on one's world view) is/are present, determining not only the input, but also the output of one's identity. Bearing the importance of the multidimensional nature of identity in mind, Part III of this book (Chapters 9–11) is devoted to the theme of language and ideality, with a particular focus on the concepts of power and agency (for more on various aspects of identity, also, see Coulmas, 2013; Leary & Tangney, 2012).

The world of the 21st century is said to be more 'liquid' than 'solid' and more 'fragmented' than 'concrete' (Ritzer, 2010). The liquidity of the 21st century is due to many reasons, including the enormous flow of information, goods, capital, and, most importantly, peoples (with their languages and cultures) across national borders. Although immigration is by no means a new phenomenon, the flow of people that is now on the move tends to be much higher than before. Thus, today, for many people, identity is no longer a solid tree with roots in one geographical space, but is, rather, more liquid and fragmented. Yet, the questions, as I posed elsewhere (Borjian, 2016) and I am reposing here, are as follows: How does the individual define oneself when the self is no longer rooted in one's original space? How is the individual defined by others—those in whose land, physical-social environment or nation the individual now resides as the foreign other? Within this zone of human contact, are the two sides of the interaction equal in terms of power and/or agency? If not, then what type of issues and challenges does the individual encounter?

The fragmentation of identity as the consequence of a border-crossing and its impacts on the individual are the central theme of Joseph Sung-Yul Park's paper (Chapter 9). Park's chapter provides a much needed dimension to our discussion of globalization; that is, the psychological aspect of globalization and its impacts on the individuals who have crossed the expected borders (geographical, socio-cultural and/or linguistic), either voluntarily or involuntarily. Using his own experiences of living as a trans-migrant Korean-American (who works as a professor in Singapore), Park explores how one's name can be seen as a site of tension where global relations of power mediated by language get played out through one's life. Using his own name as the frame of reference, he examines the three different components of his name: his first name (Joseph) signifies his US-born status, his middle-name (Sung-Yul) is a trace of his Korean identity marginalized by its position in the middle and his last name (Park) is a Romanized Korean surname, which reveals South Korea's desire for the modern West. In Park's view, our subjective experiences of names are rooted in material and historical conditions of globalization, including the asymmetry of power that has long existed between the countries of the Global North and those of the Global South.

In Chapter 10, Birgit Brock-Utne uses her identity as a springboard to reflect on the linguistic inequality that, in her view, has long existed in the world. Brock-Utne, who lived in Norway, had a mother who was German and a father who was Norwegian. She was originally brought up bilingually in Norwegian and German but explains what it meant to her identity that the language of her mother was so hated in Norway during and right after the war. She remembers that her mother and grandmother did not dare speak German in the street. They spoke English, a totally foreign language to her. This experience left its marks on her mind, making her aware of the existence of linguistic inequity and injustice in her surrounding world—themes that have become central to her research and have taken her to many places, especially to different parts of Africa. She has herself experienced what it means to have your own language, which is part of your identity, looked down upon. After so many years of independence, the language of instruction in African schools is still a foreign language; that is, the language of the former colonial rulers. African children, as Brock-Utne argues, are being punished for speaking their mother tongues.

The language education policy of postcolonial contexts opens a new facet to our discussion of globalization: that is, globalization—unlike what we have been told by its globalist supporters (Friedman, 2005; Fukuyama, 1989)—has not been a radical break away from modernity or colonialism (not at least for all locales and peoples of the world). Nor has it been, as rightly argued by Joseph Stiglitz (2007), a 'zero-sum game' in which everyone could win. "Does globalization hop rather than flow?" is a question posed by George Ritzer (2010: 10), who argues that "globalization flows more easily through the developed world, [. . .] whereas it bypasses many locales in the less developed world or even skirts them completely" (p. 11). In the case of the medium-of-instruction policy in African schools, it seems that globalization has been hopping rather than flowing, for the old language policies of the colonial era are still intact, shaping the linguistic identity of the African children, who have not crossed any national borders to be a subject to linguistic marginalization and/or assimilation. Social justice through multilingual education and inclusive language education policies have been examined thoroughly by many other scholars, including Alidou et al. (2011), Brock-Utne (for a list of her work, see Chapter 10 of this volume), Mazrui and Mazrui (1998), Mazrui (2004), and Tollefson and Tsui (2004), to name but a few.

Chapter 11 is written by Humphrey Tonkin, a seminal linguist, who is known internationally for his pioneering research on various aspects of language, including language problems and planning, multilingualism, world languages, language and literature, and, last but not least, the international language Esperanto (on the latter topic, see Tonkin, 2009). Perceiving Esperanto as an earlier wave of linguistic globalization, in his eloquently written chapter, Tonkin invites the reader to join him as he reflects on his engagement with the Esperanto language that came to him in 1954, when he was a boy in a British boarding school. Although globalization has been praised, or blamed, for its deterritorialization of languages and speech communities, as Tonkin reminds us, deterritorialization is not a novel phenomenon to Esperanto, whose speech community has never belonged to a certain geographical territory. Likewise, Tonkin problematizes the notion of 'linguistic community' by viewing it not as a fixed and static construct but rather as a hybrid and fluid site, which evolves and re-evolves over time. A similar view is articulated by Alamin Mazrui (2007: 2), who argues that "hybridity is an antithesis to the essentialism," which challenges the validity of any given property, including the essentialist notion of cultural or linguistic identity. Having a fluid-hybrid lens toward language and speech community, Tonkin argues that the real owners of any language are the speakers of the language. In the case of Esperanto, its speakers have not only naturalized a language that was originally 'planned,' but have also taken ownership of the language: today's Esperanto has evolved beyond its original form, created by Leyzer Ludwik Zamenhof 130 years ago.

In addition, Tonkin's chapter reflects on other aspects of identity, including given/inherited versus made/achieved identity. Although English was his first language, Tonkin chose to go beyond his inherited linguistic identity to become a speaker and user of Esperanto, which attests to the power of individuals, human agency, and one's ability to choose, select and shape one's linguistic identity. As an alternative language, Esperanto has not only brought him into contact with a worldwide community of Esperantists, but it has also offered him a different perspective on international political divisions, particularly on the Cold War. Nonetheless, Tonkin argues that the rise of English and the concomitant decline of other languages threaten human agency, or 'our essential freedom to enjoy multiple identities—to be different at different times and in different ways,' using his own words.

References

Alidou, H., Glanz, C. & Nikièma, N. (2011). Quality multilingual and multicultural education for lifelong learning (A Special Issue). *International Review of Education*, 57 (5/6), 529–785.

Blommaert, J. (2006). Language policy and national identity. In T. Ricento (ed.), *An introduction to language policy: Theory and method* (pp. 238–54). Malden, MA: Blackwell Publishing.

Borjian, M. (2016). Issues and challenges in constructing identity in an adopted home: Being an Iranian professor in America. In A. Komisarof & H. Zhu (eds.), *Crossing boundaries and weaving intercultural work, life, and scholarship in globalizing universities* (pp. 105–17). New York: Routledge.

Coulmas, F. (2013). *Sociolinguistics: The study of speakers' choices*. Cambridge: Cambridge University Press.

Friedman, T. (2005). *The world is flat: A brief history of the twenty-first century*. New York: Farrar, Straus and Giroux.

Fukuyama, F. (1989). The end of history and the last man. *The National Interest*. Retrieved April 23, 2016 from: www.wesjones.com/eoh.htm.

García, O. (2009). *Bilingual education in the 21st century: A global perspective*. Malden, MA: Wiley-Blackwell.

Gramsci, A. (1999). *Selections from the prison notebooks* [edited and translated by Q. Hoare & G. N. Smith]. London: ElecBook.

Leary, M. & Tangney, J. (eds.) (2012). *Handbook of self and identity* (2nd edition). New York: The Guilford Press.

Makoni, S. & Pennycook, A. (2007). *Disinventing and reconstituting languages*. Clevedon: Multilingual Matters.

Mazrui, A. M. (2004). *English in Africa after the Cold War*. Clevedon: Multilingual Matters.
Mazrui, A. M. (2007). *Swahili beyond the boundaries: Literature, language and identity*. Athens, OH: Ohio University Press.
Mazrui, A. & Mazrui, A. M. (1998). *The power of Babel: Language & governance in the African experience*. Chicago: University of Chicago Press.
Ritzer, G. (2010). *Globalization: A basic text*. Malden, MA: Wiley-Blackwell.
Sartre, J. P. (2007). *Existentialism is a humanism* [translated by C. Macomber]. New Haven: Yale University Press.
Stiglitz, J. (2007). *Making globalization work*. New York: Norton Company.
Tollefson, J. & Tsui, A. (2004). *Medium of instruction policies: Which agenda? Whose agenda?* Mahwah, NJ: Lawrence Erlbaum.
Tonkin, H. (2009). Where art and nature meet. In E. Todeva & J. Cenoz (eds.), *The multiple realities of multilingualism: Personal narratives and researchers' perspectives*. Berlin: Mouton de Gruyer.

9

MY NAME

An Autoethnographic Reflection

Joseph Sung-Yul Park

Introduction

My name is Joseph Sung-Yul Park. At least that is how I present myself formally (for instance, it is the name as it appears in my passport) and professionally (as it appears under the title of this chapter above). But, it is also not my name. I say this because your name is supposed to be you, a familiar string of sounds that identifies you and that you can call a home; yet my name only gives me a feeling of awkwardness and insecurity. It is not that I do not like the name that has been given to me by my parents. It is that my name, composed of three foreign and clashing elements, seems to constantly remind me of the liminal and uneasy position I occupy as a transnational Korean-American. Born in the US, having grown up in Korea, having received higher education in the US, living and working in Singapore but maintaining various familial, cultural and professional ties with both Korea and the US, I live a life on the border, and it feels like my name is always there to underline the uneasiness and anxiety of my in-betweenness through its cacophonous clanging of component parts.

Originally I had hoped that this juxtaposition of name-elements would have the opposite effect, offering me flexibility and adaptability that would make me recognizably at home in both countries and beyond. The English name 'Joseph' was supposed to allow me to slip in easily and soundly into the US society, while 'Sung-Yul' would indicate to Koreans that I remain one of their own. But instead, what I am left with is an obtrusive baggage that gets stuck in the doorway each time I try to navigate the border between Korea and the US. Rather than making me more authentic and unnoticeable, my name highlights my foreignness and difference, both in the US and in Korea, representing in symbolic terms the residue that I am. In this way, my name betrays me, denying me a home and a true sense of belonging.

In this chapter, I would like to talk about the psychological and subjective dimension of globalization. As Hall (2014) points out, social theorists of globalization often characterize our era as one of insecurity, instability and anxiety. With growing cross-border mobility, deterioration of a sense of national and communal belonging and the prevalence of the neoliberal ideology in which we are positioned as individuals, each responsible for one's own fate, subjects in globalization are increasingly made to feel insecure, lost and fearful. But here, I focus on subjectivity not just because it is an essential aspect of globalization, but because it is also a window for observing how the historical and political conditions that drive globalization find their manifestations in our personal lives. In particular, I show how the intersection of language and globalization serves as a useful juncture for considering the subjective consequences of those conditions. For this purpose, in this chapter I reflect on several scenes in my own life in which my name has led me to confront the material and historical groundings of my transnational trajectory.

Subjective Experience of Names

It is not uncommon to find people from East Asia, who already have a name in their own language, adopt another name in English. This is particularly so in the context of globalization, where those people come into greater contact with Western culture and heavily invest in English language learning. In China, for instance, the practice is so prevalent that Chinese American journalist Huan Hsu was surprised to find that his not having an English name was a source of bewilderment to the Chinese he interacted with in Shanghai (Hsu, 2009). It is often assumed that picking up an English name is motivated by a desire to mix easier with English speakers from the West and to signal an alignment with Western identity and culture. Academic research on this topic has added more sophistication to this view. For example, Li (1997) suggests that English names used among Hong Kongers may be a pragmatic strategy to achieve a more egalitarian interaction in bicultural and bilingual context. Henry (2012) considers the cultural basis of such behavior by pointing out how adopting an English name is deeply embedded within traditional Chinese practices through which a person's name is determined. And Kim (2007) discusses how the varying social positioning and cultural expectations of Korean immigrants to Canada may lead to different choices regarding whether to adopt an English name or not.

What I want to talk about here, however, is the deeper subjective implications for having names that are perceived as 'English' or 'Korean.' Names are not merely labels that individuals freely pick up or reject like masks as it pleases them. Names call us into being. In other words, they interpellate—as a police officer might hail us on the street by shouting, 'Hey, you there!' and making us turn around and become an individual answerable to and subject to the authority of the law (Althusser, 1984:48). Here, I am not just talking about the fact that names are used to call or refer to us. Names also place us in particular junctures of historically rooted relations of power, pressing us to become particular kinds of persons. In this sense, names position us as historically constituted subjects.

For instance, what counts as an English name in the first place? After all, only a small portion of what is recognizable as 'English names' can be traced back to Old English roots, with many coming from languages as diverse as French and Hebrew (Tan, 2001). Underneath the fascination about East Asians taking up English names lies an ideology that conceives the world in terms of neatly demarcated languages, which in turn represent distinct people and their cultures—Koreans are defined by their Korean culture and their Korean language, which neatly differentiate them from Americans who speak standard American English, for instance—even though the modern history of cultural and linguistic contact problematizes such boundaries, particularly in the increasingly globalizing world of today. Indeed, it is through such differentiation, through such acts of boundary making, that a sense of 'being Korean' is constituted, against the image of a modern, advanced, Western 'Other' (Park, 2012; 2015). Adopting a name in a particular language, then, is to be subject to the ideologies that presume the distinctiveness of that language as well as the historical conditions that gave rise to and reproduce those ideologies.

Considering the subjective experiences of living with names, variously understood as belonging to different languages and cultures, then, is to look into the historical and political conditions that make up the subject hailed by those names. It is through such experiences that the relations of power which shape and reproduce multiple forms of inequality on global and local levels come to exist in embodied ways. By reflecting on such experiences, we learn that globalization is not simply about smooth flows of people, culture and ideas across borders that can be facilitated by an act as simple as acquiring a global language like English or taking up a new name in English—for those experiences recount to us how the weight of history and social relations do not get washed away by the currents of globalization, but continue to exert itself on our shoulders.

Name of the Other

Joseph is not a name that I picked up for myself; it is a name that was given to me by my parents, who were both graduate students studying in the US in the 1960s. My mother once said it was derived from St. Joseph, the patron saint of the sick and dying (she was not Catholic, but she attended a Catholic university in the US). I do not think my parents ever questioned whether my sisters and I should be given English names in addition to Korean ones. When we were born in the US, they immediately gave us English names, as most Koreans living in the US were doing back then. As they spoke English to us at home, naturally those English names were what they used to call us. Even after we returned to Korea in the early 1970s and Korean replaced English as the home language, our English names were still used more frequently than our Korean ones. But outside of the home, as I interacted with other Koreans at school and elsewhere, my English name was mostly kept hidden, until I returned to the US to pursue my graduate studies.

Back in the US, where Joseph had become my publicly known name again, one of my fellow graduate students from Japan once asked me, 'Why do Korean people have English names?' It might have been an innocent factual question inquiring the reasons for the cultural difference between Koreans and Japanese, where Japanese people are much less likely to adopt English names than Koreans (for that, Heffernan, 2010, proposes some explanations). But, to me it was a deeper, scathing question that foregrounded the reason of the discomfort that my English name generated for me in Korea. It pointed to the unnaturalness of the act of picking up an English name, something that cannot be just explained by Korean 'culture,' due to its political nature in a context where English and the US stands for a distant but powerful Other.

Ever since the US military occupied the southern half of the Korean peninsula following the fall of Japanese colonialism in 1945, the US exercised an enormous influence on South Korea. Due to Korea's geopolitical significance, located at the intersections of Russia, China and Japan and situated at the front line in the contest with communism, the US maintained continuous control on South Korea through military, economic, and cultural influence and by condoning a series of military regimes that thwarted the country's democratization. South Korea's ruling elites maintained their power by building their connections with and asserting their loyalty to the US, and oppressing voices of criticism towards the role of the US in Korea. Even though the Cold War subsided and South Korea's procedural democracy stabilized, the American influence over Korea still persists, through neoliberal conditions of the global economy and the enduring power of the conservative elites of Korean society.

In this context, taking up an English name in Korea cannot be an innocent act of appropriation. Regardless of one's intent, it cannot be free from suspicion of others who might view it as evidence of an opportunistic desire to profit from an affiliation with those in power. When my parents gave me a name in English, certainly they were hoping I would be able to benefit from my US-born heritage and my familiarity with English. My parents had come to the US when Korea was barely recovering from the total destruction of the Korean War, and they were among the very few privileged Koreans who gained the opportunity to study in the center of the modern world. The American degrees they acquired would later secure my family a stable middle-class life back in Korea with a valued cosmopolitan flair. The English name they gave to me was a symbolic way of passing down this privilege—a marker of my provenance in the US, a reminder that I should one day return there to retrace my parents' path. Indeed, here I am, having acquired a doctoral degree in the US, and living a career in the global academic scene in which English is the dominant language of operation.

The name Joseph thus invokes for me layers of global, national and familial histories and the place I occupy within them. It indicates the classed privilege I was inherited within the space of Korea's modern history, and the distance that it implies from the arduous struggles of the Korean people against dictatorship, imperialism and economic inequality. It also narrates the deep embodied nature of my position, cultivated by my memories of childhood interaction at home and sustained through my transnational middle-class upbringing. In this sense, this English name places me in a particular time-space, leaving me to confront, through my own life, the questions of power and inequality that still overshadow Korea's relation with the US and the world.

Anxiety of Being Unpronounceable

Sung-Yul is another name that my parents gave me. In Korean it is 성열 [sʌŋjʌl], and when I introduce myself to other Koreans, this is the name I give them, never Joseph. But even though it is supposed to be a given name with equal status to Joseph, in the context of my full name it is placed second, occupying the awkward position of a middle name, a notion that does not even exist in Korean. This reduces my Korean name into a diacritic for my English name, a distinguishing mark that differentiates me from others who might also be called 'Joseph Park.' My Korean name is thereby absorbed into a format familiar to Americans, something they would be able to recognize and understand. In this sense, the place of my Korean name reflects an anxiety—an insecurity about being accepted into the cultural order of the English-speaking world, a desire to be called upon in English.

This anxiety is also reflected in the way my Korean name is represented through Romanization. It is actually a terrible instance of Romanization, for no one (including Korean speakers) seems to be able to pronounce it (typical first guesses are [sʌŋjul] or [suŋjul]). My excuse for this bad Romanization is that I decided on it before I started to study linguistics. I remember having a discussion with my father about the Romanization of my name right before I was to return to the US for the first time after more than 20 years of living in Korea. My father emphasized the importance of Romanization, saying that it is crucial that Americans know how to pronounce your name. The model he gave was none other than Syngman Rhee, South Korea's first president, who avoided the problem of representing the high back unrounded vowel of his name with an ingenious <y>: 'That way, anyone can pronounce it,' my father said. But we were unable to come up with something as clever as the president's, so reluctantly we settled on Sung-Yul, along with the unsightly hyphen to mark the syllable boundary, (injudiciously) hoping it would be clear enough for Americans.

The problem with the Romanization of my name is that it is actually more of an Anglicization. Instead of following a formal system of Romanization (such as the revised Romanization system of the Korean government, which would give Seong-yeol; or the McCune-Reishauer system widely used outside of Korea, which would result in Sŏng-yŏl), it represents the vowel with the grapheme <u>, attempting to build upon the way it is often pronounced in English (in words such as *sung* or *lung*). I am not alone in this choice, as it is a common practice found among many other Koreans, such as the figure skater Kim Yuna, whose given name is [yʌna]. The prevalence of this strategy of Romanizing Korean names based on English can also be evidenced in many names, such as those of past presidents Kim Young-sam and Roh Moo-hyun, the first syllables of whose given names are [jʌŋ] and [mu], respectively.

Seo (2000) is right to argue that choice of Romanization is always a political choice, for one must decide whose linguistic assumptions about grapheme-to-phoneme correspondence should be privileged. If so, Koreans' impulse to identify Romanization with Anglicization cannot simply be attributed to the fact that English is the only foreign language taught mandatorily to all students in the national education system and thus the one most familiar to them. I want to suggest that it reflects an underlying identification of the US with the modern and global, a source that one must emulate in order to be recognized as having an authentic and legitimate place in the world. If insecurity is primarily about a perceived distance between one's own place and where one desires to stand, then the constant elevation of the US as the ideal center of the global order places Koreans in an unending state of insecurity (Park, 2012). They must constantly wonder and worry how the speaker of American English will view them, whether their name would be pronounced correctly, whether their name will be remembered, whether they would be recognizable as a person rather than as some nameless, insignificant alien figure.

My father's praise of Syngman Rhee is no coincidence in this regard. The first Korean to receive a PhD from a US institution of higher education (Princeton), Rhee ascended to power through his political connections with the US and his fluency in English, and while he is criticized for his dictatorship and unwillingness to purge elites who collaborated with Japanese imperialism, among his supporters he is still idealized as a 'good bilingual' who managed to translate himself successfully into the English-speaking modern world without compromising his Koreanness (Choi, 2014). Continued reverence for Rhee demonstrates the persistence of the Korean belief that successful representation of oneself in the eyes of the English-speaking West is a sign of legitimacy in the global world. Thus, while Heffernan (2010) rightly points out that the Chinese and Korean practice of adopting an English name is not motivated by the desire to make one's name easier for Westerners to pronounce, that desire that is often invoked to explain such practice is real. Being unpronounceable, uncallable and unrecognizable by the Western, or American, Other is a fear that Koreans continue to struggle with, as the historical-political conditions of Korea still position the US as the cultural center of the world.

Embracing the Surrogate

Park is my surname, family name, or what in Korean is called *seong*. The importance of *seong* in the Confucianism-entrenched Korean culture cannot be emphasized enough. *Seong* is not really a separate 'name' to begin with; and it certainly does not come 'last.' The conspicuous initial character of one's name, it fuses with a person's given name to be an inalienable part of how the person is identified. 'I'll change my *seong*' is an epithet that one utters when swearing for the veracity of some statement; the sheer blasphemy of the action promised in case the statement turns out to be untrue serves as a guarantee of its truthfulness. The fact that women in Korea do not change their surname when married has nothing to do with feminism; it merely testifies to how the essential patriarchic bond that one's *seong* forms with the person is, as an inheritance from one's father, stronger than any new identity that may be offered by a husband (cf. Zhu, 2016). Naturally, the 1939 ordinance of the Japanese colonial government that forced Koreans to change their *seong* to Japanese style *ssi* was one of the most humiliating moments of colonialism for Koreans.

It is surprising, then, that Park is not really my surname after all. While I noted the terrible Romanization my Korean name is subjected to, my *seong*, when rendered in Romanized form, becomes something entirely different. While some people use Bak to capture the original pronunciation of [b̥ak̚], Park is by far the most common form used by people of this *seong*, even though this is obviously an adoption of a preexisting English name that can approximate the sounds of the surname (for instance, there is no [r] sound in my surname at all). In a culture where one's *seong* is considered one of the most inalienable and immutable aspects of the person's identity, one might find it surprising that such adoption of an English name is hardly questioned.

Perhaps this should not be a big deal. In many cultures, people have multiple names over the course of their lives, and it is not unusual at all for someone to be known by different names to different groups (Jacquemet, 1992; Rymes, 1996). Why is it problematic if a Korean surname is represented through a different name in English, especially when there is some traceable phonological similarity between the two names? What strikes me as odd, however, is the obliviousness of Koreans to the potential contradiction underlying this choice. Nearly 4 million people in Korea share this surname, making it the third most populous *seong* (after Kim and Lee), and over 95% of them use Park to represent it, so this is clearly not some odd choice by a quirky minority; yet this use of an English name to replace a Korean surname is rarely problematized. In the discussion forum on the Romanization of Korean surnames organized by the National Institute of Korean Language (2009), the institution in charge of promoting and standardizing the Korean language, participants displayed concerns about the inconsistencies in the way people were Romanizing their names, but nothing was said about the contradiction of Koreans willingly modeling their names upon English ones despite the significant cultural values they associate with surnames.

I, for one, admit that I never gave as much thought to my Englishized surname as I did to my two given names, for it has never bothered me that every non-Korean is calling me by a name that is not my own. Even when I felt nervous about revealing my English name among Koreans or informing non-Koreans about how to say my Korean name, writing down my surname as Park never made me squirm, not in Korea, not in the US, not elsewhere. In fact, there were occasions in which I felt mildly annoyed when some American English speakers called me 'Parks,' a common variant of the English name that I am emulating—as if my name is really [p^{h}ɑrk] and I have the right to be called that way.

I believe that Koreans' obliviousness to the gap between their *seong* and the way it is represented is a powerful illustration of how deeply naturalized is their desire for the English-speaking West. Despite the strong ethnolinguistic and nationalistic value attached to cultural heritage in Korean society, using English names as the model for Korean names virtually escapes critical scrutiny, demonstrating how beliefs in English as the normative order of the world are taken for granted. I do not mean to say that language ideologies ought to be consistent and such contradictions should not be tolerated. But if anxieties and insecurities are important elements of being positioned as a subject, so are the ease and comfort with which one overlooks the contradictions that underlie one's practice. The naturalness by which I embrace the surrogate for my surname, for this reason, forces me to critically reflect on the feeling of tension and confusion that I experience between my two given names.

Conclusion

We do not experience globalization in the abstract. We experience it through our lives, feelings and sense of being, where material and historical consequences of globalization take root to find their concrete articulations. Through some vignettes from my own life, I tried to suggest above how names can serve as a powerful illustration of this. Ideologies that define and dictate the boundaries of language work against the greater mobility and linguistic contact of our lives under globalization, thrusting upon us the weight of historical relations that are built upon those ideologies. To move across different names associated with different languages, to balance multiple names and to find ways to string them together across linguistic spaces, then, is to confront the relations of power and inequality that are reproduced and sustained by those ideologies. In my own case, my name that straddles English and Korean conjures up ideologies that demarcate a boundary between the two languages, and those ideologies in turn call me into a social space where the English/Korean binary stands in for multiple other hierarchical distinctions along the lines of nationality, ethnicity, class, native-speakerness and legitimacy. My name, thus, positions me at a particular historical juncture of Korea's relation with the modern world, revealing one cross-section of its contradictions and inequalities, a space that I embody through my experiences, feelings and desires.

The evolving trajectory of my transnational life brings me more opportunities for reflecting on this. For instance, living in Singapore, where appropriation of English and English names has long constituted a well-established element of its lively multilingualism (Tan, 2001), encourages me and teaches me to accept my own name more. But at the same time, it also reminds me of the historical situatedness of the significance names carry. Obviously, forms of names themselves do not have determinate meanings that fix us into a particular social position. What matters is the social and material relations that lie behind the name to fill its form with meaning, and that reproduce their presence every time that name is called out. For this reason, my name also serves me as a lens for observing the world. The tensions and sensitivities that my name instill in me transform into an impulse to look for the historical nuances and subjective experiences that constrain and color the way we call each other and label ourselves, leading me to wonder, as I encounter new worlds through my border crossings, what collective memories and unshared narratives might be resonating through the sounds of others' names.

Questions for Discussion

1. Reflect on some of the feelings you have regarding your own name. In what way might they be related to the widely held beliefs about languages in your community or culture?
2. If you were to move to and live in a different country or culture, would you adopt a different name? Explain your choice.

Author Profile

Joseph Sung-Yul Park is an associate professor in the Department of English Language and Literature at the National University of Singapore. His work studies the intersection of language and globalization, transnationalism and neoliberalism, with a particular focus on the politics of English as a global language. He is the author of *The Local Construction of a Global Language* (Mouton de Gruyter), and co-author of *Markets of English* (Routledge, with Lionel Wee).

References

Althusser, L. (1984). Ideology and ideological state apparatuses. In L. Althusser, *Essays on ideology* (pp. 1–60). London: Verso.

Choi, L. J. (2014). Fragile bilinguals: Rescaling "good" and "bad" South Korean bilinguals. Unpublished PhD dissertation. University of Illinois at Urbana-Champaign.

Hall, K. (2014). Hypersubjectivity: Language, anxiety, and indexical dissonance in globalization. *Journal of Asian Pacific Communication, 24* (2), 261–73.

Heffernan, K. (2010). English name use by East Asians in Canada: Linguistic pragmatics or cultural identity? *Names, 58* (1), 24–36.

Henry, E. (2012). When Dragon met Jasmine: Domesticating English names in Chinese social interaction. *Anthropologica, 54*, 107–17.

Hsu, H. (2009, April 27). The name's Du Xiao Hua, but call me Steve. *Slate*. Accessed July 12, 2016, from: www.slate.com/articles/arts/culturebox/2009/04/the_names_du_xiao_hua_but_call_me_steve.html.

Jacquemet, M. (1992). Namechasers. *American Ethnologist, 19* (4), 733–48.

Kim, T. (2007). The dynamics of ethnic name maintenance and change: Cases of Korean ESL immigrants in Toronto. *Journal of Multilingual and Multicultural Development, 28* (2), 117–33.

Li, D. C. S. (1997). Borrowed identity: Signaling involvement with a Western name. *Journal of Pragmatics, 28*, 489–513.

National Institute of Korean Language (2009). 성씨 로마자 표기 방안 마련을 위한 토론회 [Forum for developing a system for Romanization of *seong*]. Accessed July 12, 2016, from www.korean.go.kr/front/board/boardStandardView.do?board_id=6&mn_id=19&b_seq=228.

Park, J. S. (2012). English as border-crossing: Longing and belonging in the South Korean experience. In V. Rapatahana & P. Bunce (eds.), *English language as Hydra: Its impacts on non-English language cultures* (pp. 208–20). Bristol: Multilingual Matters.

Park, J. S. (2015). Structures of feeling in unequal Englishes. In R. Tupas (ed.), *Unequal Englishes: The politics of Englishes today* (pp. 59–73). New York: Palgrave Macmillan.

Rymes, B. (1996). Naming as social practice: The case of Little Creeper from Diamond Street. *Language in Society, 25* (2), 237.

Seo, B. (2000). 로마자 표기법의 식민성과 탈식민성 [The coloniality and postcoloniality of Romanization systems]. 창작과 비평 109: 300–10.

Tan, P. K. W. (2001). Englishised names? *English Today, 17* (4), 45–53.

Zhu, H. (2016). "Where are you from?": Interculturality and interactional practices. In A. Komisarof & H. Zhu (eds.), *Crossing boundaries and weaving intercultural work, life, and scholarship in globalizing universities* (pp. 147–59). London: Routledge.

10

LANGUAGE AND IDENTITY

Reflections by a Cultural Commuter

Birgit Brock-Utne

> *Since we were considered as French 'a part-entière', nothing but French was taught. The whole curriculum was based on France and anything that was French, whereas Comorian, our mother tongue, was never considered to be a suitable medium of instruction.*
>
> (Bakar, 1988: 184)

Introduction

I have devoted my life, work and scholarship to the promotion of linguistic equality and social justice, especially in Africa. This position has emerged as the consequence of my own personal, professional and scholarly life. In this chapter, I draw on my lived experiences as a cultural commuter in order to reflect on instances of linguistic inequality and injustice that I have seen both in partly forgotten yesteryears and in the current years of the 21st century.

German-Norwegian

My mother was German. My father was Norwegian. They met in Berlin in 1937. She was teaching German at Humboldt Universität. He had just finished his law degree and had been given a year by a rich uncle to study German, which was the first foreign language in Norway at the time. It was a beloved language by academics, professionals and people of power. My parents fell in love, married and moved to Norway. It was the right time for my mother to get out of Germany. She had just been requested to sign a paper where it said that she was committed to teach the Nazi ideology. She was very much opposed to the Nazi ideology and refused to sign the paper. She was told that if she did not sign, she would lose her job. My father rescued her. Her parents rejoiced with her, since they looked at Norway as a peaceful country and felt that it would not be involved in any war.

My parents decided that their children should be brought up bilingually. I was born in 1938 and my mother spoke only German to me the first two years of my life. My father spoke Norwegian. I learnt the two languages simultaneously. My father had a job where he traveled a lot so I was more often with my mother. I was alone with her when the war broke out in Norway on the 9th of April 1940. My father was fighting the Germans in the north of Norway. Shortly after the outbreak of the German occupation, there were rumors that Oslo would be bombed. The inhabitants of Oslo were evacuated in big lorries to farms outside the city. One farmer who owned his farm came to greet us and said we could sleep in the hay in his barn. And he had a crib for me. I was placed in the crib with hay under and above me, like a Christ child. My mother tried to get me to sleep, but I was used to her always singing German lullabies for me at bedtime. So I said: "Sing doch Schlaf Kindchen Schlaf" ("Please sing 'Sleep, little child sleep'")—one of my favorite lullabies. But she just hushed and tried to explain that she could not sing that song tonight. I could not understand why and insisted louder and louder and all the time in German: "Sing doch! Warum singst Du nicht?" ("Please sing. Why don't you sing?"). My loud voice—in the end, I screamed—made people gather around the crib. One of them asked in a rather unfriendly tone: "Why is this girl screaming in German?" My mother answered in her far-from-perfect Norwegian and with a German accent: "I am very sorry, but I am German. I am very much against the Nazis. I am married to a Norwegian and so far we have brought this girl up to become bilingual. My husband speaks Norwegian to her, I speak German. But from this day she shall not hear a German word until the war is over."

My mother kept her promise. Linguistically it was not the right thing to do, but considering the political situation, her decision is understandable. I was ten when I again got immersed in the German language. In 1948 my lovely German grandmother came to us for three months. She was a widow now. She had lost everything in the war; her big house with all valuables had been bombed. Her only child, her son-in-law and her two grandchildren were in Norway. At home, my parents and my grandmother spoke German. I picked the language up again. I enjoyed so much sitting with my grandmother, talking with her, listening to her read poetry and learning to write German.

I remember one particular incident from her stay. I was walking in the streets of Oslo with my mother and my grandmother. I heard them speak a language which I did not understand a word of. I got annoyed and asked why they spoke this strange language. Did they not want me to understand? The strange language was English, a language we did not start learning before the 6th grade. I was in 4th grade. My mother explained to me that the language we spoke at home, and I felt as part of my identity, was a language which was looked down upon in Norway. It was not a popular language. We should not speak it outside our home.

When I started secondary school and we learnt German in school, many of my schoolmates had been told by their parents to get the lowest possible grade in that subject. I always got good grades in German.

The fact that the tongue of my mother and my beloved grandmother, a language that was part of my identity, was trampled upon, was a tough emotional experience. It helped me, however, later in life to understand the emotions African children go through when they are punished for speaking their own language in school, when their language is denigrated (Thiong'o, 1986; Bakar, 1988; Brock-Utne, 2000, 2009, 2014, 2015, 2016; Brock-Utne & Qorro, 2015; White, 1996).

English as a Foreign Language Versus Having It as the Language of Instruction

When I was 19, I got a one-year scholarship to Stanford University. It was a scholarship donated by the students at Stanford to ten international students, two female and eight male students. We shared rooms with the American students, were exposed to their culture, their dating practices, their slang and table manners. Elsewhere I have written about the cultural shock it was for me with my continental European table manners to experience the way Americans were eating only with their fork (Brock-Utne, 1995). Had I eaten that way at home, I would have been sent to the kitchen. Among my American classmates it was a normal way of eating. Later in life, I became accustomed to eating with chopsticks like the Chinese and Japanese do and eating with my right hand, like I first learnt in India and later in Africa.

I attended both undergraduate and graduate classes and mostly got Bs in the undergraduate classes and As in several of the graduate classes. I had no problem, whatsoever, following the lectures and participating in the discussions, which all took place in English. It was the first time I had experienced having English as the language of instruction. I had learned English as a foreign language in the two last grades of primary school (grades 6 and 7) and the five years of secondary school. My English teachers had been excellent teachers, building up a vocabulary slowly and introducing grammatical elements progressively. I had also spent five weeks in Britain in the family of some relatives. That gave me some practice in talking daily English but not in writing it. In the US my everyday as well as academic vocabulary was expanded daily. The point in telling about my encounter with studying in English is that learning English well in school from teachers who are experts in teaching English as a foreign language is the best preparation one can have for studying in that language later. This experience has been important to draw on when I have worked the last twenty years with the language-of-instruction issue in Africa (Brock-Utne, 2000; 2014).

In his book *Decolonising the Mind,* the Kenyan author Ngugi wa Thiong'o (1986) uses an autoethnographical approach to the language issue when he describes his own experiences growing up in Kenya and being forced to have English as the language of instruction. He writes that language supplemented the sword and the bullet of the colonizers as the means of European subjugation of Africa:

> But the night of the sword and the bullet was followed by the morning of the chalk and the blackboard [. . .]. The bullet was the means of physical subjugation. Language was the means of spiritual subjugation. (Thiong'o, 1986: 9)

He then goes on to tell movingly about his own school experience. His mother tongue, Gikuyu, was the language of all the evening teach-ins around the fireplace when he was young, and the language used with friends and in the fields where he worked. In his first school years, he went to a school run by nationalists grouped around the Kikuyu Independent and Karinga Schools Association. The language of instruction in this school was Gikuyu, so for the first four years of his schooling there was harmony between the language of his formal education and the language he spoke at home, in the fields and with his friends. He tells that after the state of emergency in Kenya in 1952, all the schools run by patriotic nationalists were taken over by the colonial regime and placed under District Education Boards chaired by Englishmen, and English was made the language of instruction. His own mother tongue, Gikuyu, was not deemed fit to be used as a language of instruction. He tells how one of the most humiliating experiences was to be caught speaking Gikuyu in the vicinity of the school. The culprit was given corporal punishment—three to five strokes of the cane on bare buttocks—or was made to carry a metal plate around the neck with inscriptions such as *I AM STUPID* or *I AM A DONKEY*. Sometimes the culprits were fined money they could hardly afford. And how did the teachers catch the culprits? Thiong'o tells how a button was initially given to one pupil, who was supposed to hand it over to whomever was caught speaking his mother tongue. Whoever had the button at the end of the day had to come forward and tell whom he had got it from, and the ensuing process would bring out all the 'culprits' of the day. Thus, children were turned into witch-hunters and traitors to their own linguistic community.

African students are still being punished for speaking their own language. This is an attack on their identity. On the 18th of May 2010, the Tanzanian newspaper *Majira* told about a Form II student, Charles Wabea (16) from Luchelele secondary school, who died while performing a punishment meted out to him by his teacher for speaking Kiswahili in class. He was to dig 20 buckets of soil from a pit, and the pit collapsed on him.

Living and Working in Africa

From 1988 to 1992, I was a Professor of education at the University of Dar es Salaam in Tanzania. These years formed a steep learning curve for me and sent me through several intellectual shocks. My first shock had to do with the language issue. I had read that there were 120 languages in Tanzania and been told by people in the NORAD office in Dar es Salaam that there was not much point in learning Kiswahili, because the language of instruction both in secondary school and at the university was English and all the meetings would take place in English. They also told me that many of my colleagues and students would be speaking other languages like Kihaya or Kichagga anyway. Already in the first tea break, I noticed that all my colleagues spoke Kiswahili. The same was true of my students. They came into the lecture hall all speaking Kiswahili.

I gave some lectures in educational psychology with about 250 students in the lecture theatre. To make them more active, I wrote some questions on the blackboard and had them discuss the questions for some minutes in buzzing groups of four to five students. I soon discovered that all the groups had switched to discussion in Kiswahili, even though I had written the questions down in English. Under my periods of doing student-teacher supervision in secondary school, I noticed the lively atmosphere in the classes taught in Kiswahili (at that time not only the subject Kiswahili, but also the subject *siasa*[1] were taught in Kiswahili) and the passivity of the students and aggressiveness of the teachers when the teaching was conducted in English. Two of my PhD students (Mwinsheikhe, 2007; Vuzo, 2007) and myself (Brock-Utne, 2007) noticed that when the teachers were teaching in English, they frequently punished the students, mostly by having them stand all through the lesson. They never punished the students when the teaching was in Kiswahili. The teachers themselves were not aware of this fact before we pointed it out to them.

When tutoring my many Tanzanian students both in Tanzania and Norway, I found that they were all very proficient in Kiswahili. After I learnt the language, I did most of my tutoring in Kiswahili. Some of my students had grown up with Kiswahili as their mother tongue, their first language. This was the case for all students from Zanzibar and very many who had grown up in Dar es Salaam. Others had grown up with another Tanzanian language as their most familiar language and learnt Kiswahili as a second language. I also had students who grew up with several Tanzanian languages at the same time, and to them terminology, like 'mother tongue,' 'first language' and 'second language,' did not make sense. The following is an excerpt from one of my PhD students who originally grew up with another Tanzanian language than Kiswahili:

> I experienced language barriers from early years of my schooling. When I started grade one, I was forced to juggle between my mother tongue, which is Kihaya, and Kiswahili (the LoI [i.e., Language of Instruction] in primary school). I grew up in a village where Kiswahili was not spoken. I was prohibited from using my mother tongue within school surroundings as well as in the classroom. To some extent it was difficult to learn through Kiswahili, especially in lower grades; but little by little I got used

> to Kiswahili. After primary education I went through new experiences of learning through English. This shift was very challenging as I was supposed to learn all subjects through English except for Kiswahili, 'elimu ya siasa' (Civics) and religion. English was an unfamiliar language for most of the students in my class. We survived in the system by depending on translations and code-switching. Teachers used to explain almost everything in Kiswahili to make us understand the subject contents well. The teaching of the subject 'English' was dominated by teacher centred instruction, teaching of grammar, test taking, and memorization. In some cases English was taught through Kiswahili. In other subjects, teachers did not pay attention to helping students to learn English; they concentrated on teaching subject contents. (Bakahwemama, 2016: 11)

Another PhD student of mine tells how he grew up with three Tanzanian languages simultaneously. He spoke one language—kiVinza—with his father and the whole clan of his father, and another one, kiHa, with his mother and her whole clan. They all lived in the same compound, and he went back and forth between the family members shifting languages according to whom he spoke. The languages of his mother's clan and his father's clan were not very different. They were more dialects of each other but the pronunciation differed and some words could be found in one of the languages, not in the other. From an early age, he spoke Kiswahili with all his friends. All these three languages became part of his identity. He was brought up trilingually and could not say what was his 'mother tongue,' first, second or third language (Kimizi, 2009). He also tells of his friend James:

> My parents languages seem to be more dialects of the same language, yet they are different dialects and I speak them both. My friend James, whose parents were among our neighbours, had, however a more complicated linguistic situation than mine. His father was a Chagga and his mother a Ha. kiChagga and kiHa are absolutely different languages in all linguistic aspects. But my friend James could speak both languages proficiently as they were both used at home at the same time. There were twelve family members in his home, six of whom were Chagga, close relatives of his Dad and the other six were Ha, close relatives of his Mom. At the beginning the harmonising language between the family members of James was kiSwahili. After some time of living together, however, all family members became familiar with, and users of, all three languages, kiChagga, kiHa and kiSwahili. My friend James and his brothers and sisters, who were born in such a linguistic context, acquired all three languages simultaneously during their childhood at home. For them, too, it is difficult to determine which is their mother tongue, first language or second language. (Kimizi, 2009: 199)

Adama Ouane (2009), from Mali, the former Director of the UNESCO Institute of Lifelong Learning in Hamburg, also tells that he grew up with three different African languages simultaneously and, like Kimizi, cannot tell which one is his 'mother tongue' or first language. Ouane (2009) also criticizes Western theories of language learning in a multicultural setting:

> As an experienced language learner and 'multilingualist' I question the suitability of current approaches to language learning to serve multilingual settings. Official monolingualism and regulated binary bilingualisms are undermining the ground or the spread of multilingualism. Linguists and specialists promoting multilingual education have so far failed to construct more suitable approaches for language learning and teacher development, which become practices of multilingualism. Western theories of multilingualism, which are influenced by the monolingual, compartmentalising habitus bar the understanding of the multilingual habitus such as the one in African everyday life. (Ouane, 2009: 169)

The fact that most Africans are multilingual has struck me many times. Many of the concepts employed by Western linguists, formed on the basis of the situation in Europe, Canada or the US, do not make sense. Kimizi comments, based on his own experiences:

> To many of us the whole bilingual debate seems strange since the term 'bilingualism' seems to be used only when one of the languages is a European language. James, who speaks two very different African languages kiHa and kiChagga would not be called bilingual according to the way the term transported to Africa, is often used. The use has been taken over by Africans without much reflection. (Kimizi, 2009: 199)

In a book edited by Kwesi Kwaa Prah and myself (Prah & Brock-Utne, 2009), the authors discuss the inadequacy of many Western language learning theories when applied to the African continent and the necessity of working for a paradigm shift in the thinking on bilingual/multilingual education in Africa. Most theories on bilingualism are from the US, Canada, Europe and other industrialized countries and have been formed on the basis of experiences in this part of the world. They do not fit the situation in Africa. Concepts, like mother tongue, first and second language learning, bilingual teaching additive and subtractive bilingualism, immersion and submersion programs, early and late exit, maintenance and transition programs, are concepts taken from the West, partly applied to affluent situations in Canada, partly applied to immigrant and minority children from third world countries being integrated into school life in the affluent West. Neither of the situations resembles the situations in Africa. Most Africans are at least bilingual in African languages. Yet they are, as Kimizi

(2009) correctly observes, not called bilingual unless one of the two languages is a foreign language.

Normally, when the concept 'bilingual' teaching or 'second language learning' is used, it means using the African child's mother tongue or familiar African language as a stepping-stone to the use—also as the language of instruction—of an ex-colonial language. The fact that children learn best when they understand what the teacher is saying is overlooked. So is the fact that the ex-colonial languages are foreign languages to most Africans. They are in reality minority languages, but given a prestige far above that of minority languages in Europe.

Literacy In Whose Language and Whose Script?

The last half of 2002, I was a Visiting Professor at the Centre for International Cooperation in Education (CICE) at Hiroshima University. It came as somewhat of a surprise to me that hardly anyone I met, apart from my nearest colleagues at the Centre, spoke any English. I gave talks at Kyoto University and at a couple of universities in Tokyo, and my talks were translated into Japanese. I had gotten all my slides translated into Japanese, and when students asked me questions, they did so in Japanese and the questions were translated into English for me to understand and answer. I felt a frustration by not being able to talk with people, so I enrolled in a Japanese beginner's class. I also bought a book in English called *Japanese Made Easy*. It was written in Latin script. With the help, especially of that book, I was able to learn some phrases and to converse a little. I saw that it was possible to write Japanese in Latin script, but that is not what is done, and even suggesting it seemed as cultural imperialism. I concentrated on learning to speak some Japanese. Since each written sentence in Japanese has words from three writing systems (Hiragana for the words of Japanese origin, Katakana for the words of foreign [mostly English] origin and Kanji [the Chinese writing system]), it takes a long time to learn to read and write. I saw that there would not be time to learn to read and write in the fall term I was there.

I love doing workouts, aerobics, Zumba and the like in classes with other people and to good music. I enrolled in a gym which was located within a supermarket and where there were lots of classes I could attend. My oral Japanese was now good enough for me to have some small talk with the women in the Onsen we frequented after the workout. One day, when I came to the gym, the whole supermarket was closed. There was a big sign in Japanese which I recognized to be from the gym where I did my workout, but I was unable to read it. I knew there was another entrance to the supermarket and went there. Also that entrance was closed, and I encountered the same sign. So I had to go back home unable to do my workout that day. Next day, when I came to the gym, I asked the girl at the reception why the gym had been closed. She told me that the gym had not been closed. "Did you not see that we had put up a sign telling members of the gym to go through the garage?" And I had to answer her: "But I cannot read and write your language." Then she replied: "Oh, so sorry, we had completely forgotten that you are illiterate." And she was right, I am illiterate—in Japanese script. The episode told me something about literacy. Who is literate in whose language and whose script?

In an article on illiteracy in Sierra Leone, Kingsley Banya (1993: 163), writes:

> Only about 25% of the country's population were [in 1961] literate in English, which is the official language. However, most people are literate in Krio, which is the lingua franca of the country [. . .] in absolute numbers there has been a tremendous expansion in the number of illiterates. As the population has increased, the number of literate people has not kept pace; 85 out of every 100 Sierra Leones are now illiterate.

Banya classifies as illiterate those Sierra Leoneans who cannot write and read English, even though they may read and write Krio, the lingua franca of their country! If a native Englishman who reads and writes English, but not any other language, were likewise classified as illiterate, there would be many illiterates in the English-speaking world.

Taking the Experiences of Africans Into Account

The so-called sandwich programs through which many Africans get their higher education in the US, Canada or Europe frequently school the students in Western theories, send them back home on fieldwork collecting raw data and have them write up the data according to the Western theories (Brock-Utne, 1999). This practice does not contribute to the building up of an African way of knowing. Even when the African is studying or working in an African university, the practice of relying on Western theories to put data into is still there. In an article discussing the problems of validity and reliability in qualitative research within education in Africa, I attempt to show that the African researcher knows his/her environment better than any expatriate and will be more likely to ask the right questions provided that s/he is allowed to ask them and is not forced to work with questions of concern to Western donors, and provided that s/he trusts her/his own experiences and uses those to form concepts instead of merely transferring concepts formed in the West, which are based on experiences in the northern hemisphere (Brock-Utne, 1996). I argue for the need for secondary research that reanalyzes from an Afrocentric viewpoint many of the accounts written by Western travelers and anthropologists. I, further, argue for the use of an autobiographical approach to secure data of high ecological validity.

I mention an example of an African scholar who wanted to write a paper on the albino children in Tanzania. Instead of using autobiographical experiences from parenting albino children in Africa, the researcher consulted books in differential psychology written in the US and texts in anthropology about the status of albino children in Africa written by European travelers and anthropologists. These were the books he found in the library. He did not use his own experiences from parenting albino children. The researcher would have made a more interesting piece of research using an autobiographical approach based on grounded theory (Nitsch, 2015).

Narrative Study of Lives in Africa

In an article based on case study research of lives in South Africa, Coetzee, Elliker and Rau (2013) introduce the program The Narrative Study of Lives in Africa. Such a program provides a platform for establishing and strengthening a significant component of the training of social and human scientists. The essence is epistemologically related to indigenous knowledge, cultural transmission and community engagement, and it contributes towards a democratization of knowledge.

One of the primary aims of this program is to explore ways to listen to the voices of ordinary people. The Narrative Study of Lives in Africa attempts to sensitize students to description and understanding of aspects of their own social reality, its unique context and the need to participate in social transformation and reconstruction. This type of research is needed all over Africa, not only in South Africa.

Questions for Discussion

1. Have you yourself or close friends or family had similar experiences described in the first part of this chapter, i.e., a language being looked down upon, in your life (or theirs)? If so, describe these experiences.
2. What do you see as the main reasons why the language of instruction (LoI) in Africa does not change in a way where children would be able to study through their mother tongue or another familiar African language?

Author Profile

Birgit Brock-Utne is affiliated to the University of Oslo as a Professor in Education and Development (www.uv.uio.no/iped/english/people/aca/bbrock/index.html) and also works as a consultant around the globe. She speaks Norwegian, German, English, Kiswahili and French. In 2011 she was the President of BAICE (the British Association of Comparative and International Education). She was the Norwegian coordinator of the Language of Instruction in Tanzania and South Africa project (www.loitasa.org). She is currently one of the Norwegian coordinators of the TRANSLED project, which builds capacity at the State University of Zanzibar (SUZA) and at UDSM. www.uv.uio.no/iped/english/research/projects/brock-utne-transled/index.html E-mail: birgit.brock-utne@iped.uio.no

Note

1 'siasa': a social science subject closely connected to the ideology of CCM, Nyerere's party, was taught in Kiswahili.

References

Bakahwemama, J. (2016). Change of language of instruction in the teaching of science and mathematics in grade five in Zanzibar: What was the reasoning behind the policy change? Ph.D. thesis. University of Oslo.

Bakar, A. S. (1988). Small island systems: A case study of the Comoro Islands. *Comparative Education, 24* (2), 181–91.

Banya, K. (1993). Illiteracy, colonial legacy, and education: The case of modern Sierra Leone. *Comparative Education, 29* (2), 159–71.

Brock-Utne, B. (1995). Reflections of a cultural commuter. In J. Bystydzienski & Estelle P. Resnik (eds.), *Women in cross-cultural transitions* (pp. 121–32). Bloomington: Phi Delta Kappa Educational Foundation.

Brock-Utne, B. (1996). Reliability and validity in qualitative research within education in Africa. *International Review of Education, 42* (6), 605–21.

Brock-Utne, B. (1999). African universities and the African heritage. *International Review of Education, 45* (1), 87–104.

Brock-Utne, B. (2000). *Whose education for all? Recolonization of the African mind*. New York: Falmer Press. Reprinted in 2006 in Seoul by Homi Publishing and Africanabooks.

Brock-Utne, B. (2007). Learning through a familiar language versus learning through a foreign language: A look into some secondary school classrooms in Tanzania. *International Journal of Educational Development, 27* (5), 487–98.

Brock-Utne, B. (2009). The adoption of the Western paradigm of bilingual teaching—why does it not fit the African situation? In K. K. Prah & B. Brock-Utne (eds.), *Multilingualism—An African advantage. A paradigm shift in African language of instruction polices* (pp. 18–51). Cape Town: CASAS.

Brock-Utne, B. (2014). Language of instruction in Africa—the most important and least appreciated issue. *International Journal of Educational Development in Africa* (IJEDA), *1* (1), 4–18.

Brock-Utne, B. (2015). Language, literacy and development in Africa. In L. Makalela (ed.), *New directions in language and literacy education for multilingual classrooms in Africa* (pp. 15–38). Cape Town: CASAS.

Brock-Utne, B. (2016). The ubuntu paradigm in curriculum work, language of instruction and assessment. *International Review of Education*, Vol. 62. Retrieved February 8, 2016 from: DOI10.1007/s11159-016-9540-2.

Brock-Utne, B., & Qorro, M. (2015). Multilingualism and language in education in Tanzania. In A. Yiakoumetti (ed.), *Multilingualism and language in education: Current sociolinguistic and pedagogical perspectives from Commonwealth countries* (pp. 19–30). Cambridge: Cambridge University Press.

Coetzee, J. K., Elliker, F. & Rau, A. (2013). Training for advanced research in the narrative study of lives within the context of political and educational transformation: A case study in South Africa. *Forum Qualitative Sozialforschung / Forum: Qualitative Social Research*, 14 (2). Retrieved April 12, 2015 from: www.qualitativeresearch.net/index.php/fqs/rt/printerFriendly/1972/3516 1/12.

Kimizi, M. M. (2009). From a Eurocentric to an Afrocentric perspective on language of instruction in the African context: A view from within. In K. K. Prah & B. Brock-Utne (eds.), *Multilingualism—an African advantage: A paradigm shift in African language of instruction policies* (pp. 195–219). Cape Town: CASAS.

Mkwizu, M. (2002). The pedagogical implications of using English in teaching civics in Tanzanian secondary schools. Master thesis. University of Oslo: Institute for Educational Research. Unit for Comparative and International Education.

Mkwizu, M. (2003). The pedagogical implications of using English in teaching civics in Tanzanian secondary schools. *Education in Africa*. Vol.12. Report no. 5. 2003. Oslo: Institute for Educational Research. Unit for Comparative and International Education.

Mwinsheikhe, H. M. (2007). Overcoming the language barrier: An in-depth study of Tanzanian secondary school science teachers' and students' strategies in coping with the English/Kiswahili dilemma in the teaching/learning process. Ph.D. dissertation, University of Oslo.

Nitsch, W. (2015). Africanizing grounded theory studies? *CERM-ESA Core-Paper* No. 25.

Ouane, A. (2009). My journey to and through a multilingual landscape. In B. Brock-Utne & G. Garbo (eds.), *Language and power: The implications of language for peace and development* (pp. 164–72). Dar es Salaam: Mkuki na Nyota Publishers.

Prah, K. K. & B. Brock-Utne (eds.) (2009). *Multilingualism—an African advantage: A paradigm shift in African language of instruction policies*. Cape Town: CASAS.

Thiong'o, N. (1986). *Decolonising the mind: The politics of language in African literature*. Nairobi: Heinemann.

Vuzo, M. (2007). Revisiting the language of instruction policy in Tanzania: A comparative study of geography classes taught in Kiswahili and English. Ph.D. dissertation, University of Oslo.

White, B. W. (1996). Talk about school: Education and the colonial project in French and British Africa (1860–1960). *Comparative Education*, *32* (1), 9–25.

11

NATURALIZING A PLANNED LANGUAGE

Esperanto and the Promotion of Linguistic Diversity

Humphrey Tonkin

Introduction

In this chapter I will tell the story of my encounter with the international language Esperanto and the way in which it has changed how I think and feel about language. I have been speaking and using Esperanto for over half a century; it has brought me into contact with people and ideas very different from those I would have encountered through the English language, and perhaps any other conventional ethnic language. All languages carry with them differences of affect and of cultural assumptions. This is certainly true of Esperanto, how I think and feel about language and particularly, its relation to globalization.

The Beginning

I am not sure what brought me to Esperanto in 1954. It occurred after I was banished to the library at my British boarding school for unruly behavior in German class. I was angry at myself for learning so little German and, I think, annoyed at the world for serving that language up as though World War II had never happened. Wartime austerity, perhaps coupled with a reluctance to feature the Nazis, had prevented the publisher from producing a new edition of our textbook. So, as Britain sought its path in a postwar world, as populations displaced by the war gradually found their way home or into permanent exile, and as the ugly bombsites of London were filled little by little with new buildings, in my textbook the Germans were still drinking coffee along the Unter den Linden, walking their dogs, visiting the opera, moving freely from one Frankfurt to the other, oblivious of Hitler or Stalin and their ilk. In this now fictional world, Dresden still stood, Nuremberg was just a quaint medieval city and no one had heard of Bonn.

I wanted to know more about the real Germany—the Germany of 1954. But I also wanted to show my teacher that I was capable of learning another language—one different from his German. So whether my motive was high-minded or base, whether I cared about the current state of Germany or simply resented the need to manipulate three grammatical genders and make adjectives and nouns agree, I cannot be sure. But the moment in history, or my own adolescent development, or the politics of the classroom, or (most likely) sheer 14-year-old obstinacy, drove me to select a new language to learn—and I arrived at the international language Esperanto.

The Esperanto textbook in the school library offered simplicity, logic, and, perhaps most appealing of all, autonomy. Here was a language I could learn on my own. More than that: Esperanto was not just a constructed language but seemed in effect to afford the learner the ability to construct his or her *own* language, using the building blocks available. Never mind that I had no one to talk with: this experience was about reassuring myself that I could learn a language, about my ability to talk to *myself* in this language. For me, Esperanto began as a kind of inner dialogue.

In truth, I sometimes wonder whether it was the *lack* of German that drove me to Esperanto—simple grammar, no annoying speakers to confuse me, no need to engage with an existing culture belonging to someone other than myself—and of course no need to come to terms with the language of the people who bombed our family out of our house and whose malign behavior had been daily reiterated on the radio during the years when I was coming to consciousness. Esperanto, by contrast, was just a language, or so it seemed. I did not yet know that Esperanto would ultimately hasten my understanding of both the German language and the Germans, giving me confidence in my language skills and a new awareness of the relations among peoples.

Esperanto was a safe space for a confused adolescent. I dug into learning the language. I wrote to the British Esperanto Association in London to find out more. It turned out, of course, that Esperanto did indeed have speakers: it was not a language known only to me. These speakers were scattered across the world, but contacts provided by Esperanto organizations made it easy to reach them. So I plunged into correspondence with Esperantists all over the world, most of them young people like me. A new world was revealed. Although I followed a correspondence course, I learned the language primarily through letter-writing—with some fifty people in all. My correspondents and I helped one another to express ourselves, correcting one another's grammar and expressing our curiosity about other countries and peoples, unmediated by the often demonizing opinions of others. Not even teachers stood between my correspondents and me: I was an autonomous interpreter of what I read.

Thus, Esperanto was for me a relatively benign form of adolescent rebellion—against teachers for whom most of what we learned (starting with adjective-noun agreement) was either right or wrong and seldom both or neither, and against our elders in general (though my family displayed an equanimous and generally supportive indulgence of my newfound enthusiasm). Through Esperanto, I was negotiating my own personal globalization, one correspondent at a time—a globalization perhaps stimulated by the plausible arguments of those teachers and elders who wanted to build a better world, to forgive and to show compassion. They taught me about the new United Nations, about a new Europe, even as they sought to make me (and perhaps themselves) understand how it could be that Britain and its allies had been fighting insurrections in Malaya and Kenya and staging a full-scale war in Korea.

Yet even these constructive sentiments were a form of rebellion in the tight world of the British public school, where winning often seemed more important than coexisting and ridicule of difference more important than embracing it for its own sake. Indeed, that was the paradox that absorbed me: a prudent and studious child who avoided confrontation, I found myself seemingly perpetually engaged in defending myself against ridicule. Why learn a pretend language 'that no one spoke'? Why lose myself in the unmanly world of grammatical intricacy (this was a boys' school, after all, and languages were for girls)? Why nurture a belief that matters were not settled, that a world full of ambiguity was all the richer for it?

Some of my friends felt as I did about international affairs. Before long, we had formed a little group of like-minded internationalists who studied the language together, read books in Esperanto and presented a united front against detractors. Most of the group members dropped by the wayside after they left school. But I was launched on a lifetime as an Esperantist.

This simple narrative, as I retell it (see also Tonkin, 2009), shows me now that I was dealing with what I would in due course learn were language attitudes—views of language as markers of views of the world, assumptions about the nature of language itself and of particular languages and their speakers. I was perhaps bothered by the context-free, or contextually erroneous, approach to German and looking for a different linguistic space. Esperanto, as I learned it and used it, in effect erased itself: it was not so much a marker of identity as a way to free myself from the tyranny of identity.

Nor was this language—as perhaps the doubters around me seemed to believe—based on the assumption that everyone was the same across the world. What appealed to me about Esperanto was the accessibility of difference: my correspondents were all human, to be sure, but they were also profoundly different, and willing to share these differences. I am not suggesting that our correspondence was particularly profound—only that it was not based on prior assumptions about either nationality or human universals. We were communicating in a language largely devoid of such assumptions—driven by a certain youthful optimism.

An Alternative World

Esperanto came into the world in 1887, the work of Leyzer Ludwik Zamenhof, a Polish Jew, in what was then the Russian Empire. Born in 1859, he was 28 years old when he published his language, in a slim volume under the pseudonym Doktoro

Esperanto—a name that soon became identified with the language itself. Published in Warsaw with the financial assistance of Zamenhof's new in-laws and the bureaucratic help of his father, who served as Czarist censor for Hebrew and Yiddish, the book was ten or more years in the making, so Zamenhof was not much older than I was when he started work on his language: Esperanto was, and in many respects still is, a language of young people (a recent app for learning Esperanto, Duolingo, has been downloaded by almost a million people).

The Esperanto language was inspired by Zamenhof's conviction that the interethnic strife that he witnessed on the streets of the city of Bialystok, in northeastern Poland, where he had grown up, could at least be mitigated if people had a language in common. As we look at Nairobi or Los Angeles, today, we are apt to imagine that urban multilingualism is very much a phenomenon of our own day, but, as William McNeill (1986) and many others have clearly established, cities have always been multilingual and multiethnic. What Zamenhof witnessed on the streets of Bialystok may not have been a manifestation of what today we might, with Jan Blommaert (2013), call 'superdiversity' so much as raw anti-Semitism.

Korzhenkov and others (Korĵenkov, 2011; Korzhenkov, 2010; Schor, E., 2016) have established that two ideas commingled in Zamenhof's mind at the time: a strong belief in the brotherhood of man (to give it its 19th-century term) and revulsion at anti-Semitism. As an ophthalmology student in Moscow and Warsaw (whence he transferred following the assassination of Czar Alexander II and the pogroms that followed) he grew actively interested in Zionism, publishing essays, organizing his fellow students and proposing a Jewish homeland, first in some "uninhabited" part of the United States, then in Palestine. He was also an enthusiast for Yiddish, leaving behind him a manuscript grammar of that language, apparently the first ever. Thus, specific ethnic identity and universalism vied for attention in his thinking. His close contemporary and near neighbor Eliezer Ben-Yehuda (born in what is now Vitebsk Oblast, Belarus, in 1858) focused his attention on a language for Jews, which became in due course Modern Hebrew, while Zamenhof turned to the creation of a language of humankind—in effect, a Yiddish for all humanity.

Zamenhof's goal—significantly—was not the creation of a perfect language. Many people before him, and indeed after him, tried to create ideal international languages that everyone might learn (Eco, 1995; Okrent, 2009). The Catholic priest Johann Martin Schleyer had done just that a few years before when he created Volapük. A sure sign that philologists in love with complexity are the worst people to create usable languages (Schleyer's language was complicated and hard to learn and use), Volapük had initial success, but eventually collapsed under its own weight and the zeal of reformers, as Schleyer clung to its original version with all the tenacity of sole authorship (Garvía, 2015). Zamenhof was interested in what gradually became a vision of spiritual unity—branded as unrealizable idealism even by many of his fellow Esperantists. But the fact that he saw his language more as a medium of communication than as a work of art meant that he shared the language freely with his followers, indeed worked hard to persuade them to own it and develop it, rather than acting as sole proprietor. One might argue that he sought to make us all Jews: Esperanto was a kind of Yiddish for all, performing a similar role as a lingua franca. But it was Latin that Zamenhof took as his model: while the parallels are not complete, Esperanto is in many respects a kind of simplified Latin, etymologically and morphologically allied to that model, while incorporating elements that are quite non-European in nature (Parkvall, 2010; Gledhill, 1998; Janton, 1993).

This is not to say that there was no tension between Zamenhof's philosophy of spiritual universality and the notion that the language belonged to all, and could be used for all purposes. Almost from the beginning (the first World Esperanto Congress took place in 1905) there were disagreements between Zamenhof on the one hand—this rather wild Litvak from Eastern Europe—and the progressive bourgeois element that adopted his language in Germany and France on the other. The battle over the 'neutrality' of Esperanto eventually drove Zamenhof to abandon a leadership position in the Esperanto movement to devote himself to religious and ecumenical issues, thereby giving the language and its growing community freedom to develop as it might. Nor was Zamenhof's openness proof against divisive, though ultimately unsuccessful, efforts at reform (Gordin, 2015).

'Neutrality' was and is an issue among Esperantists. The 1920s saw an outpouring of enthusiasm for Esperanto in the new revolutionary Soviet Union, and in the workers' movement in general—leading in due course to a split between the highly centralized Soviet movement, with its vision of Esperanto as the language of the proletariat, and the workers' movement in the west, likewise wedded to Esperanto as the people's language but more pragmatic, cosmopolitan and fragmented in its approach (Lins, 2016a). Esperanto seized the attention of Japanese reformers as the movement for modernization swept that country in the early years of the century (Konishi, 2013; 2015). It became associated with westernization in China, and particularly with the anarchist movement (Müller-Saini & Benton, 2006a; 2006b; Lins, 2008). The bourgeois movement, meanwhile, clinging to political neutrality, was caught in the vise of fascism in Germany, making concession after concession to the authorities, all to no avail. In Stalinist Russia, the internationalism of the early years of the revolution gave way to virulent nationalism: the Great Purge of the late 1930s sent Esperantists to the firing squads or to the farthest reaches of Siberia.

I brought little of this knowledge with me to Esperanto. Most of what went on under Stalin became apparent only after the collapse of communism in the late 1980s and early 1990s; and Zamenhof's Jewishness, and particularly his spiritual radicalism, was downplayed over the years, in part by Zamenhof himself, eager not to burden Esperanto with extraneous misrepresentation. I knew that Zamenhof died, allegedly disillusioned by the war, in 1917, and that virtually his entire family was wiped out in the gas chambers of Treblinka. But in 1954 the world had still to come to grips with the full horrors of the Holocaust.

In essence, Esperanto, as I began to acquire it, offered a kind of alternative world. If my initial impressions were of a language spoken by none, and therefore, mine to play with, my later view, as I engaged with the Esperanto movement, was of a community of idealists, eager to make the world better, often unrealistic in their expectations and their ability to influence events. Here there was a contradiction: Esperanto was available to all, for all purposes (thus the German High Command used it for propaganda purposes in World War I, China and Viet Nam denounced American atrocities in the Viet Nam War in Esperanto, and companies like Fiat in Italy and Philips in the Netherlands employed it in advertising campaigns), but the core of the organized movement consisted, at least as far as I could see, of people who believed in world order and in human rights. Indeed, the Universal Esperanto Association, the principal international Esperanto organization, wrote an affirmation of human rights into its constitution even before the Universal Declaration of Human Rights came into being in 1948. So I could test my consciousness of these values in the relatively sheltered environment of the Esperanto community—a less contentious atmosphere than that of public school Britain in 1954–55, yet also an intellectual staging-area for voicing these ideas among my contemporaries and teachers without the sense of isolation often endured by the idealist.

I was inspired in part by my reading. In addition to readings for beginners, my texts included the poems of Zamenhof, one of them, *"Mia Penso"* ("My Thought"), describing the feelings of isolation experienced by the idealist. While there are better poets in Esperanto than Zamenhof (the role and quality of Esperanto literature are an important element in the cultural life of the community: Sutton, 2008; Tonkin, 2002; 2012; Gubbins, 2012; Minnaja & Silfer, 2015), these early poems have served as inspiration for many, who perhaps recognize these sentiments in themselves. Built into the very culture of Esperanto (open though it may be for all) is this sense of making a way in a world all too often hostile to ideas, particularly ideas for improvement. In its alternative linguistic system, Esperanto in effect offered me an alternative value system: the gods of my Esperanto-speaking world were intriguingly different from the gods of my English-speaking world.

In alternative worlds the stakes are low. The speaker of Esperanto, abandoning the mother tongue, can fight the battles of internationalism in a protected environment, and is always free to return to a more everyday existence. Thus, we are free to fail in an Esperanto environment (I refer not to the language but its ideas) without the same sense of failure in the mother tongue environment, so we can take risks in the one without recrimination in the other. We, all of us, balance our lives with alternative pursuits and varied cultural registers, and all languages offer the potential for alternative identities. Esperanto provides an extreme form of this dualism.

Naturalization

Many people believe that advocates of Esperanto want to replace other languages with Zamenhof's. On the contrary, most Esperantists believe fervently in the right to use one's own language; they believe in linguistic diversity, with Esperanto as a bridge across languages. Esperanto floats on top of languages—on top of (and conserving) linguistic diversity.

I admired those who could move freely from one language to another. Languages did not enjoy much prestige in the British schools curriculum. As one commentator on the UK's exit from the European Union recently put it, "We are not multilingual; we are not part of Europe." This part of my British identity, this particularly insular kind of exceptionalism, I yearned to put behind me; I wanted to be able to negotiate my way in a multilingual environment. By the time I came to German, I had already studied Latin. Later that language became part of my scholarly life, along with basic Italian. And I had gathered a fair knowledge of French, which I continued to study during the rest of my schooling. Esperanto, easy to learn and pronounce, and suited to self-instruction, offered an alternative way to fluency.

Yet my path to fluency was long, given the distractions and obligations of youth. Recently a staff member at the Universal Esperanto Association's office in Rotterdam found a letter I had written to the Association in 1957, two or three years after I began learning. Reading it today, I am struck by how stilted it is. Although I had begun speaking the language and listening to it, in 1957, my spoken language was probably as awkward as my written language.

However, in 1958, I attended my first international youth meeting and, almost overnight, spoken Esperanto became a normal part of my linguistic repertoire. Among people my own age, from many different countries, conversation became an extraordinary and enlightening experience. Esperanto conversation creates a particular kind of existential space: sitting with half a dozen people from half a dozen countries and languages, one becomes less aware of one's own origins and yet unencumbered by anyone else's. It is a space where meaning can be negotiated among equals quite differently from its negotiation in the languages of nationality, which situate us within a particularized cultural space.

If this existential space is different from that encountered in other languages, in other respects Esperanto resembles those languages. For example, much of what is current in today's written and spoken Esperanto is the creation of its present-day speakers and was unknown to Zamenhof: Esperanto may have started as the creation of a single individual, but ownership rapidly shifted to the collective, where its speakers were free, within certain bounds of received practice (like the speakers of all languages), to build on to it as they saw fit and as their *Ausbau* (to borrow Heinz Kloss's term) proved acceptable to the community at large. Some processes were endogenous (Tonkin, 2001): discovery of latent qualities in the language (and often the functional application of the law of necessity and sufficiency), primarily in its grammar, but also in its combinability into compound words of essentially new semantic value (what we might call neomorphisms). Others were exogenous: the introduction of new words and expressions from outside, often contested, but also often successfully assimilated (neologisms). The general tendency in word-formation has favored simplicity: for example, the elimination of nonessential affixes. This process occurs socially, generally without overt reference to grammar—because Esperanto speakers, like speakers of other languages, give little or no *conscious* attention to the rules of grammar in the creation of new expressions, even though these expressions follow the existing rules.

The sheer exuberance of Esperanto contrasts with its common definition as a *planned* language. In fact, one of the distinctive characteristics of Esperanto is its abundant wordplay (Melnikov, 2008; 2015; Fiedler, 1999; 2002), brought on perhaps by a certain sense of freedom that the speaker of Esperanto enjoys. Linguists often refer to Esperanto as a *constructed* language or *planned* language, occasionally as an *artificial language*, sometimes as an *auxiliary* language (Blanke, 1987). Each carries its political and ideological burden, and each has only an indirect and largely irrelevant applicability to the language as it exists today. To speak of an *artificial* language, for example, is to contrast it, by default, with a *natural* language, a particularly misleading metaphor used all too frequently by specialists in linguistics, promiscuous lovers of analogy. All languages are artificial in that they are made by art, and all are in some measure constrained by their own history and usage; none is natural, except in the sense that it appears to grow spontaneously—a characteristic as identifiable with modern Esperanto as with any other language. And *auxiliary* implies *incomplete*—a kind of aid or crutch. With 130 years of use behind it, Esperanto has long since surpassed that designation (Blanke, 2009).

Not only did Zamenhof extract his ideas of language from existing languages, but he also laid down a structure for language change that seems to follow the same rules as other languages. What today's speaker of Esperanto is doing with the language is what speakers of all other languages do: they choose their words to make their communication interesting and convincing; rhetoric in Esperanto is the same as rhetoric in any other language. Esperanto, like other languages, is in this sense a language of art.

So when I refer in my title to the *naturalization* of Esperanto, I am employing a shaky metaphor. It suggests that a language has an existence of its own. In truth it is not the language that is living, but its speakers.

But the term *naturalization* is not a bad term to define the process whereby I, as an individual, acquired Esperanto: it became a part of my linguistic nature. And my *individual* acquisition of the language seemed to parallel the history of the language itself—from planned building blocks to complex architectonics, and from an idea to a living reality. Ontogeny recapitulates phylogeny, at least as far as Esperanto is concerned: to learn Esperanto as an individual is to relive its history as a collective. The sense of artificiality is soon left behind as rules are internalized; compound words and expressions become simple, assimilated into the lexis like all other morphemic components in the language. Zamenhof created building blocks; the users of Esperanto lived in the house (or perhaps, as L2 speakers, visited the hotel . . .) that resulted.

So it is with individuals. When, years ago, I explained Esperanto word-formation to an audience in Chicago, a questioner expressed dismay that the opposite of the word for 'happy' in Esperanto, *feliĉa*, had no independent existence but was formed simply by applying the prefix 'mal-,' denoting the opposite of something. English, the questioner suggested, was so much richer because it had a separate word, *unhappy*. Obviously (and quite appropriately) the questioner had a fully formed notion of unhappiness in his mind that existed independently of the notion of happiness. Just as *happy* and *unhappy* occupy semantic spaces that in practice barely touch, so do *feliĉa* and *malfeliĉa*. (I should perhaps add that Esperanto now has numbers of words for 'unhappy,' like *trista*, which entered the language independently of, and later than, Zamenhof.)

At the same time, Esperanto began as a 'prescriptive language' (as Edwards 2012 uses that term) and will remain so: Zamenhof's early prescriptions for the language were pulled together into what was called the *Fundamento*, the indivisible body of basic rules that apply in all instances and (in theory at least) are inviolable. The Esperanto Academy is the theoretical guardian of this *Fundamento*. In practice, however, usage extends beyond these prescribed limits. As a community of L2 speakers (there are a few L1 speakers but their number is very low and their status is contested: Fiedler, 2012), and occasional speakers at that, many have an imperfect command of the language—creating problems of definition for linguists wishing to study Esperanto usage (How do we define the fluent speaker?).

Even among those who are widely regarded as speaking the language well, we find examples of L1 interference (in phonology, word choice, grammatical construction and so on), but, given the affirmative desire to understand and be understood, and the flexibility of the language, the interference seems to have minimum effect on comprehension. While I know of no formal study of the phenomenon, competent speakers of Esperanto can also distinguish, and apply, a range of registers, depending on the circumstances. Back in 1958, in my first youth meeting, I discovered expressions and turns of phrase exclusive to young people—elements in an incipient youth dialect that has grown stronger today. Though the forces that tie Esperantists together as a community exceed those that fragment them linguistically, the latter are not wholly absent.

Thus, in Esperanto as in other languages, identity and usage are near-allied. But identity in Esperanto is different in one major respect from most other languages. First, it is an L2 identity, an alternative in that sense. But, second, it does not imply identification with an ethnic group or with a group in which a particular ethnic identity is understood. Present-day L2 English is perhaps the closest equivalent: we can no longer easily argue, in a world in which English is regularly used as a vehicle to plot revolution against the English-speaking powers, that to speak English is to assume a distinctive set of values. But, if geographically based languages imply some form of identification with culture and ethnicity, Esperanto by its very nature implies ideological rather than ethnic unity. This hypothesis has been tested in recent years in several sociological studies. What emerges from them is a picture of a generalized internationalist and cosmopolitan ethos, linked to a pluralistic notion of globalization (a world that is unified in its respect for diversity), but a sharp division between those who see Esperanto as a phenomenon to be enjoyed for its own sake and those who are loyal to Esperanto as a social movement seeking social change (Galor & Pietiläinen, 2015). I have described it in my own work as a distinction between a self-sufficient community and a developing movement (Tonkin, 2006). In the Esperanto world, tension between these two views sometimes produces internal conflict.

A New Politics

My first visit to Germany took place in 1959, when I passed through that country en route to Poland. The occasion was the World Congress of Esperanto, in Warsaw, the first time the World Congress had been held on the other side of the Iron Curtain. Stalin's death in 1953 and Khrushchev's denunciation of his cult of personality in 1956 brought a gradual thaw in Eastern Europe, including the Esperanto movement—the suppression of the Hungarian Revolution of 1956, notwithstanding. Poland led the way, seizing the occasion of the centennial of Zamenhof's birth to invite the congress and attracting participants from both east and west. Nineteen years old, I was among them, thereby beginning a relationship with the Esperantists of Eastern Europe that lasted until the wall came down thirty years later.

In the highly politicized environment of Eastern Europe, it was almost impossible to operate an organization independently of the state, and state-sponsored organizations were obliged to recognize and assist in the state's policies. While the Esperanto associations of Eastern Europe varied both in their histories and in their present circumstances—and some countries were unwilling to rehabilitate Esperanto at all (notably Romania and Albania)—they represented a significant element in the community of speakers of Esperanto (Blanke, 2007). Their relationship with the politically neutral Universal Esperanto Association was troubled: the association was never quite sure whether they were acting on behalf of Esperanto and tolerated by the state, or acting on behalf of the state and using Esperanto to do so.

Western intelligence suggested the latter; but, for my part, I was never fully convinced. I doubted whether the entity described as western intelligence had actually learned the language to find out. It seemed to me that the primary purpose of most people's loyalty to Esperanto in the countries behind the Iron Curtain was to establish and maintain links with the outside world: Esperanto flourishes where communication is restricted. These Esperanto speakers were not overtly disloyal to their countries: their interest was primarily apolitical. Whereas most international organizations operating in the years right after World War II split apart into separate western and eastern entities under the pressure of the gradual sovietization of Eastern Europe in the years 1946–50, the Universal Esperanto Association did not. It held together, in my view, primarily because its members were linked linguistically and acted pragmatically: they could, in the most literal sense, speak the same language (Lins, 2016b). This political resilience fascinated me—not because I myself was attracted by Marxism, but because it seemed so unlike what I read in the papers or heard from my elders. I will not say that I became an expert on Eastern Europe (I am no political scientist), but I took it upon myself to read about it and to visit it, and I nurtured my friendship with East European Esperantists in Poland, Hungary, Bulgaria and elsewhere, some of whom I had met for the first time in Warsaw.

I became active in the leadership of TEJO, the World Esperanto Youth Organization, joining its board in 1961, the year in which my fellow Cambridge students and I organized TEJO's annual congress at a school in Berkshire. We invited representatives of Poland, Bulgaria and Hungary to attend, generating considerable interest in the local community. In 1963, I was again in Eastern Europe—in Hungary, where I conducted a series of interviews with Esperanto's greatest poet of the day, Kálmán Kalocsay, a professor in Budapest's medical school; and in Bulgaria for the congresses of TEJO (in Vratsa) and the UEA (in Sofia)—with a side visit to the Bulgarian coast.

Later, in 1974, I was elected president of the Universal Esperanto Association, a role in which I served for upwards of a decade. My old college tutor wrote to tell me that he had heard I had become 'Pope of Esperanto;' he was not entirely wrong. My new role took me frequently to Eastern Europe and to other parts of the world. But by that time, while I of course continued to improve my language skills, much as we all do in our languages native and acquired, I spoke Esperanto essentially as fluently as I speak English, and my linguistic development, though not my social development or my organizational skills, showed little documentable change. And, thus, I became a naturalized citizen of the world of Esperanto, with, I like to think, a different perspective on the world at large—a perspective that has held me in good stead ever since.

The point about 'the world at large' is that it remains a diverse and multifaceted world, indeed that its very cultural diversity is what makes it appealing and challenging. The forces of globalization, paradoxically, both allow us to explore it and threaten to homogenize it. Some years ago, in an essay on language and globalization (Tonkin, 2003), I suggested that, even if English is to become our global lingua franca, it is important that, underneath this lingua franca, we preserve linguistic diversity and, with it, cultural diversity. Personally, I derive considerable pleasure from the fact that I have learned so much about the world by flying under the radar, as it were: by seeking out speakers of Esperanto in many settings rather than losing myself in an English-speaking world where I enjoy a position of strength that inevitably distorts my perceptions. The rise of English and the concomitant decline of other languages threaten our essential freedom to enjoy multiple identities—to be different at different times and in different ways. And it offends against our sense of linguistic egalitarianism—a concept that lies at the heart of Esperanto.

Conclusion

I believe that scholars interested in issues of language and identity, linguistic community, globalization and political and social history should pay attention to Esperanto. Traces of Esperanto are to be found everywhere in the interstices of history, so that a knowledge of the story of Esperanto becomes a branch of a liberal education. The movement itself, and the language that inspired it, was a product of an earlier globalizing wave following the invention of the telegraph, the beginning of international organizations, and the misguided idealism of an imperialism that sought to 'civilize' the 'savage.' It intersected with the League of Nations, provided insight into the policies of the Soviet Union, gave James Joyce some of the wordplay of *Finnegans Wake*, and inspired efforts at writing reform in China. Roberto Garvía, in the introduction to his recent book on the "struggle for an international language" (Garvía, 2015), reminds us that the young George Orwell, eager to improve his French, moved in with his Parisian aunt Nellie Limouzin, only to find that she was living with a leader of the Esperanto workers' movement and the couple conversed in Esperanto. Was Newspeak Orwell's revenge against Zamenhof and his wayward aunt? Who knows? I like to think that Orwell moved to the library and learned French in protest.

Questions for Discussion

1. It is often said that Esperanto has succeeded as a language (it is, after all, widely used as a means of communication by its global community) but has not succeeded as an idea (it has not been adopted as a major language of wider communication). Why is that so?
2. If language is an important element in defining identity, how might linguistic identity function differently in the case of Esperanto from the way it functions in other languages?

Author Profile

Humphrey Tonkin (M.A. Cambridge, PhD Harvard), has been successively Professor of English at the University of Pennsylvania, President of the State University of New York at Potsdam and President and University Professor of the Humanities at the University of Hartford. He has served as president of the Universal Esperanto Association, and chaired the Council for International Exchange of Scholars, the Canadian Fulbright Commission, and the board of the Center for Applied Linguistics. He was editor-in-chief of the journal *Language Problems & Language Planning* and now edits the series Studies in World Language Problems. His publications include books and articles on literature, international studies, Esperanto and service-learning.

References

Blanke, D. (1987). The term 'planned language.' *Language Problems & Language Planning, 11* (3), 335–49.

Blanke, D. (2007). *Esperanto kaj socialismo? Pri la movado sur la 'alia flanko'*. 2nd edn. New York: Mondial.

Blanke, D. (2009). Causes of the relative success of Esperanto. *Language Problems & Language Planning, 33* (3), 251–66.

Blommaert, J. (2013). *Ethnography, superdiversity and linguistic landscapes: Chronicles of complexity*. Bristol: Multilingual Matters.

Eco, U. (1995). *The search for the perfect language*. Oxford, UK & Cambridge, MA: Blackwell.

Edwards, J. (2012). Language, prescriptivism, nationalism—and identity. In C. Percy & M. C. Davidson (eds.), *The languages of nation: Attitudes and norms* (pp. 11–36). Bristol: Multilingual Matters.

Fiedler, S. (1999). *Plansprache und Phraseologie: Empirische Untersuchungen zu reproduziertem Sprachmaterial im Esperanto*. Frankfurt/Main: Peter Lang.

Fiedler, S. (2002). *Esperanta frazeologio*. Rotterdam: Universala Esperanto-Asocio.

Fiedler, S. (2012). The Esperanto *denaskulo*: The status of the native speaker of Esperanto within and beyond the planned language community. *Language Problems & Language Planning, 36* (1), 69–84.

Galor, Z. & Pietiläinen, J. (2015). *UEA en konscio de esperantistoj*. Dobřichovice, Czech Republic: Kava-Pech.

Garvía, R. (2015). *Esperanto and its rivals: The struggle for an international language*. Philadelphia: University of Pennsylvania Press.

Gledhill, C. (1998). *The grammar of Esperanto : A corpus-based description*. Languages of the World/Materials 190. München & Newcastle: LINCOM Europa.

Gordin, M. D. (2015). *Scientific Babel: How science was done before and after global English*. Chicago: University of Chicago Press.

Gubbins, P. (ed.) (2012). *Star in a night sky: An anthology of Esperanto literature*. London: Francis Boutle.

Janton, P. (1993). *Esperanto: Language, literature, and community*. Albany, NY: State University of New York Press.

Konishi, S. (2013). Translingual world order: Language without culture in Post-Russo-Japanese war Japan. *Journal of Asian Studies, 72* (1), 91–114.

Konishi, S. (2015). The science of symbiosis and linguistic democracy in twentieth-century Japan. *INDECS: Interdisciplinary Description of Complex Systems, 13* (2), 299–317.

Korĵenkov, A. (2011). *Homarano: La vivo, verkoj kaj ideoj de d-ro L. L. Zamenhof*. 2nd edn. Kaliningrad: Sezonoj / Kaunas: Litova Esperanto-Asocio.

Korzhenkov, A. (2010). *Zamenhof: The life, works and ideas of the author of Esperanto* [translated by I. Richmond]. New York: Mondial.

Lins, U. (2008). Esperanto as language and idea in China and Japan. *Language Problems & Language Planning, 32* (1), 47–60.

Lins, U. (2016a). *Dangerous language 1: Esperanto under Hitler and Stalin*. London: Palgrave Macmillan.

Lins, U. (2016b). *Dangerous language 2: Esperanto and the decline of Stalinism*. London: Palgrave Macmillan.

McNeill, W. H. (1986). *Polyethnicity and national unity in world history*. Toronto: University of Toronto Press.

Melnikov, A. S. (2008). *Vortludoj kaj luda komunikado en Esperanto*. San Marino, Moscow, Rostov-on-Don: Akademio Internacia de la Sciencoj.

Melnikov, A. S. (2015). *Gvidlibro tra Esperantio*. Rostov-on-Don: Author.

Minnaja, C. & Silfer, G. (2015). *Historio de la esperanta literaturo*. La Chaux-de-Fonds, Switzerland: Literatura Foiro.

Müller-Saini, G. & Benton, G. (2006a). Esperanto and Chinese anarchism 1907–1920: The translation from diaspora to homeland. *Language Problems & Language Planning*, *30*, (1), 45–73.

Müller-Saini, G. & Benton, G. (2006b). Esperanto and Chinese anarchism 1907–1920: The translation from diaspora to homeland. *Language Problems & Language Planning*, *30*, (2), 173–92.

Okrent, A. (2009). *In the land of invented languages*. New York: Spiegel & Grau.

Parkvall, M. (2010). How European is Esperanto? *Language Problems & Language Planning*, *34* (1), 63–79.

Schor, E. (2016). *Bridge of words: Esperanto and the dream of a universal language*. New York: Metropolitan Books, Henry Holt.

Schubert, K. (ed.) (2002). *Planned languages: From concept to reality*. Brussels: Hogeschool voor Wetenschap en Kunst.

Sutton, G. (2008). *Concise encyclopedia of the original literature of Esperanto*. New York: Mondial.

Tonkin, H. (2001). Esperantologio eksogena kaj endogena. In S. Fiedler & H. Liu (eds.), *Studoj pri interlingvistiko / Studien zur Interlinguistik* (pp. 307–25). Prague: Kava-Pech.

Tonkin, H. (2002). The role of literary language in Esperanto. In K. Schubert (ed.), *Planned languages: From concept to reality* (pp. 11–35). Brussels: Hogeschool voor Wetenschap en Kunst.

Tonkin, H. (2003). The search for a global linguistic strategy. In J. Maurais & M. A. Morris (eds.), *Languages in a globalising world* (pp. 319-333). Cambridge: Cambridge University Press.

Tonkin, H. (2006). *Lingvo kaj popolo: Aktualaj problemoj de la Esperanto-movado*. Rotterdam: Universala Esperanto-Asocio.

Tonkin, H. (2009). Where art and nature meet. In E. Todeva & C. Jasone (eds.), *The multiple realities of multilingualism* (pp. 191–208). Berlin & New York: Mouton de Gruyter.

Tonkin, H. (2012). Esperanto poetry. In R. Greene (ed.), *The Princeton encyclopedia of poetry and poetics*. 4th edn. (pp. 457–58). Princeton, NJ: Princeton University Press.

PART IV

Language Death and Birth

INTRODUCTION

Language Death and Birth

Maryam Borjian

> *[L]anguage death is not an isolated phenomenon confined to ancient empires and remote backwaters. It is going on before our very eyes in all parts of the world.*
>
> Daniel Nettle & Suzanne Romaine (2000: 4)

> *And in the case of the evolution of a language into a new variety, what is the relationship between language death and language birth? Can these processes be considered as two facets of the same process?*
>
> Salikoko Mufwene (2004: 204–5)

An alarming outcome of globalization is the rapid endangerment and death of many minority languages worldwide. According to an estimate provided by Google's Endangered Language Project (2016), out of the 7000 languages that are spoken in the world today, 50% will not outlive the turn of the century. This well-documented trend has, in turn, caused linguists to be concerned about the homogenizing outcomes of globalization, with its universalization of the English language, on the one hand, and the weakening of minority languages, on the other. Through research (for example, Crystal, 2000; Fishman, 1991; Nettle & Romaine, 2000), we have learned about the phenomena of language shift, decline and death; causes for language endangerment; why we should care and what can be done about it. Field linguists, like Abley (2003) and Harrison (2007), traveled to the heart of a number of minority speech communities in different parts of the world as a means to add a human face to the phenomenon of language death by bringing the voices of the speakers of many dying languages to a world audience. Perceiving unjust language policies as the main driver of language decline, Stephan May (2001) took us to the heart of nation-states to highlight the hierarchical nature of the national language policies, through which the 'national,' 'official' language(s) were sanctioned, whereas all other languages of the nation-state were minoritized. Perceiving language death and language birth as the two 'facets of the same process,' Salikoko Mufwene (2004) added a new dimension to our understanding of endangered languages; that is, the birth of new varieties within every language as the consequence of language evolution. That is a very important factor that is often overlooked in research on endangered languages (for a similar point, see Ulrich Ammon, Chapter 3 of this volume). Bearing the importance of all these aspects in mind, Part IV of this book (Chapters 12–14) is devoted to the theme of language death and birth.

In Chapter 12, Daniel Kaufman points out that while the rapid spread of English throughout the world has been commented upon widely in connection to globalization, the large-scale presence of speakers of endangered languages in megacities of the world, including New York, has, generally, gone unnoticed. In Kaufman's view, linguistic and ethnic diversity in New York City is still very poorly understood, despite being one of the city's most celebrated 'selling' points. When attempting to identify the city's linguistic riches, writers fall back on a small handful of national languages. Yet, Kaufman argues that in New York City there are far more languages than the government census is able to count. Where do these languages come from? Who are their speakers? Are they being transmitted to children? These questions were the main reasons for the formation of the Endangered Language Alliance (ELA) that Kaufman co-founded in 2010 in New York City. The ELA is a nonprofit organization dedicated to documenting and helping to sustain the many languages of the New York area through collaboration with immigrant communities. In his chapter, Kaufman travels through time, taking the reader through the journey of his life: from his childhood in New York City to his undergraduate studies in the Philippines, where he encountered multilingualism, linguistic diversity, inequality and the linguistic scars of colonialism, all of which left their impressions and became the main reasons for his establishing the ELA. Kaufman and his ELA team should be credited for taking language-related matters outside academic circles and placing them at the heart of public domains, including in the media, libraries, museums and community centers.

"An Alaskan Language Odyssey" is the title of Chapter 13, written by Bob Holman with Sam O'Hana. As a celebrated American poet, language activist, founder of Bowery Poetry Club in New York, and also host of the PBS endangered language–focused documentary film, *Language Matters with Bob Holman*, Holman received funding from the Ford Foundation to pursue language-revitalization-focused outreach activities in Alaska. In this chapter, he invites the reader into a one-month series of outreach activities (September–October 2015) in Alaska's schools, libraries, heritage centers, arts centers, museums, prisons, churches and community meetings, in locations ranging from Juneau to Arctic Village to Nokolaevsk. The chapter provides a vivid description of the multilingual poetry readings that Holman organized in Alaska, and includes poems by two Alaskan poets that were read, analyzed and used for inspiration at these workshops. These poems help the reader add a face and voice to the theme of endangered languages, many of which may disappear by the turn of this century. In Alaska, as Holman argues, he found a place poised for transformation in support of indigenous language speakers' rights and educational language reform. In his view, Alaska is uniquely positioned to heal the tragic wounds of the state's colonialist history by restoring the importance of indigenous languages both to broader society and in the lives of individual speakers. The chapter concludes with a poem written by Holman during his journey in Alaska, which captures the odyssey of Alaskan languages through his eyes and creative language, utilizing aspects of oral tradition, including praising participants by name, illuminating morals through stories, and creating a history from the voices of the participants, among others.

Classified as 'definitely endangered' by UNESCO in 2010, Western Armenian is the focus of Chapter 14, written by Jennifer Manoukian, a translator of Western Armenian. Of the many reasons for the endangerment of Western Armenian, the most notable is the Armenian Genocide, which began in 1915. It was then that speakers of Western Armenian had to leave their ancestral lands in the Ottoman Empire to find themselves new homes in the Middle East, Europe and the Americas. It was then, too, that Western Armenian became a de-territorialized language, whose speakers had to live in various geographical spaces, in which their language was minoritized. So the questions are as follows: What are the issues and challenges faced by speakers of minority languages in the 21st century? Should we narrow the focus only to the endangerment of minority languages (language death), or should we, as rightly argued by Mufwene (2004), be open to the new possibilities that are emerging within languages and speech communities—such as the rise of new varieties (language birth)—as the consequence of language evolution? Applying a poststructuralist approach, Manoukian's chapter tackles the fascinating phenomenon of the rise of new speakers and, consequently, new varieties within the Western Armenian speech community and language.

Born to an Irish-American mother and Armenian-American father in New York, Manoukian did not learn Western Armenian as a mother tongue, but rather came to it as a university student; thus, she joined a generation of 'new speakers' of Western Armenian, who were born and raised in diaspora, speaking another dominant language. The challenge that she encountered is that the very variety of Western Armenian spoken by her and the younger generation of speakers is not recognized by the older generation within the speech community. Hence, the questions she poses are; Who is a legitimate speaker of the language, and what factors should determine legitimacy? In revitalizing endangered languages, Manoukian argues, there is a tendency to look to the past for sources of linguistic legitimacy, for the past is perceived as 'authentic,' whereas, the present is perceived as 'adulterated.' Yet, she problematizes such a perception by arguing that the rise of new speakers in many minority languages, including in Western Armenian, suggests that we need to redefine static notions of linguistic legitimacy and speech community, for today, as rightly argued by Ofelia García et al. (2013) and Humphrey Tonkin (Chapter 11 of this volume), the linguistic community can no longer be perceived as a 'homogeneous whole' but rather as a 'heterogeneous site' that is 'fluid,' 'hybrid' and 'dynamic.' Hence, new speakers, as Manoukian argues, should be perceived as the legitimate owners of the language, for attempts to revitalize endangered languages rests in the hands of the younger generation.

The case of Western Armenian and the issue of linguistic legitimacy are also relevant to the internationalization of the English language. Today, English is no longer a territorialized language but rather belongs to the world community; thus, the question remains: Whose variety should be regarded as the legitimate variety of English? This is a theme that Jan Svartvik and Geoffrey Leech (2006) examined in depth in their book *English: One Tongue, Many Voices*.

References

Abley, M. (2003). *Spoken here: Travels among threatened languages*. New York: Houghton Mifflin Company.

Crystal, D. (2000). *Language death*. Cambridge: Cambridge University Press.

Fishman, J. (1991). *Reversing language shift: Theoretical and empirical foundations of assistance to threatened languages*. Clevedon: Multilingual Matters.

García, O., Zakharia, Z. & Otcu, B. (eds.) (2013). *Bilingual community education and multilingualism: Beyond heritage languages in a global city*. Bristol: Multilingual Matters.

Google's Endangered Language Project. (2016). Retrieved April 24, 2016 from: www.endangeredlanguages.com.

Harrison, D. (2007). *When languages die: The extinction of the world's languages and the erosion of human knowledge*. Oxford: Oxford University Press.

May, S. (2001). *Language and minority rights: Ethnicity, nationalism and the politics of language*. Edinburg: Longman & Pearson Education.

Mufwene, S. S. (2004). Language birth and death. *Annual Review of Anthropology*, *33*, 201–22.

Nettle, D. & Romaine, S. (2000). *Vanishing voices: The extinction of the world's languages*. Oxford: Oxford University Press.

Svartvik, J. & Leech, G. (2006). *English: One tongue, many voices*. New York: Palgrave Macmillan.

12

KEEPING THE LANGUAGE ARK AFLOAT IN NEW YORK CITY

Daniel Kaufman

Introduction

I have spent the last seven years in New York focused on documenting threatened linguistic diversity. While my passion has always been for the structural aspects of language, my motivation has extended beyond the languages themselves and into the vaguer territories of ethnic and individual identity. Linguists, over centuries, have shown that human languages are intensely complex and beautiful natural objects in their own right. But languages are also a bridge to a particular way of being for their speakers. The connection between what we speak and how we identify ourselves turns out to be one of the more slippery aspects of language, as it is best understood through experience. The notion of 'grounded identity' is perhaps useful here. We can understand 'grounded identities' as those that developed organically over time and anchor us to places and peoples. Languages, as the collective product of historical communities, represent unique communal identities. Through choices in our daily language use, we identify with one or another community. Those choices, collectively, have consequences not only for the fate of the languages themselves, but also for our own social orientation. My goal has been to give a platform to communal identities in distinction to the larger, manufactured 'macro-identities' that are foisted on us from a variety of angles. In traditional communal identities, I see a sliver of hope for the future. In the constructed (national, religious, racial) macro-identities that are now enjoying such a strong resurgence throughout the world, I see, more often than not, xenophobia and fascism.

These types of motivations are difficult to articulate, and they have not featured prominently in the larger academic discourse on language diversity or endangered languages, which has typically centered on the loss of knowledge (e.g., Crystal, 2000; Nettle & Romaine, 2000; Dalby, 2003; Harrison, 2007; Harrison 2010;

Hagège, 2009; Evans, 2010). Most likely, this is because the academic discourse around language endangerment is still dominated by linguists, such as myself, who are not living through the loss of their own heritage language. It is also no doubt easier to discuss a discrete piece of botanical, environmental or grammatical knowledge at risk of being lost than it is to describe the changes wrought by language loss on communal or ethnic identities. The general public, furthermore, seems more sympathetic to the notion of rescuing scientific knowledge than supporting threatened identities. For those in the field, it is critical to consider competing motivations and perspectives on language death, as these largely determine our approaches in remediating it. If loss of knowledge (from a universal perspective) is viewed as the gravest consequence, then extraction of that knowledge becomes the utmost priority. If, on the other hand, it's loss of identity that moves us, then we will concentrate our efforts helping maintain those languages as intergenerational vehicles of identity.

Note that the seemingly contradictory perspectives above are not really at cross-purposes. Even those in the deepest trenches of what can be considered a 'knowledge extraction industry' are happier knowing that these languages are being transmitted to children within healthy, well-grounded communities. In an ideal world, the communities themselves can also make use of scholarly publications and archival materials created by outside academics for their own purposes. But with limited resources allotted to these tasks, one perspective will inevitably enjoy more support than the other. At this point, efforts at language documentation clearly enjoy greater material support than efforts at revitalization and language maintenance. I am caught between these two streams. On one hand, I feel an overpowering imperative to record everything linguistic around me that may be lost by the end of this century; I have a strong interest in how language varies across time and space and the scientific significance of that variation. On the other hand, it was questions of identity that formed my entry point to the study of language, and those questions have accompanied me ever since. In the following, I explore these latter questions of identity and language through three phases of my life, my adolescence in New York, my university days in the Philippines and my return to New York. I draw connections between these three phases to three aspects of globalization: (1) the rise of highly diverse megacities, a process which has been accelerated by the diminishing returns of small-scale agriculture; (2) the effects of electronic communication on minority languages; (3) new population movements and new levels of interconnectedness between global cities and remote countryside.

A Globalized City before Globalization

My parents were both born in Haifa, a northern city in what was then Palestine under British rule. Their first language was (revived) Hebrew, although they also grew up hearing Yiddish, Polish and German inside the house and Arabic, among other languages, outside the house. The household I was born into in Greenwich Village in 1975 was often filled with their friends, mostly Israeli artists with origins in Yemen, Iraq, Lebanon and Morocco, as well as many Ashkenazi Israelis born in in the time of the British mandate. I had, thus, grown up hearing Hebrew only as spoken by my parent's generation and in the various Middle Eastern dialects that now seem to be largely lost among younger speakers. Having no real contact with Hebrew speakers my own age, Hebrew became for me strictly a language of older people. My habit then, as is that of most children with immigrant parents, was to always answer in the dominant language regardless of context. This pattern continued until adolescence, at which point I began to reconsider my own ethnic identity. Because language was the most immediate window into my cultural heritage—my family was not religious or traditional in any standard sense—it was through language that I began. A Manchu language activist, cited in a recent article in the popular press (Johnson, 2009), sums up the feeling succinctly: "At some point you realize that the first language you're speaking isn't your mother tongue ... You feel like an orphan. You want to find your mother." I started looking for my 'mother' in a very unlikely place: a translation of Bergsträsser's (1928) *Einführung in die semitischen Sprachen* (Introduction to the Semitic Languages). While being an odd place for anyone to find their roots, this seemed to me just what I was looking for. Hebrew became not just a vehicle of communication for the older people in my household but an ancient connection to Aramaic speakers of Syria and Arabic speakers of the Middle East, as well as to speakers of Tigre and Mehri, languages I had never even heard of before. It connected me to places and peoples that were at once far away but at the same time around the corner, in the stores that dotted my neighborhood's streets and that contained speakers of Egyptian Arabic, Lebanese Arabic and even the more distantly related Tamazight. With his comparative grammar sketches, Bergsträsser sought to open the doors of scholarship onto a proto-Semitic past. My adolescent self, on the other hand, wanted to step through this door to embrace a historically grounded identity that I had felt was lost to me. While this sounds eccentric, it was also very much in line with the local milieu. In particular, African-American youth in New York City were then at the peak of embracing the symbols, imagery and identity of Ancient Egyptian civilization. I never drew a direct connection to this discourse at the time, but in retrospect, the collective African-American search for a 'mother' in Ancient Egypt must have influenced my own search for a 'mother' in the Ancient Middle East. The positive outcome for me of this reorientation was that I went from being somewhat embarrassed at being spoken to in Hebrew outside the house to making every effort to speak and respond in the language. This was an awkward process of several years that involved, among other things, relinquishing the linguistic power of being the more fluent speaker in family negotiations and arguments. But it was ultimately successful, as I managed to salvage my own heritage language from personal obsolescence. Even though I remained suspicious of many aspects of Jewish nationalism, the ability to read the words of my ancestors in the original gave me a tremendous sense of continuity and direction at the time. I found that Jews, in particular, were extremely fortunate in New York City to have such easy access to our roots, not only as found in books, but as living traditions. I would go, for instance, to the Romaniote synagogue on Broome Street, where they maintained endangered Jewish liturgical traditions from Yanina, Greece, and occasionally to Syrian synagogues in Brooklyn to hear the *maqams* of Damascus and Aleppo. One could reconstruct thousands of years of Jewish history, liturgy and song just within the radius of a few miles. If only all communities had such resources available, I thought, there would be a future for authentic diversity in this city, not only a diversity of nationalities and 'national cultures.'

I later discovered that many of those active in language revitalization have similar personal stories. Many had to bring back their own language on a personal level before they could bring it to others, and many sought to recreate lost connections, to the land, the ancestors and other peoples. These shared experiences helped me understand their struggle on a more meaningful level. We wished to share the personal strength that we gained from our efforts with those who have fewer resources and opportunities to continue their linguistic heritage.

My early days in New York highlighted the positive side of a globalized city before globalization. The newer elements associated with globalization, such as hyper-connectedness, had yet to make their debut. The next chapter of my life took me to the Philippines for four years and was to have a lasting impact on my views of language, identity and society.

The Philippines: A Multilingual Eden?

After stepping through the Semitic door that Bergsträsser built, I developed a strong general interest in linguistics through Edward Sapir's (1921) classic work *Language*, which I read surreptitiously under the desk during many of my high school classes. The work was meant as an introduction to the study of human language, but it focused, in particular, on the tremendous typological diversity displayed by Native American languages, especially the unique ways in which these languages package information in words and the unfamiliar semantic categories that they make use of. Sapir's book opened up a new horizon of intellectual interest for me and led me to spend many hours poring over grammars of various languages in the Mid-Manhattan library. In this exercise, my interests settled on Philippine languages, perhaps because of their initial accessibility from a linguistic perspective, or perhaps because I enjoyed the sound of Tagalog on the Filipino shows I would occasionally catch on cable TV. Through a friendship with a young Filipino chess hustler who plied his trade in the park near my house, I immersed myself in Tagalog and gained some degree of conversational fluency. At the same time, I was on my way to exhausting the offerings in anthropology and linguistics at Hunter College, where I enrolled after high school, and this led me to take a plunge, which at the time seemed rational only to me. In 1996, I moved to the Philippines to finish my BA in linguistics at the University of the Philippines and gain a deeper understanding of Philippine languages.

The country is home to over 175 indigenous languages belonging to the Austronesian family in addition to varieties of Philippine English, two varieties of a Spanish-based creole and various varieties of Chinese and other non-indigenous languages. One of the first things that struck me was how vibrant regional languages were among young people and that they were spoken with pride on the campus of the national university. Students of every province formed regional organizations within the university and use of anything but the regional language during official meetings seemed unthinkable. Nonetheless, the intense multilingualism of daily life did not extend into written communication, which was still typically carried out in English. Even now, one can travel quite far in Manila without seeing any trace of public signage in Tagalog/Filipino asides from the ubiquitous hand-painted, *Bawal umihi dito*, "Urinating here is forbidden." Little support existed at the time for regional languages in any official capacity. Print materials in regional languages almost completely comprised of tabloids, comics and religious tracts. The largest regional languages, Ilokano, Cebuano and Hiligaynon, have long-standing popular literature magazines (*Bannawag, Bisaya* and *Hiligaynon*, respectively) but very few of the other 170-plus languages have any existence at all in print. Most surprising was the lack of a single quality newspaper in Tagalog/Filipino, despite the short-lived attempts that were made every several years. For the millions who could not read an English language newspaper, there were only sensationalist tabloids with semi-nude movie stars on the cover. It was quite clear that the reason these languages thrived as spoken vernaculars was not due to any particularly benign language policy but rather due to the failure of the national language to take hold. The haggling and negotiating over the national language of the Philippines was a protracted process which inspired more than a few protest movements on the part of non-Tagalog regions. The debate over the national language was never definitively settled, and English still wins out over Tagalog in many domains. The Tagalog language was always seen by other ethnolinguistic groups as belonging exclusively to the Tagalogs and not any more worthy of becoming the national language than their own. At its most acrimonious, the national language debate even made reference to 'Tagalog imperialism,' a charge which can still occasionally be heard today. The upshot of this failure was that Tagalog never became a real threat to the majority of indigenous Philippine languages. Most surprisingly, the lack of a definitive language policy left educators at all levels to their own devices with regard to language choice in the classroom. In the best cases, teachers would code-switch between the local vernacular, Tagalog and English, allowing the students to comprehend the material while introducing them to the languages of higher education. In the worst cases, teachers would use English exclusively and thereby exclude children who had no previous exposure to it. I had met several young, bright menial laborers in the university who had claimed that they were essentially forced out of high school by their lack of English comprehension. They had the bad luck of ending up with an *Inglesera* teacher who insisted on using English exclusively in the classroom.

The flourishing multilingualism of the Philippines was, thus, more a result of benign neglect than anything else. As an undergraduate student, I was under the impression that this represented the norm for highly multilingual countries. The notion of language endangerment was still a vague and distant thing. To be sure, there was a vast number of Philippine languages without official status, prestige, print materials or other resources, but they were still embraced by their speakers as a means of daily communication, just as in the past. I could not imagine it any other way. On further inspection, though, the bright patina of multilingualism bore a dark underside that became apparent only as time went on. Despite its status and support, the national language was still very much a second-class citizen to its colonial competitor, English.

The Philippines was annexed by the United States in 1898 and remained an American colony for 48 years before gaining independence in 1946. Despite well over half a century of independence, there are still many sectors of Philippine society and domains of communication where English dominates. National Bookstore, the country's largest bookstore chain, devotes roughly 90% of its space for books in any given store to English literature. Businesses of all types greet their customers in English. Forms and applications are entirely in English. The recently elected president, Rodrigo Duterte, who has challenged the United States far more than any of his predecessors, still uses Philippine English predominantly when addressing the Filipino public. It is thus hard to imagine how the millions of non–English speakers navigate a country that is operated almost entirely in the former colonial language.

The effects of globalization on linguistic diversity can be easily misunderstood as involving a small handful of global languages devouring the smaller languages of the world. But this is clearly not the normal case. It is national languages, whether they are global or not, that are displacing local languages in any given country. The effects of globalization on language loss have been indirect, but pernicious all the same. One very concrete effect of the outward orientation has been that local languages can be allotted only an insignificant time in the school system (if at all) due to the increasing pressure to teach English, or another 'global' language. While great gains have been made over the last few decades for the inclusion of indigenous languages in the education system (in countries like Mexico, Bolivia and elsewhere, where they were previously banned) an even greater push for increasing English education has resulted in many of these language programs having only a symbolic value. This has generated a dangerous sense of complacency as the languages are now visibly 'in the schools' but this inclusion is not producing new speakers. There is no evidence, in fact, that two hours a week of language classes (as is often the case) can do anything substantial towards revitalization. The Internet has further fueled an outward-looking (national or global) orientation at the expense of valuing local languages and cultures. This process obviously began long before globalization proper, but the delivery mechanisms have become so much more effective that it seems appropriate to treat the era of globalization as a discrete phenomenon.

Despite the negative impacts of globalization, the Internet and electronic communication more generally brought important positive changes, as well. Unlike previous media such as television and radio, the Internet is very much a two-way street; it is far easier for a layperson to create a webpage or post a video than it has ever been to broadcast on the radio or television. In the Philippines, the Internet was only starting to become visible after I arrived in 1996.[1] As the use of email spread and the number of Philippine webpages increased, the impact on language use appeared transformative. First of all, the Philippines took up electronic communication through the Internet and texting with a fervor that has yet to be fully understood. The so-called EDSA II revolution, which ousted president Joseph Estrada in 2001, appears to have been mobilized by mass text messaging. As reported by Lichauco (2001), 30 million text messages were being transmitted daily in the Philippines in the same year, twice as many as in all of Europe combined. Vincente (2003) attributes these remarkable numbers in part to the psychological escape that texting provides from broken infrastructure and corruption. Another reason is offered by Philippine sociologist Josephine Aguilar (as cited by Lichauco, 2001), who frames text messaging as a "high-technology veil, protective, yet provocative" in a society where face to face communication is regulated by conservative social conventions. In my observations, the casual (or 'veiled') nature of electronic media seemed to offer strong support to regional languages that were not previously being used by the younger generation in writing. The modern, transient and spontaneous nature of electronic media seemed to encourage use of vernacular languages in a way that was rare for traditional writing. The norm outside the university was that writing was a domain of English but casual speech was the domain of Tagalog or the local regional language. Through texting, average Filipinos were, in most cases for the first time, writing as they spoke.

Patterns of language use in older media are still remarkably conservative. Television programs produced in the Philippines were a mix of English and Tagalog, with the purest Tagalog on television ironically being found in the dubbed soap operas from Mexico. Nowhere could the strange linguistic division of society be heard as clearly as on the radio, which was completely segregated by language. FM stations were almost exclusively English-medium while AM radio was largely transmitted in Tagalog and regional languages. FM radio hosts not only spoke English but a kind of American English that made every effort to hide any trace of Philippine origins. Some of the more stubborn radio hosts would come to loggerheads with callers who were not comfortable in English. In these cases, the hosts, eliciting a comment or message from the caller, would repeat themselves again and again in English before finally giving up on the illusion that they were broadcasting from America and switching to Tagalog. A close parallel can be drawn with today's call-center workers. Call centers have grown on a massive scale in the Philippines. The employees answer questions and solve problems for American customers throughout the night. Like the DJs on FM radio, call-center workers suppress their identity and often tell customers explicitly that they are based in America (Friginal, 2009: 26). While English appeared to have opened doors of economic opportunity to some extent, it also seemed to reenforce a colonial mind-set in which indigenous languages were inferior.

This was the environment in which I formed my understanding of language in society. The systematic marginalization of the underprivileged through colonial era language attitudes opened my eyes to meaning of 'language rights.' It struck me as fundamentally wrong that only those who had the best access to a colonial language could navigate through their own society freely. Why should any domain of life be off limits to one's mother tongue? There was no reason why a colonial language should enjoy a perceived aura of intelligence and sophistication while indigenous languages were essentially left to rot. Simultaneously, the benign effects of the language policy vacuum showed me that the most crucial ingredient for multilingualism to flourish was simply a lack of coercion. As modest as this sounds, it turns out to be exceedingly rare.

New York City and the Endangered Language Alliance

On returning to New York City after completing my doctorate in linguistics at Cornell, I began to take a fresh look at the linguistic situation of my own hometown. I had become increasingly curious about the indigenous Mexican population in the city, a population that had increased exponentially since the 1980s with waves of migration from the Mexican states of Guerrero and Oaxaca. These two states, located on the southwestern coast of the country, contained the vast majority of Mexico's considerable linguistic diversity. The country has roughly 280 indigenous languages belonging to 11 distinct language families, representing a massive degree of diversity both in the sheer number of languages as well as in their genetic distinctiveness. But in New York, the indigenous Mexicans are not known for their diversity or history. They constitute an underclass of menial laborers who are largely marginalized and ignored. Because many are undocumented and most work excessively long hours, they have had only a minimal cultural impact on the city at large, despite their numbers. The local public, however, seems to entertain a strong interest in the historical civilizations of Meso-America. To take one example, a major exhibit on Aztec art was put on several years ago at the Guggenheim Museum and drew enormous crowds and positive reviews. But few of the visitors would have known that the descendants of that civilization were alive and well, working long shifts throughout the delis and restaurants of the city, where they continue to speak modern varieties of Nahuatl. Ironically, those who are most aware of the presence of this population are often those who persecute them the most in their new home. Those Mexicans who identify as 'mestizo' (non-indigenous, monolingual Spanish speakers) all too often hold a colonial view of their indigenous neighbors. Unfortunately, for many mestizos, indigenous languages are not associated with the great civilizations of pre-Columbian Meso-America but rather with ignorance and poverty. One of the stronger public expressions of anti-indigenous sentiments had come from the Puerto Rican New Yorker politician, Herman Badillo, a vocal champion of the Hispanic community and then the chairman of the City University of New York (CUNY). In response to a question about immigrant students who lacked formal education in their home countries, he said:

> The problem is that in Mexico and Central America, there has never been a tradition of education [. . .]. They're pure Indians: Incas and Mayans, who are about, you know, five feet tall, with straight hair. And when they speak about 'La Raza' they're not talking about the Spanish language, they're talking about the original Indian language. And therefore it's far more complicated problem than the problem that we're used to dealing with but nobody seems to want to face up to it. (Putnam, 1999)

Outrage ensued and apologies were soon dispensed (Arenson, 1999; Haberman, 1999), but the statement lay bare prevalent attitudes towards indigenous people on the part of more established segments of Latin American immigrant population (a fact which was lost on most reporters at the time, e.g., Haberman, 1999). The prominence of language as an identifier in Badillo's statement was especially revealing. If even the chairman of a well-respected university system considered indigenous languages a relic of the past, one could only imagine the discrimination this population faced and still faces in the school system and workplace.

It was clear that New York City could use an organization that advocated for its many indigenous and threatened languages under a single umbrella. My exploration into indigenous Mexican communities was the beginning of a more general push towards creating a united front of marginalized linguistic communities in the city. These efforts were formalized in 2010 with the launching of the Endangered Language Alliance (ELA) as a nonprofit organization.

Almost as soon as we began, we serendipitously landed on the front page of *The New York Times* in an article on endangered languages in New York City (Roberts, 2010). This began a long string of reports and articles on what had hitherto been a largely ignored phenomenon: urban centers have been absorbing endangered languages and cultures as linguistic and cultural diversity is flattening out in rural areas. Our organization advocated a new role for the global megacity as a Noah's ark for the world's threatened linguistic diversity. In this role, we have begun to show how strategies for documenting linguistic diversity can be adjusted to diaspora settings as urbanization proceeds at its exponential pace. The most important result from our early publicity was that legions of New Yorkers emerged from the woodwork to tell us about their own endangered languages. They came from

Tajikistan, Guatemala, Costa Rica, Croatia, Gabon, Nigeria, Taiwan and Ossetia, among other countries. They spoke languages that in many cases even we had never heard of. Many had been waiting to share their languages with their own communities, but did not have the resources. Most were surprised that someone outside their community would care about their language.

Within a few months we had the largest urban network for endangered languages in the world. Equally importantly, an enormous wave of volunteers offered their services to the cause. They wanted to do whatever possible to help record, map and document these languages. Our first meeting, at Bob Holman's Bowery Poetry Club (the author of Chapter 13 of the present volume), was a unique event bringing together young people wanting to help with older people wanting to share their endangered languages. We divided the volunteers into neighborhood groups. Their job was to survey as many neighborhoods as possible to better understand the city's true linguistic diversity. The US census has historically been the only source of data on languages in New York City, but their methods are (by necessity) so limited that we have only the most superficial picture of what languages are really spoken here. The volunteer street surveys not only uncovered the regional vernacular languages of certain local communities, they also found a number of new collaborators who were eager to work with us to document their languages. At the busiest point of that year, we had seven language groups meeting once a week each with volunteers for the purpose of documenting their languages. In many cases, volunteer students went on to write papers and theses based on these meetings. In other cases, these collaborations even developed into support for revitalization efforts.

The anthropologist Claude-Lévi Strauss was quoted as saying, "all the essentials of humanity's artistic treasures could be found in New York" (Cohen-Solal, 2000). At this point, however, the city's gain seems like the world's loss. As environmental pressures increase and agriculture ceases to be a viable source of livelihood, the global countryside empties out into urban centers. In some areas, like the Mixteca region of Mexico, these changes have been so extreme that many villages have been completely abandoned by everyone except those too old to leave. We can marvel at a city that now resembles a cultural Noah's ark, but the causes behind this ark's diversity are nothing to celebrate. The economic consequences of globalization have been responsible in part for these circumstances, but has the new level of interconnectedness also provided us with a means of fighting back? As I suggest below, electronic communication turns out to be globalization's silver lining.

Prospects for an Urban Multilingual Future

Joshua Fishman (1966) concluded from his survey of immigrant communities that, in the vast majority of cases, heritage languages are not transmitted beyond two generations. Exceptions to this come from those insular communities such as the Yiddish-speaking Hasidic community and the German-speaking Amish community. What hope then is there for New York's smaller languages, in particular, those who are threatened even in their places of origin? Given the lack of financial resources and official support for smaller marginalized languages, the answer would seem to lie in the creation of new social spaces dedicated to language transmission. A particularly good example has been New York's Latvian community, which founded a summer program for their children in the 1980s when they were convinced that their country was on the brink of obliteration at the hands of the USSR. Even though the existential threat has passed for the time being, the summer program continues until today and is highly effective in creating fluent Latvian speakers in a city where they are a tiny minority. For communities with fewer resources, such as the indigenous Mexicans' communities, the creation of 'transmission spaces' has to be approached more creatively. There is hope for the creation of urban language nests, even if this proceeds in an informal, grassroots manner. It was only through such grassroots efforts that the famous language nest programs began among the Hawai'ians and the Māori. Facilitating such programs is our next frontier.

More immediately, however, we have been working to counteract the brain (and tongue) drain in remote communities by creating digital media in New York that can positively impact language transmission back home (Kaufman & Perlin, forthcoming). Together with the apparent positive impact of texting and the Internet discussed earlier, venues like YouTube have provided a means for immigrants to maintain a voice in their places of origin. With smaller communities, these voices can take an outsize significance. ELA's Toronto branch, headed by Anastasia Riehl, has worked with the local Harari community to create subtitled videos in their language, one of many minority languages of Ethiopia. One such video of a young Harari woman who has maintained her language in the diaspora has gained 7,000 views and extensive positive comments from the community. This is all the more remarkable considering this language is estimated to have only 20,000 speakers. It suggests, anecdotally at least, that urban centers of immigration are increasingly important platforms for speaking back to the homeland and can play a significant role in influencing language choice in younger generations.

Conclusion

From my experiences in the Philippines as well as my observations in New York, subtractive models of assimilation offered only false promises of upward mobility while reinforcing a colonial mentality. The identity component of language was further brought into stark relief through our work at ELA. Far away from their homelands, in a city where you can pretend to be whatever you want, a sizable contingent is fighting for the survival of their mother tongues. These 'language champions' became my primary inspiration over the last several years, and their fight seems especially urgent as the nation witnesses the ascendancy of a president whose primary campaign promise is to build a wall between the United States and Mexico. Signs bearing variations of the message "Speak English or Get Out" have again become a regular sight and, regardless of the election's outcome, the sentiments have been given a new legitimacy. As fits the general pattern, it is those with the least exposure to diverse populations who have the most fear of them. My hope is that the hyper-diversity of cities like New York will foster a new appreciation, or at least tolerance, in the face of these dangers, and that marginalized ethnolinguistic communities will be able to create a sustainable future for themselves, even if this means doing it here, in our ersatz ark.

Questions for Discussion

1. What are some of the positive and negative aspects of globalization with regard to language endangerment?
2. In some developing countries with multiple official languages, language choice in official contexts (including schools) is left up to individual teachers/speakers/authors. What are some of the positive and negative aspects of this *laissez faire* approach?

Author Profile

Daniel Kaufman specializes in historical, descriptive and theoretical issues in Austronesian languages with a focus on the languages of the Philippines and Indonesia. He is co-founder and executive director of the Endangered Language Alliance, a nonprofit organization dedicated to documenting and conserving the endangered languages of New York City's immigrant communities, and is also Assistant Professor at the Department of Linguistics and Communication Disorders at Queens College, CUNY.

Note

1 The University of the Philippines, for example, launched its webpage in 1997. Cell-phone service, on the other hand, had begun a few years earlier in 1991 but became affordable only around 1998. By the year 2000, however, cell-phone lines had overtaken landlines by a large margin.

References

Arenson, K.W. (1999). Officials back Badillo amid furor on Hispanic remarks. *The New York Times*, Oct. 2, 1999.

Bergsträsser, G. (1928). *Einführung in die semitischen Sprachen. Sprachproben und Grammatische Skizzen*. München: M. Hueber.

Cohen-Solal, Annie. (2000). Claude L. Strauss in the United States. *Partisan Review*, *2*, 252–60.

Crystal, D. (2000). *Language death*. Cambridge: Cambridge University Press.
Dalby, A. (2003). *Language in danger: The loss of linguistic diversity and the threat to our future*. New York: Columbia University Press.
Evans, N. (2010). *Dying words: Endangered languages and what they have to tell us*. Malden, MA: Wiley-Blackwell.
Fishman, J. (1966). *Language loyalty in the United States*. The Hague: Mouton.
Friginal, E. (2009). *The language of outsourced call centers: A corpus-based study of cross-cultural interaction*. Amsterdam: John Benjamins.
Haberman, C. (1999, October 29). NYC; When saying the obvious invite wrath. *The New York Times*. Retrieved from: www.nytimes.com.
Hagége, C. (2009). *On the death and life of languages*. New Haven: Yale University Press.
Harrison, K. D. (2007). *When languages die: The extinction of the world's languages and the erosion of human knowledge*. Oxford: Oxford University Press.
Harrison, K. D. (2010). *The last speakers: The quest to save the world's most endangered languages*. Washington, DC: National Geographic Books.
Johnson, I. (2009, October 3). In China, the forgotten Manchu seek to rekindle their glory. *Wall Street Journal*. Retrieved from: www.wsj.com/.
Kaufman, D. & Perlin, R. (forthcoming). Language documentation in diaspora communities. In L. Campbell & K. Rehg (eds.), *Handbook of Endangered Languages*. Oxford: Oxford University Press.
Lichauco, J. T. (2001, May 15). The Philippine text messaging phenomenon. *Philippine Star*. Retrieved from: www.philstar.com/.
Nettle, D. & Romaine, S. (2000). *Vanishing voices: The extinction of the world's languages*. Oxford: Oxford University Press.
Pasquali, V. (2015, November 1). The world's richest and poorest countries. *Global Finance*. Retrieved from: www.gfmag.com
Putnam, M. (1999, November). Badillo once again proves he's a pig. *The Messenger, 2* (1).
Rafael, V. (2003). The cell phone and the crowd: Messianic politics in the contemporary Philippines. *Public Culture, 15* (3), 399–425.
Roberts, S. (2010, April 29). The lost languages, found in New York. *The New York Times*. Retrieved from: www.nytimes.com/2010/04/29/nyregion/29lost.html
Romaine, S. (1988). *Pidgin and Creole languages*. London: Longman.
Sapir, E. (1921). *Language: An introduction to the study of speech*. New York: Harcourt, Brace and Company.
Vincente, R. (2003). The cell phone and the crowd: Messianic politics in the contemporary Philippines. *Public Culture 15* (3), 399–425.

13

AN ALASKAN LANGUAGE ODYSSEY

A Reflection by a Poet

Bob Holman with Sam O'Hana

> *Of the 6,000 languages in the world, it is estimated half will vanish by the end of this century. The die-off parallels the extinction of plants and animals. But we have laws to protect endangered species—who will save our languages?*
>
> *Language Matters with Bob Holman*
> PBS documentary, 2015

Introduction

The 21st century has brought many issues and challenges for the world's languages and cultures. The English language has gone global, finding itself home in all parts of the world. But at the same time, we have seen the weakening, loss and death of many minority and indigenous languages in their own homes or places of origin. The language crisis of the world has been well-documented by many linguists (Abley, 2003; Evans, 2010; Crystal, 2000). Language is the essence of all poetry, and as a poet, I see part of my job being to bring awareness to what is lost when we lose a language and doing what I can to help speakers keep their mother tongue thriving. Linguists and non-linguists alike are becoming language activists; the global language crisis has been a major focus of my work for the past twenty years.

After the endangered language-focused documentary *Language Matters with Bob Holman*,[1] a film by David Grubin, aired on PBS in January 2015, I received funding from the Ford Foundation to pursue relevant language-revitalization-focused outreach activities. From September 15th to October 18, 2015, I visited sites across Alaska, in Juneau, Kotzebue, Barrow, Arctic Village, Ft. Yukon, Fairbanks, Homer, Nokolaevsk, Kodiak and Anchorage. Events took place at schools, libraries, heritage centers, arts centers, museums, prisons, churches and community meetings. Outreach methods included film screenings, Q&As, multilingual poetry readings and workshops and classroom visits. In this paper, I invite the reader to join me on my journey to Alaska as a means to reflect not only on the odyssey of Alaskan indigenous languages, but also to get a taste of what actually goes on at one of these outreach activities, a bilingual Iñupiatun-English Poetry Workshop in Kotzebue, just above the Arctic Circle. In addition, the paper includes two poems from Alaskan poets as a means to add a face and voice to poets of the many areas of the world where languages are endangered. The paper closes with my poem, "An Alaskan Language Odyssey," which I wrote to commemorate my stay in Alaska and to reflect on the many issues and challenges of Alaskan languages in the 21st century.

Poet as Language Activist: Networks of Solidarity

Poets have been using language rent-free for thousands of years. It's payback time.
Bob Holman

A poet's job in US culture is generally defined as 'one who writes/teaches poetry.' For me, that job also includes being an activist for poetry itself, making films, producing events, running a record label, administering poetry nonprofits[2] and other activities intended to help relocate poetry into everyday life. Much of this poetry activism has been involved with spoken word: hip hop, poetry slams, performance. Spoken word *is* poetry, a type of poetry, connected to the world's oral traditions, for word as art was humanity's first poetry. And since endangered languages are almost universally oral languages, respecting these mother tongues also respects the deep roots of spoken word (for more on this topic, see Bringhurst, 2004; 2008; Ong, 2000).

In 1989, I imported the idea of Marc Smith's Poetry Slam in Chicago to the Nuyorican Poets Café on New York's Lower East Side, where it became a living metaphor for multiculturalism and helped popularize one of the great grassroots art movements of the twentieth century. Not in my wildest poetic imagination did I foresee this advocacy of spoken word leading to a month in Alaska spreading the gospel of language continuity 25 years later. But, in a way, that is what happened. I went to Alaska to further the outreach of the PBS documentary I made with David Grubin, *Language Matters*, which begins in Australia with Charlie Mangulda, the last speaker of Amurdak; then travels to Wales, where Welsh has made an astonishing comeback; and finishes in Hawai'i, where Hawaiian is on the upswing but in a difficult situation.

It was a great moment of public awareness for the Language Movement when PBS broadcast the film—the first national broadcast of a film on this topic. But the Alaska tour of *Language Matters* spoke directly to individuals about what is lost when a language disappears and what it takes to keep a language alive in a place where the effects of language loss are lived every day. For those engaged directly in language revitalization, the screenings and discussions offered new ideas and support for their work. My visit also connected Alaskan language communities with others around the globe via the Endangered Language Alliance—a nonprofit organization dedicated to documenting and conserving the endangered languages of New York City's immigrant communities (for more, see Chapter 12 of this volume)—building a network of solidarity among languages that generally have no cultural connection.

My Alaskan odyssey included a dozen film screenings and as many workshops, half a dozen poetry readings, hosting a poetry slam and other programs. We begin in Kotzebue, Alaska, September 23, 2015, as I prepare for this evening's Iñupiatun-English Poetry Workshop.

Approach to Alaska: The Preparation

Right now it is 10 a.m. and I am sitting alone in the Kotzebue Heritage Center Meeting Room, letting the workshop that will fill this space tonight spill out of the walls and exhibits. The possibilities! The taxidermied polar bear in the corner is giving me hints for the bilingual Iñupiatun-English Poetry Workshop. But, to what extent will it actually be bilingual? Well, that depends on who shows up.

My main contact in Kotzebue has been Tim Argetsinger, Iñupiaq Language and Cultural Manager at NANA Regional Corporation, the Iñupiat-owned regional corporation created under the Alaska Native Claims Settlement Act (1971). Tim speaks Iñupiatun and was instrumental in setting up the workshop. He hopes to bring some Elders, first-language Iñupiatun speakers, tonight—but there are no promises. Hinton and Montijo (1994, cited in Yamamoto, 2007) estimate that there are 3,000 speakers of Iñupiatun (the Alaska dialect of the Inuit language), just over half the Iñupiat population. *Iñupiatun* is the spoken language of *Iñupiat*, the ethnic group. 'Iñupiat' means 'the real people' [*inuit* 'people' plus *-piat* 'real, genuine']; Iñupiaq is the singular form meaning 'a real person.' The name of the language, Iñupiatun, means 'to be like an Iñupiaq.' The word 'Iñupiaq' is used to refer to a person of this group ['He is an Iñupiaq'] and can also be used as an adjective ['She is an Iñupiaq woman'].

I had arrived in Kotzebue straight from Juneau, where linguist Alice Taff had been my first point of contact. She zipped me straight to Mendenhall Glacier, where I saw a bear, an eagle and a raven: the omens were good. Now I was carrying greetings direct from Juneau's Tlingit community, from poet/language activists, like Nora Marks Dauenhauer and X̱'unei Lance Twitchell. I will pass those on tonight while screening Nora's poem "For My Grandfather, Jim Nagat'w, Blind and Nearly Deaf" from the film I made for PBS in the mid-90s, *The United States of Poetry*.

I have tried to break down the prejudice about a 'poetry writing workshop' by inviting different sectors of the local population, including John Creed's Creative Writing class at the local University of Alaska satellite campus, the workers at the

FIGURE 13.1 "Within a Half Hour of Landing in Alaska, I'd Been Visited by a Bear, an Eagle and a Raven: The Omens Were Good."

museum, my climatologist roommates at the bunkhouse, and the people eating next to me on Restaurant Row (the three restaurants in town).

Tiffany Creed, who works at the local University of Alaska campus, had suggested a poem by a local poet, Stephen Bolen, a member of the 49 Writers Collective (Alaska is the 49th state of the USA). And I had two poems of Joan

Naviyuk Kane in Iñupiatun. Without Joan's Iñupiatun poems, the center of the bilingual poetry workshop would not hold. Kotzebue had also had some recent history that I can include: President Barack Obama visited here two weeks ago to promote the ecological significance of the Arctic to outsiders.

Next came a key preparation for the workshop—handouts! Handouts inspire poets, and attending a poetry workshop makes you a priori a poet. I had picked out nine poems, not intending to cover them all, but to take home, look at later and think, *Ah! Poetry!* Ryan Sherman of the National Park Service, who had picked me up at the airport and showed me around, was also a wizard at the copy machine, reproducing the gorgeous covers of the poetry books, one by Vivian Faith Prescott and two by Joan Naviyuk Kane (2013). When running a workshop with a varied population, visuals are a great complement for text density.

The Hide of My Tongue: Ax L'óot' Doogú, Vivian Faith Prescott's book (2012), is the first poetry book I have seen dedicated completely to the issue of language revitalization. The cover is a multicolored close-up of a totem pole with striking reds, greens and whites—it appears abstract at first, and then snaps into fierce animal imagery. Vivian is part Sami, the indigenous people of Scandinavia, and was adopted into a Tlingit clan; she has a Tlingit daughter, too. Her poems tell the story of language loss from many angles, including persona poems that read like oral histories. Every minority language has its own horror story of language eradication by colonists—mouths washed out with soap, having to wear a hat or badge of some kind if caught speaking in mother tongue. Nicholas Evans (2010) does a great job describing this in his book, *Dying Words: The Hide of My Tongue*, which tells these stories with page-after-page insistence. It concludes with a study guide—a Tlingit language primer by Lance Twitchell.

I will leave a copy of Vivian's book at the Kotzebue Library and with every community on my journey, playing Johnny Appleseed with this relevant text. The other poems in the handout are from Joan Naviyuk Kane's two most recent books, *The Cormorant Hunter's Wife* (2009), with its cover featuring work by Siberian Yupik sculptor Susie Silook, and *Hyperboreal* (2013), with its ghost-blue landscape, which contains poems in Iñupiatun.

The contemporary poetry workshop is in part the spiritual successor of the poets' collating parties of the 1960s and 70s. Then, we would all meet up for a home-cooked meal in someone's apartment and put together books from mimeographed pages laid out in stacks. I will never forget the whiff of the ink, but the whole process had its own distinctive smell: we were producing our own linguistic legacy. The poets would shuffle round the table, building each book page by page, adding covers at the end. A huge stapler pushed staples through the stack, and there you have it—a book. It was a party with a purpose now revived in Kotzebue, circling the table, creating handouts.

I handwrite Nora's poem on a giant tablet the size of the whiteboard easel, including her name. On screen, we will hear a whistling-wind and music soundtrack and see images of waves and seaweed. Nora delivers the poem in close-up, hair blowing, glasses sprayed with saltwater. We will discuss all three versions of the poem: spoken word, written word, and digital media, and how including the name of the maker is different but important in all contexts. The poem is in English, but uses oral poetry techniques to make its points.

For My Grandfather, Jim Nagat'w, Blind and Nearly Deaf

Nora Marks Dauenhauer

I was telling my grandfather
about what was happening
on the boat. My father
and his brothers were trying to
anchor against the wind
and tide.

I could smell him, especially
his hair. It was a warm smell.
I yelled as loud as I could,
telling him what I saw.
My face was wet from driving
rain.

I could see his long eyebrows,
I could look at him and get
really close. We both liked this.
Getting close was his way of
seeing.

What a treat it had been, making the film of Nora twenty years previous, meeting a poet central to Tlingit oral tradition, who had also translated Wang Wei and Edward Estlin Cummings (a.k.a. e.e. cummings) into Tlingit. Nora's late husband, the linguist and poet, Richard Dauenhauer, had helped us translate her poems into English. I had taught this poem in an Endangered Language Poetry Workshop at Columbia University, as well as at the Jack Kerouac School of Disembodied Poetics at Naropa. One of the students did not show up for class that time, so all twenty of us went over to his bedroom and yelled really loud, *Ch'a tlákwdáx si. áat, tlél ch'as yá táakw*! "It didn't just start yesterday," a line that Nora speaks in the film. That woke him up—in two languages. Nora was the first person I had written to in Alaska, but I knew she was not in good health. Then, Lance Twitchell, who visits her every week for Tlingit conversation and to work on a documentary he is making of her, informed me that she wanted to participate in a poetry reading with me at Kindred Post, held in an old post office in Juneau. *OMG*, as they say (or *text*, actually). It was a terrific reading—we even made the cover of a local newspaper, the *Capital City Weekly*.

"We Should All Greet Each Other in Iñupiaq!": The Poetry Workshop

As the workshop time drew nigh, we had to make a crucial decision: How many tables? I like a sitting-around-a-table workshop, so everybody can write and talk (not to mention Google, these days). I suggest two large tables, enough to accommodate ten chairs. When the first people walk into a workshop, you want them to relax, think *All right, just a few of us.* Straight away, however, eight students from the local high school arrive, and as we are getting more tables out. Then, Tim Argetsinger enters with three Elders. Next some local government representatives show up—we wind up with five tables and twenty-three people crowded around. I warm up the group, talk about poetry and orality, when Hannah Atkinson, Cultural Resource Specialist at the Center, seizes the day, and, Sharpie in hand, bum-rushes the notepad!

"We should all greet each other in Iñupiaq!" she proclaims, and writes on the board *Kīna atqiń? Uvaŋa* _____. (*ŋ* in *Uvaŋa* is an ng sound): "What's your name?" "My name is ______." I am surprised, for many workshoppers have Iñupiaq names. Lorena Williams, an Elder whose Iñupiaq name is *Kapniaq*, takes a moment to describe how she had hoped for a while that she would not have to do "this language business" anymore. "It takes up a lot of my time," she says, "and doesn't seem to be going anywhere." She recounts her life's experience as a speaker of Iñupiatun: first as a birth-language forbidden to her by the English-speaking teachers at her school, then the stirrings of revitalization during the 60s, when Alaskan Native corporations were being founded and a kind of indigenous cultural renaissance began, and now, a cultural treasure in high demand as the benefits of language revitalization become known. As a young girl, she was told *not* to speak her language in order to better assimilate, and now she is being told she *must* speak her language in order for it to survive. Her husband, Whittier Williams Jr., speaks next. Lorena darts her hand to remove his ever-rolling toothpick, which seems to be knitting something in his mouth (language?)—but he is too fast. The stories roll out from him, too—about a friend in grade school so intimidated by English he could not say the words for "May I go the bathroom?" so peed his pants.

There's a deep engagement with language in the room, and we have not even gone a'round the table introducing ourselves yet. By the time I say *Uvaŋa Bob*, we have bonded. I will not get my Iñupiaq name until tomorrow, at the immersion school—*Uqaq*, 'Tongue.' It must be time for Nora Marks Dauenhauer—greetings from the Tlingit nation. We watch her speak her poem on screen, then, with a flourish, I uncover the easel revealing the poem as text. Many of the difficult-to-dissect intricacies of the oral tradition become analyzable: internal rhymes ('tell/smell/

yell'), shifts in scale ('anchoring against the tide,' 'I could see his long eyebrows'), engagement with all the senses. I make a point of how orality, literacy and digital each have pros and cons, how the poem is received differently in each consciousness.

Next, we read this poem by Kotzebue poet Stephen Bolen.

301 Shore Avenue

Still, now; the torn tin-wrapped two-story structure stands:
Towards a century ago; its tired timber and stone-age material met
To hold each other unconditionally;
To vanquish Kikiktagruk's seasons.
Legendary: a hunting-guide, a bush-pilot, a man;
Family spent and shared time and more time.
Liquor and grub given to many at "Marie's":
Before the hunt; Roy Rogers ate,
Hunger found Hank Williams Jr.,
Then Mr. Lincoln bagged the record bear: polar.
Floors plywood; careful were the feet of children.
Covered by linoleum; stairs steep, it changed.
Generations abandon their native hallways,
Sheltering memories of lives; so many,
We were raised by those rooms.
Upstairs at the *front-room* windows we all sat as children,
No matter the day, no matter the Sun.
None of us are around to cherish the crashing shores' whispers anymore,
Every one of us left;
All of us, but one.
She's with her home; they grow old alone,
Boxes and boxes; packed and stacked high.
It's almost deserted: haunting; she's fervid,

I wish we all hadn't left you . . . Mother of mine.

We read the poem as a group, each person taking a line, creating a sense of community. Other elements of orality emerge: whenever a proper name is mentioned, a place referred to, there are nods and *uh-huhs*, a sort of call and response, generally led by the Elders. "Not since Roy Rogers," comments a young student, whose personal history of Kotzebue has now been extended, thanks to the poetry of Stephen Bolen.

"I Saw Him" —A Discussion Among Elders

The topic of my 'advance man,' Barack Obama, comes up, and when Ernie, the third Elder, mentions his own recollection, "I saw him. He was in an SUV. It was dark," I pounce. "Haiku!" I shout, and this spontaneous oral-to-text poem goes up on the board:

Obama

I saw him
He was in an SUV
It was dark

There is silence. It is that magic moment in a workshop where words spoken in the air become a poem when written down. And in this bilingual situation, power and race and income disparity, language and commerce and poetry are all meshed in what is now a poem, thanks to Ernie. Yes, we *are* all poets now, and it is time to use paper and pen. Words splash on paper as gossip is passed about. Lorena's Obama poem recalls an Eskimo kiss Barack received, as stereotype meets reality meets poetry.

All the Big Shots got on stage
Somehow the Town Beauty got there too
Everybody shook his hand, but she
Gave him the Eskimo Kiss

The kiss in Lorena's poem leads to a discussion from many viewpoints. Did anyone think real political change might come from it? Obama, the first president to visit north of the Arctic Circle, is a native of the US's other outlying state, Hawai'i. These are the only two states that have an official language along with English. I bring up another Hawai'i–Alaska connection: Lance Twitchell is a Linguistics PhD candidate at University of Hawai'i, Hilo, studying with Larry Kimura, godfather of the Hawaiian language immersion program. Lance's three children are reaching school-age years, and it is crucial for him to get the Hawaiian model implemented. Despite renewed efforts at language teaching, many children in that situation begin their school years speaking only English (Dalby, 2003).

After this language lecture, things move to the more sensational—were there snipers on the rooftops and submarines in the bay during Obama's visit? I am about to say, "Now this is the stuff of poetry!" when Ernie speaks up again. "I just wrote a poem," Ernie says. The room stops. Ernie proceeds to read a completely formed poem addressing the birds of the Kotzebue environs—their calls, their geometries of flight, their nesting and eating habits. In each line is a word in Iñupiatun. Somehow, Ernie had followed the instructions of my final assignment before I even gave them! One minute we are talking snipers on the rooftop and the next Ernie is bringing Kotzebue to life in a poem, through birds as varied as the people sitting around the table. It is poem as intervention: a moment of full participation, as if Ernie had plucked the poem from our group discussion, and it galvanizes the entire workshop.

This affords a perfect transition to a handout poem in English and Iñupiatun by Joan Naviyuk Kane. The Elders get tremendously excited, begin speaking their native tongue. The rest of the class is spellbound, overhearing a stream of Iñupiatun in all its glottal richness. Each Iñupiatun word in the poem brings up an association. The Elders muse over 'Uyaġauramik,' which Joan translates as 'a shard of rock.' The Elders know that the 'shard of rock' is King Island, a one-mile-wide islet between Alaska and Russia with an abandoned Iñupiat village on it; and indeed, Joan's relatives are from King Island, and, as the locals can tell, so is her dialect. Next come stories of the sealskin kayaks, the perilous trip just to get from one island to another. The Elders talk about visits by the 'Diomeders' with their strange accents, the people from the twin islands of Big and Little Diomedes, one Russian, the other American. Because the International Date Line is drawn through the mile-and-a-half passage between them, they are sometimes called Tomorrow and Yesterday. Nora's Tlingit phrase is brought up: the Iñupiat Elders' stories "didn't just start yesterday." With more efforts at language revitalization, they won't end tomorrow, either.

The discussion centers on King Island dialect, the way identity and language are so connected, the slight changes from place to place, the 'taste' of the different accents, as Lorena says. How they miss the sweet dialect of Barrow— "people don't travel like they used to." Sealskin kayaks are less common today, as are people speaking native languages. They talk about how powerful Iñupiatun words are more condensed—Joan's poem is 37 words in English, 19 in Iñupiaq. The Elders are speaking like college professors: Does 'daughter' rhyme with 'asunder'?, they ask. They discuss the Iñupiatun word 'niaquŋ,' which Joan translates as 'head.' The Elders say in their dialect it can mean 'headache' and now the poem takes on even more meanings. The non-speakers in the class are hypnotized.

Joan's English and Iñupiatun versions are nowhere identified as translations. You read an English poem, turn the page, and there is an Iñupiatun poem that seems to have the same structure and line breaks. You must check back and forth to ascertain they are the same poem. "Yes," Lorena says, "It is a translation." Except, Walter adds, "I see how 'Innate' is the English title for 'Ilu.' But we think different in our Iñupiaq." I asked what he would say for 'Ilu.' "Guts," he says, "We'd just say guts."

And with that, the cold streamed in and the years peeled back and we were all in our sealskin boats struggling against the wind to make it home.

An Alaskan Language Odyssey

The poets' job is never complete until the poem is written. And a poem is not written until someone reads or hears it—so it is up to you, dear reader, to complete this poem. This idea comes from the oral tradition, and I wrote the following poem to chronicle my trip through Alaska's languages trying to maintain a sense of orality in written form. It is a praise poem for one thing, a tradition I learned from the Gambian griot, Papa Susso. Part of that tradition is to *name* important people, and in this poem I do—mentioning people who are engaged in language revitalization efforts throughout Alaska. The poet can bring attention to this work, *but it is these people who do the real work, keeping languages alive.*

Sing to me of Alaska, O Muse! Sing of treasured languages,
Heard only by the Ancients! Sing of languages rising,
Ever to be heard!

Iñupiaq, Siberian Yup'ik, Central Alaskan Yup'ik,
Alutiiq, Unangax, Dena'ina, Deg Xinag, Holikachuk,
Koyukon, Upper Kuskokwim, Gwich'in, Tanana,
Upper Tanana, Tanacross, Hän, Ahtna, Eyak,
Tlingit, Haida, and Tsimshian!

Hear Tlingit! Here Juneau!
Nora Marks Dauenhauer! X̲'unei Lance Twitchell!
Speaking/recording poems and stories that never end.
Nora in her 90s speaking Tlingit—essence poetry!
Lance, in his 30s with 3 children under the age of 6,
Studies for Linguistics PhD in Hawai'i—
His kids will learn Tlingit in a school he will create
Like the Pūnana Leo that Larry Kimura, Kauanoe Kamana,
And Pila Wilson and others started in Hilo!

Hear Juneau story of linguist Alice Taff
Teaching language as identity is health.
If you don't know who you are
You wander a lost landscape,
Try to find yourself in alcohol and addiction.
Speaking your Mother Tongue, you know who you are.

Sing, Juneau! Woosh Kinaadeiyi poetry slam!
Reading with Nora at Christy NaMee Ericksen's Kindred Post
Juneau, glacier clutching mountains, Tlingit is rising!

Hear Iñupiaq! Here in Kotzebue!
Obama is my advance man, his visit just two weeks ago.
Tim Aqukkasuk Argestsinger, NANA language activist says,
"What use is your language being 'official' if it's dying?"
Here where tundra meets sea, a hundred miles from Russia,
A poetry workshop at the Northwest Arctic Heritage Center,
With three Elders and the poems of Joan Naviyuk Kane.

Barrow, northernmost point of US!
Snowstorms sweep in September!

I arrive on first day of whaling season. Auspicious!
Three bowheads are brought in, maximum daily catch,
Will feed three extended families through the entire winter.
On the beach, the animals are treated with respect, Iñupiaq spoken,
Passed from one generation to the next, as life itself
Is carried on. Or you can pay $20 for a 5lb bag of potatoes.
Language Matters is screened at the town's living room,
Tuzzy Public Library, David Ongley, Culture Warrior, Director.

Here, Fairbanks! The story: Allan Hayton,
Speaking to me in Gwich'in because he must speak
Aloud to keep the sounds alive in his ears.
Let's go to Immersion Class, he says one day.
So we visit a woman and her two children.
Allen sets a timer for an hour.
For an hour the children hear Gwich'in only
Smiling in the language of who they are
Ready for a chapter in Leanne Hinton's *Bringing
Our Languages Home* (Hinton, 2013).

FIGURE 13.2 Allan Hayton Speaking Gwich'in at a Language Immersion Class in Anchorage.

Fairbanks! Moose stew and caribou meat!
Singing church hymns in Gwich'in
Yeendoo ji' dhandaii danh
Zhik gwįįzhrįį nihtat ts'at tiidadaa.
(In the sweet by and by
We shall meet on that beautiful shore.)

Fairbanks! The university linguists are the people's linguists!
Hear the story of Larry Kaplan, Gary Holton, Siri Tuttle, all
Who see the continuation of Alaskan languages
Not as part of their job, but as the job itself!

Hear the Poetry Slam, multi-culti, futuristic! Hail Effie Kokrine Charter School!
And here the story of poetry workshop at Fairbanks Youth Facility,
Poems blaze freedom for these young men, poems as salvation,
Hip hop bravado next to a poem of silence
And waiting while on a bear hunt. Where is my language? ask the young poets.
The language is silent and waiting. Poetry holds a place.

And here in the wilds,
Hear the story of tiny prop plane dropping me off in Arctic Village,
Where I sleep on Gwich'in Immersion Classroom floor,
The lights on a motion sensor
A blast of light every time I roll over
Waking me in a room of ghosts.

Hear the tale of the new Caribou Fence, complete with website!
http://www.vgfn.ca/heritage/ and video! https://vimeo.com/121193920
The project brings work to this village of 400
Brings history alive recreating ancient hunting method:
Funnel of felled trees direct caribou to hunters waiting with spears.
Gwich'in words for caribou, for caribou fence, for strings-
Woven-in-air-to-catch-caribou-antlers
Bro, in his marijuana watch cap, rifle slung across his back,
Shows up near sunset—he'll take me to caribou fence for gas money.
I climb behind him on his muddy four-wheeler.
I've been told the fence is just a short way out of town,
But we make our way into the wilderness, pine trees dotting
Frozen landscape, crunching 'cross ice creeks, half-frozen lakes,
Snow drifting silence and solitude, true Alaska and still traveling
45 minutes later

I worry about getting back in time to show the movie, sun lowering,
Cold draping my body. We reach a hill where under snow the trail
Is solid ice. The 4-wheeler slides, I get off, we must walk. No,
I say, we must return, the Caribou Fence will be a mirage of history.
I freeze on the long return, when Bro, nearing the village,
Rifle bumping against my chest, turns and shouts,
"Do you want to have your photo taken?" I laugh. He seems the last guy,
This the last place, to suggest a photo opportunity. "Sure."
And –what?! There it is, just off the trail, just out of town—the Caribou Fence!
The one Allan told me about, a living recreation of the past.
"But this is it!" I shout, "What I wanted to see! the Caribou Fence itself!"
"Oh," Bro shrugs, "thought you meant the Old Caribou Fence."

Hear the story of the $25 door prize. 15 people have a chance at the prize,
Arctic Village premier of Language Matters. People ask questions. I press
Spacebar, stop film to discuss Last Speaker of Amardak in Australia, say.
We all have popcorn. Sarah James, Gwich'in spokesperson, so eloquent
On home turf. Again fitfully I sleep in Gwich'in classroom
Harsh motion detector Morse code light, SOS SOS.

Hear Fort Yukon radio station story
DJ Vera Englishoe loves to speak her Gwich'in
But only does so because I ask her to.

Now, Homer, the town! I become poet here! Give readings, show new poem-film,
Khonsay: Poem of Many Tongues, 50 languages in 15 minutes,
Hail! Bunnell Street Gallery! I read poems as whales breach out window.
Visit Nikolaevsk, Old Russian Village, another language in Alaska's crown!

Here Eyak! Tales of Anna Nelson Harry
Lovingly recorded/translated by linguist Michael Krauss (1982),
Now all that's left. Last Speaker died 2008, but no one told the Legislature,
So Eyak is still an official Alaskan language, even though no one speaks it.
Not true! A French teenager is learning—hears Eyak in his dreams,
Like Jesse little doe Baird (2010), reviving Wampanoag in Cape Cod,
A language unspoken spoken for a hundred years

Now Kodiak Island, site of Alutiiq Museum!
Sugpiag, an Alutiiq nation, speaking that tongue!
Today mixed in with Tagalog-speaking Filipino population, some
Ilocano as well, some Thai. The fishing industry and brand-new brewery!

Poetry and language feted in the Library! Here's to April Councellar
And Michael Bach at the Museum! To Katie Baxter at the Library!
The grand mix of Kodiak!

And here's the story of City of Anchorage, Alaskan Federation
Of Natives Convention, thousands of Alaskans celebrating native
Heritage and languages. The power of these peoples inherent, inside the dances
Smiles of greetings cross cultures of the state.
Mutual support for struggle of identity, culture, language.

In 2003 Alaska voted to have an Official Language: English.
It took eleven years for legislature to add twenty more, the indigenous languages
That have been here "forever" ("Ch'a tlákwdáx si. áat, tlél ch'as yá táakw").
Bill passed, April 2014, but a cynical government waited for AFN Convention
To sign it, so Governor gets publicity bump.
And of course, no money to support language continuity.
So it is done—without money or support of any government.
And it was here—not uncommon at AFN—someone jumped
Off roof of Convention Center into a future without language.

In Anchorage, walk Tidal Trail with Joan Naviyuk Kane,
Hearing her story, years working for an actual trip to Ugiuvak (King Island),
With helicopters and boats and a crew of shared-vision women:
In dreams begin responsibilities.

Here, Alaska, country of languages!
Language Revolution Future where the horrors of the past
Are made right with simple respect for Mother Tongues'
Knowledge, Identity, Wisdom. Lives (and money) saved
By reviving languages! Identity pays that bottom line!
Here, Alaska waits, poised to be Center of Global Language Revolution!
It is the job of the poet to help keep languages alive.

Conclusion

I found in Alaska a place poised for transformation in support of indigenous language speakers' rights and educational reform. Alaska is uniquely positioned to heal the tragic wounds of the state's colonialist history by restoring the importance of indigenous languages both to broader society and the lives of individual speakers. In 1998, Alaskans voted to pass an 'English Only' ballot initiative. A stunning reversal occurred in 2014, when, a year before my visit, Alaska's 20 indigenous languages were given official state recognition with the passage of House Bill 216—making it the second US state to do so. Today, linguists like Alice Taff et al. (forthcoming) are shedding light on positive health implications for indigenous speakers who use mother tongues. Language warriors like Professor Lance (X'unei) Twitchell have created language immersion schools modeled after those created by Pila Wilson and Kauanoe Kanoa in Hawai'i 25 years ago. Indigenous poets like Joan Naviyuk Kane are enriching culture by embracing the use of mother tongues in their work. Kane's Iñupiaq poetry lives in her work with no introduction, contextualization, or footnote. Still there is much work to be done. As Tim Argetsinger, Language Rights Director of the North Arctic Native Association (NANA) said, "What good is an official language if it is dying?"

Questions for Discussion

1. What language revitalization methods are discussed in the essay, and which do you think are most effective?
2. What is special about Alaska that makes it central to the continuity and disappearance of languages?

Author Profiles

The author of 16 poetry collections, Bob Holman has taught at Columbia University, New York University, Bard University and The New School. He has played a central role in the spoken word and poetry slam movements. A co-founder of the Endangered Language Alliance, Holman's study of hip-hop and West African oral traditions led to his current work with endangered languages. His most recent films are *Language Matters with Bob Holman*, which won the Berkeley Film Festival's Documentary of the Year award, and *Khonsay: Poem of Many Tongues*, which won the Audience Choice Award at the Sadho Poetry Film Festival in New Delhi.

Sam O'Hana is a performance and research led practitioner in transatlantic contemporary poetics, with work appearing in *Seventh Wave, The Best American Poetry Blog* and *Columbia: A Journal of Literature and Art*. A US-UK Fulbright Scholar to The New School, New York, he was the director of *The Bureau of Imaginative Proposals: A Poetics and Politics Conference* and is managing editor of *Poet's Country* journal. He currently assists Bob Holman at the Bowery Poetry Club in New York.

Acknowledgments

Special thanks are due to these individuals: Timothy Aqukkasuk Argetsinger, Stephen Bolen, Nora Marks Dauenhauer, Allan Ditònh Hayton, Joan Naviyuk Kane, Daniel Kaufman, Ross Perlin, Alice Taff, and X̱'unei Lance Twitchell.

Notes

1 *Language Matters with Bob Holman*, a David Grubin Film, aired on PBS in January, 2015. For more, see: www.languagemattersfilm.com/. Support for bringing the film to Alaska and Hawai'i, thanks to the Ford Foundation. Support for travel to Arctic Village and Ft. Yukon, thanks to the Doyon Foundation.

2 Like all the other arts, poetry has organizations that present readings and other events, workshops, publications, etc. I have worked at the St. Marks Poetry Project, the Nuyorican Poetry Café, and Bowery Arts and Science, the nonprofit that programs the Bowery Poetry Club, which I founded in 2002.

References

Abley, M. (2003). *Spoken here: Travels among threatened languages.* Boston: Houghton Mifflin.

Baird, J. L. D., Makepeace, A., Weston, J., Lampson, M., McCarthy, S., Goodman, J. & Makepeace Productions and Bullfrog Films (2010). *Âs Nutayuneân: We still live here.* Oley, PA: Bullfrog Films.

Bringhurst, R. (2008). *Everywhere being is dancing: Twenty pieces of thinking.* Berkeley: Counterpoint: Distributed by Publishers Group West.

Bringhurst, R. (2004). *The solid form of language: An essay on writing and meaning.* Kentville, N.S: Gaspereau Press.

Crystal, D. (2000) *Language death.* Cambridge: Cambridge University Press.

Dalby, A. (2003) *Language in danger: The loss of linguistic diversity and the threat to our future.* New York: Columbia University Press.

Evans, N. (2010). *Dying words: Endangered languages and what they have to tell us.* Oxford: Wiley-Blackwell.

Hinton, L. (2013). *Bringing our languages home: Language revitalization for families.* Berkeley: Heyday.

Kane, J. N. (2013). *Hyperboreal.* Pittsburgh, PA: University of Pittsburgh Press.

Krauss, M. (1982). *In honor of Eyak: The art of Anna Nelson Harry.* Alaska Native Language Center.

Ong, W. (2000). *Orality & Literacy: The technologizing of the word.* New York, London: Routledge.

Prescott, V. F. (2012). *The hide of my tongue: Ax L'óot' Doogú.* Austin, Texas, Plain View Press

Taff, A., Hall, M.Y., Martin, N. K., Hall, J., Chee, M. & Johnston, A. (forthcoming). Language and wellness. In E. Kenneth Rehge & L. Campbell (eds.), *Oxford handbook of endangered languages.* New York: Oxford University Press.

Yamamoto, A. (2007). Endangered languages in USA and Canada. In M. Brenzinger (ed.), *Language diversity endangered* (pp. 87–122). Berlin & New York: Mouton de Gruyter.

14

IN SEARCH OF LINGUISTIC LEGITIMACY

Western Armenian and the New Speaker

Jennifer Manoukian

Introduction

Prepositions have a no-fail knack for rocking my confidence in Western Armenian. I see them as a telltale sign of my newness to the language, my hesitation with its grammar and my inclination to overlay English onto a language flailing in its grips. When, in moments of linguistic desperation, I resign myself to a literal translation from English—*on* a break, rather than *in* a break; *in* ten minutes, rather than *from* ten minutes; *to* the library rather than just *library*—not only do I mentally wince at what I hear as a mistake, but I also sense my complicity in trampling on a minority language as it takes its last stand against a globalized language of power. While these literal translations may seem contrived to my ear, this linguistic fusion may, in fact, mark the beginning of a new phase in the history of the language and its speakers.

A century ago, Western Armenian was spoken by Armenians in the Ottoman Empire; today, it is the waning language of their descendants living in diaspora on six continents around the world. A century ago, Western Armenian was a language of art and science, of commerce and news, of love and friendship; today, its domains are shrinking as its perception as a relic of the past—incompatible with contemporary life—becomes more entrenched among its native speakers. A century ago, Western Armenian transcended class and generation; today, it vies for the attention of young, upwardly mobile diasporans with few practical reasons to use it.

I belong to a growing subset of these young diasporans: *new speakers*. New speakers, emerging subjects of sociolinguistic research[1], are students of minority languages who swim against the current of language shift by learning minority—often endangered—languages. In the case of Western Armenian, where the language is still inherited to varying degrees, tension among the different language varieties of new speakers and native speakers raises questions about who holds the linguistic authority to dictate how the language is spoken. In this essay, I draw upon my experiences as a new speaker—and literary translator—of Western Armenian to reflect on the concept of linguistic legitimacy and its role in imagining a future for Western Armenian in symbiosis with the dominant languages of the Armenian diaspora.

Estrangement from Western Armenian

Every few months, an email appears in my inbox and reminds me of the imperfect transmission of Western Armenian over the past century. The emails come from Armenian Americans of a certain age who, while cleaning out their basements and attics, find old letters and journals written in a language they may have learned to prattle in, but never learned to read. The enigma of fading, indecipherable script often leads them to think they have found a trove of family secrets, investing importance in words that turn out to be nothing more than a 16-year-old's class notes or accounts of a great-uncle's bouts of fatigue.

Deciphering fading script is my pastime. I am a literary translator of Western Armenian, a decoder of a language, history and culture on the brink of fossilization. Far from in demand, literary translators of minority languages are few and far between, including those from Western Armenian—a language with a diverse literary tradition unknown to many of its speakers. No one—Armenian or otherwise—anxiously awaits the memoirs, novels and short stories I translate in the way readers might await the English translation of a best-selling Scandinavian crime thriller. But this reality is not a lament. In fact, it was this reality that attracted me to translation from Western Armenian in the first place; it was the allure of discovering the hidden, the forgotten, the neglected that enticed me as an undergraduate; and it was the endless churn of possibility at the thought of a literary tradition virtually untouched by translation that has sustained my interest ever since.

Yet each time I sit across from grandmotherly women and read my translations of their relatives' old writings, I am hyperaware of our ostensible role reversal: a 27-year-old with a slight New Jersey accent telling septuagenarians—the presumed guardians of ancestral language—about their own pasts, in English. This dynamic, though, is far from startling when we consider the historical course of Western Armenian and its speakers in the United States, defined by an enthusiastic adoption of English by the children of immigrants in the mid-twentieth century and the retreat of language as a cornerstone of Armenian identity in the decades that followed (Bakalian, 1992).

The great variation in exposure to and education in Western Armenian has given rise both to different permutations of speaking, reading, writing and comprehension skills in the children of these immigrants and their descendants as well as to the possibility for the emergence of new speakers—many of whom, like me, come from families who have not spoken Western Armenian at home for two or three generations, if at all.[2]

This linguistic estrangement in the diaspora led the United Nations Educational, Scientific and Cultural Organization (UNESCO) to classify the language in 2010 as 'definitely endangered,' the third degree on a six-degree scale between 'safe' and 'extinct'. A language is considered 'definitely endangered' when children no longer learn it as a mother tongue at home (Moseley, 2010). In other words, if a six-year-old is not using the language to tattle to her mother or console a friend in tears, linguists do not pin much hope on its maintenance, growth or vitality.

The endangerment of Western Armenian hides in plain sight. Since it is still possible to visit schools that teach Western Armenian from Beirut to Los Angeles, have newspapers in the language delivered each week and overhear conversations in cities around the world, the predicament of the language does not seem nearly as dire as that of languages without a written tradition or with speakers that number in the hundreds, rather than in the hundreds of thousands.[3] Nevertheless, the language attitudes of many of its younger speakers—who need technical, philosophical and mathematical concepts explained in languages other than Western Armenian, who text their friends in languages other than Western Armenian and who respond to their parents in languages other than Western Armenian—point to the dwindling number of speakers who will be able to teach in these schools, edit these newspapers and have conversations to be overheard fifty years from now (Jebejian, 2011).[4]

The Western Armenian predicament is the predicament of a language of diaspora, confined to homes, community gatherings and inner worlds. Before Western Armenian speakers formed a diaspora, they were concentrated in the Ottoman Empire. During the nineteenth century, the Armenians of the Ottoman Empire underwent a cultural renaissance spurred by the standardization of the dialect of Constantinople, their intellectual capital (Chahinian & Bakalian, 2016). This renaissance was marked by the founding of a Western Armenian periodical press and the flourishing of a literary culture that took the language as an object to mold, refine and broaden.[5] In 1915, the Armenian genocide made a non-territorial language out of Western Armenian, sending its speakers into diaspora and sealing its fate as a minority language to be in perpetual competition with the dominant languages of its speakers' new countries.

In the minimally assimilationist countries of the Middle East, post-genocide Armenian communities—particularly in Syria and Lebanon—continued to use Western Armenian as the language of school, home and everyday life. As turmoil intensified over the course of the twentieth century, waves of Armenians from the region were drawn to Europe and the Americas, taking Western Armenian with them and re-infusing it into communities that had strayed from the language.

I learned Western Armenian from one of these linguistic re-infusers. My teacher, Asbed Vassilian, was raised in Aleppo in Western Armenian–medium schools, on Western Armenian–speaking sports teams and at Western Armenian–speaking scout camps. In the 1970s, after moving to Beirut, he fled the Lebanese Civil War for the United States, eventually settling in New Jersey, where he has taught Western Armenian at Rutgers University for more than a quarter century. For four years, his was the only voice I knew in the language. I adopted his turns of phrase, his cadences and his penchant for slipping Turkish into conversation with a sly smile. My time with him was an apprenticeship not only in the standard Western Armenian of the classroom, but also in an uncodified spoken language deemed unworthy of formal transmission. Between the classroom and the student center where we would translate together, I would hear him shed the normative grammar and engineered vocabulary he had just taught a classroom full of students and let the rhythms of colloquial language regain lost ground. In his winding stories that scaled linguistic registers high and low, I would hear the way his language—unfettered by purist ideals—was a repository for the linguistic influences that had shaped him: Turkish from his grandmother, Arabic from his adolescence spent reading the poetry of Al-Mutanabbi, French from his years in Beirut and English from his academic career as a chemist. By the time I graduated, I found myself a new speaker in training—first out of a concern for the disappearance of my teacher's variety of the language; then out of a desire to hear a Western Armenian that was colored by my own linguistic repertoire and that of other young speakers in the diaspora today.

Emergence of the New Speaker

The distinct experiences of new speakers—a classification that has taken root in the work of linguists only within the last decade—have long been folded into larger, less precise categories: second-language learners, L2 speakers, non-native speakers, heritage speakers, etc. (O'Rourke & Pujolar, 2013). The generality of these categories has not managed to capture three nuances that distinguish new speakers from apathetic high schoolers slumped in Spanish classes across the United States or that distinguish my learning Western Armenian from my learning French, Mandarin or any other non-endangered language: attitude, transmission and origin (Hornsby, 2015).[6]

New speakers are, first and foremost, students of *minority* languages and characterized by their conviction in the value of the language's perpetuation and expansion. Voluntarily choosing to learn a minority language as adults, new speakers stand in protest to the riptide of linguistic globalization, indulging a language's emotional tug over its immediate practicality. I will likely never call on Western Armenian to argue with a postal worker about a missing package, negotiate a mortgage or ask for directions in a foreign city. I will likely never call on Western Armenian out of necessity or be in a situation where it is the only language my interlocutor and I share. Yet my invisible, seemingly irrational, affinity for the language reigns supreme, blinding me to its impracticality and coaxing me into thinking, writing, reading and fretting about the future of a language that few even know exist. This blend of *concern* for a fading language, *hopefulness* for its growth and *effort* to nurture that growth defines the mindset of new speakers. In cases of minority languages that undergo formal revitalization, new speakers often form the backbone of the movement because of their staunch belief in the language's survival along with their formalized training in its mechanics—a combination lacking, to varying degrees, in native-speaking communities (O'Rourke et al., 2015).

New speakers do not learn these mechanics from their mothers' coos or from junior-year backpacking trips, but rather from a teacher in a classroom. This form of learning leads new speakers' strengths—including my own—to lay in academic and literary registers, which can cause native speakers to perceive their way of speaking as formal, artificial or overly manipulated (Costa, 2015). My vocabulary in Western Armenian is tinged by the works of the long-dead writers I translate. Thanks to their fondness for the emotionally descriptive, I can quickly bring to mind three synonyms for 'grief' and give my dictionary a rest when I come across the Armenian word for 'leprous,' but squint in incomprehension when I hear the word for 'shopping cart' or 'screwdriver.' The esoteric, patchy vocabulary set that translation creates—often words rarely heard aloud—draws attention to my new speakerhood among native speakers, prompting unexpected smiles at the mismatch between the haltingness of my conversation and the arcaneness of my vocabulary. But it is natural that in the classroom, text-based learning of new speakers would lead to great variation between their language competencies: while I may be able to read or understand a lecture on a familiar topic—yes to late-nineteenth-century Ottoman Armenian literature, no to late-nineteenth-century Ottoman Armenian economics—in Western Armenian with ease, the ease is quickly replaced with hesitations and pauses when I'm asked to write on the same theme or explain it aloud. This phenomenon—shared by learners of all languages big and small—has an added charge for new and native speakers of minority languages, because it signals the arrival of new norms for language and new strengths of its speakers. For an endangered language, newness in any form can often be seen more as a threat than as a virtue.

This newness is also embodied in the backgrounds of the speakers themselves, who do not necessarily belong to the ethnic group associated with a language. In addition to people like me with ancestral ties to Western Armenian, new speakers can be composed of linguists and language advocates of different backgrounds. This cultural variation in new speakers of ethno-national languages can serve to dismantle linguistic purism and ingrained ideologies that link language to nationalism and perpetuate insular thinking that favors language *preservation* over language *growth*. I grew up in a household that barely remembered it was Armenian at Christmas and Easter. By not sending me to an Armenian Saturday School for language or an Armenian Sunday School for religion and mythology, my Irish American mother and second-generation Armenian American father did not instill in me any of the nationalist trappings of identity that would lead me to see Western Armenian as sacrosanct, a hallowed pillar to be guarded against change. This upbringing now awards me the privilege of being a quasi-outsider, who can look at the language from a safe distance and cheer on its evolution, without a mind clouded by memories of kindergarten teachers insinuating that not perpetuating the language just as it was spoken a century ago was an insult to victims of genocide. By bringing about a reevaluation of the requisites for belonging to a linguistic group, new speakers are positioned to challenge claustrophobic norms and embody new forms of language less paralyzed by conservative discourses on language change (Garmiryan, 2015).

Discussions surrounding new speakers doubtlessly lead to questions about their supposed foil: native speakers. In recent years, the category of the native speaker has been called into question for its imprecision in describing linguistic competencies, especially in cases of minority languages in which the bundle of language competencies within a single native speaker may vary greatly based on schooling and exposure to vocabulary in different linguistic domains (Doerr, 2009). Despite the haziness of the concept, the perception that native speakers are linguistically superior still dominates among both new and native speakers, creating tension, insecurity and feelings of linguistic illegitimacy in new speakers, who often hold different—but equally valuable—strengths in the language. I am preoccupied by this tension at each encounter with a native speaker: I hesitate to correct their spelling mistakes, to brandish an arcane word in conversation and to allow the skeleton of English grammar to show through in my sentences. I have not quite wrested myself from the idea that native speakers are the absolute arbiters of language, despite being conscious of the consequences that this mentality can have on the cultivation of minority languages. The linguistic anxiety I share with many other new speakers can stunt us as we formulate the sense of linguistic legitimacy needed to be partners in the growth of the language (Costa, 2015).

The Legitimate Language of Pierre Bourdieu

The challenge of holding linguistic legitimacy—sensed and privately experienced by many kinds of language learners—was ultimately put into words and theorized by twentieth-century sociologist Pierre Bourdieu. Within his larger commentary on language as an instrument of power—rather than as a simple instrument of expression (Bourdieu, 1977)—Bourdieu develops the notion of *legitimate language*, which can help us understand the power dynamic between native and new speakers before attempting to debunk, dismantle and deviate from it.

Though his writings apply generally to the interplay between languages and their speakers—presumably between native speakers and other native speakers—we can shrink his scale to understand native and new speakers as existing in the same hierarchy of power with a "structure of linguistic production [that depends] on the symbolic power relation between the two speakers" (Bourdieu, 1977: 648).

It is this symbolic power relation that prompts me to perceive native speakers as *models* of language use, to feel "denied of the right to claim linguistic authority in the absence of biological ties to the language" (O'Rourke & Pujolar, 2013: 51), and to lack the sense of linguistic authority to be a pioneer of new language practices.

Bourdieu's idea can be extrapolated to understand the native speaker as the holder of a "monopoly [of] the legitimate use of the legitimate language" (Bourdieu, 1991: 59). As students, new speakers must certainly adopt some of the linguistic practices of "those who are dominant" (Bourdieu, 1991: 53), but the trouble arises when they are barred from staking claim to Bourdieu's concept of *linguistic capital*, or the power derived from dictating language use. Linguistic capital—paramount in fostering a sense of autonomy over language—fuels the evolution needed to keep minority languages relevant to contemporary life.

Forms of linguistic legitimacy shift as more new speakers of endangered languages emerge and spurn the idea that they must "work [to] acquir[e] a set of linguistic competencies to be subject to 'native' evaluation" (Jaffe, 2015: 41). As they work to create new norms, new speakers subvert existing systems of power by challenging the idea that the language variety of the native speaker must be considered the ideal. As this deep-seated idea fades in my mind and in the minds of native speakers, the language varieties of new speakers can lead to alternative understandings of linguistic legitimacy and, in the case of Western Armenian, can have the potential to reflect the multilingualism of the globalized lives of its speakers.

Linguistic Legitimacy in Western Armenian

In Western Armenian, the present is not just a tense; it is a form of ideological exhibitionism. A speaker's choice between the two forms of the present tense can pinpoint his or her spot on the scatter plot of linguistic purity: a conjugated verb *or* a conjugated verb plus the particle կոր (*gor*), a simultaneously maligned and coddled result of Turkish bilingualism among Armenians in the Ottoman Empire (Donabédian, 2001).

Despite odes to its vulgarity by native speakers, this remnant of centuries-long language contact has remained a staple of warm, casual conversation. In *gor* are toothy old men teasing each other as they toss die onto a backgammon board; in *gor* are mothers leaning into cribs to tickle their two-year-olds; in *gor* is the vitality of Western Armenian, the vitality in letting language be pushed and swayed by its surroundings—the mark of linguistic health (Crystal, 2000).

Gor is not a feature of the Western Armenian taught to students. A product of the classroom through and through, I use *gor* sparingly and only with an ironic smirk of dissociation and a sense of masquerading as the native speaker I am not. I hear the particle as a stamp of linguistic legitimacy that derives its power from a linguistic encounter long ago. In *gor* and other examples of language contact with Turkish, which shelter within them the history of the language, are forms of legitimacy that new speakers cannot claim. They are not part of the language variety they learn and—with the exception of Turkish-dominant new speakers—do not characterize their own modern-day experiences with language contact. Linguistic legitimacy will be at the fingertips of new speakers once traces of their linguistic encounters in the diaspora can be heard in their language variety and seen as a natural part of the evolution of language, rather than as a sign of the language's demise.

Following the path of other minority languages, such as Breton (Hornsby, 2015), Corsican (Jaffe, 2015), Occitan (Costa, 2015) and Yiddish (Hornsby, 2015), new forms of linguistic legitimacy in Western Armenian will appear as the practices of its speakers grow more distinct and complex (Jaffe, 2015). This complexity is not, however, neatly confined to new speakers. The diasporic fate of Western Armenian has created generations of native speakers with gaping holes in their linguistic knowledge, rendering the category of native speaker without qualification—native speaker in the language of the kitchen, native speaker in the language of religion, native speaker in the language of mechanical engineering—virtually meaningless in its abstraction.

New and native speakers of the 21st century are, then, equal in their greater proficiency in languages other than Western Armenian. Rare is the monolingual Western Armenian speaker, uninfluenced by the faster tempos of the other languages in his or her repertoire. It is this reality that both corrodes the ideal of the infallible, all-knowing native speaker and dispels the myth that one form of linguistic legitimacy can exist for a language used by speakers with a range of linguistic anchors: the languages of globalization that they use at school, at work and in public life.

Language contact with globalized languages is not without precedent in the history of Western Armenian. The Armenians of the Ottoman Empire were a multilingual population who, like today, did not always have uniform proficiency in Western Armenian across subjects. An Armenian of years past may have been better acquainted with artistic terms in French (Figure 14.1), legal terms in Turkish (Figure 14.2) and medical terms in English (Figure 14.3) by virtue of the fact that his—*hers* would have been more limited—life was not monocultural, that not all his knowledge originated in Western Armenian. Translating that knowledge, however, was used to develop Western Armenian, making multilingualism—today as a century ago—a boon to the language and its growth.

Given the geographic distribution of its speakers, language contact with languages of globalization has the potential to inflect Western Armenian with regional dialects based on the speakers' dominant languages. The inclination of new speakers to translate words, expressions and sentence structure from their stronger languages into Western Armenian may not only force the disintegration of ossified linguistic norms, but also be a window into the possible linguistic practices of many more speakers once Western Armenian dominance is a remnant of a bygone age.

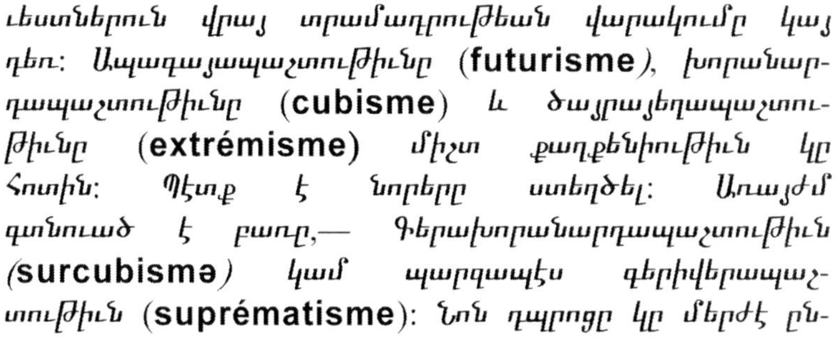
ւեստներուն վրայ տրամադրութեան վարակումը կայ
դեռ: Ապագայապաշտութիւնը (futurisme), խորանար-
դապաշտութիւնը (cubisme) և ծայրայեղապաշտու-
թիւնը (extrémisme) միշտ քաղքենիութիւն կը
հոտին: Պէտք է նորերը ստեղծել: Առայժմ
գտնուած է բառը,— Գերախորանարդապաշտութիւն
(surcubismə) կամ պարզապէս գերիվերապաշ-
տութիւն (suprématisme): Նոն դպրոցը կը մերժէ ըն-

FIGURE 14.1 From an Essay Published in Bucharest on Art in Soviet Russia that Makes use of Calqued Western Armenian Translations of the French Avant-Gardist Terms in Parentheses (Tashian, 1926: 262). Courtesy of Vazken Davidian.

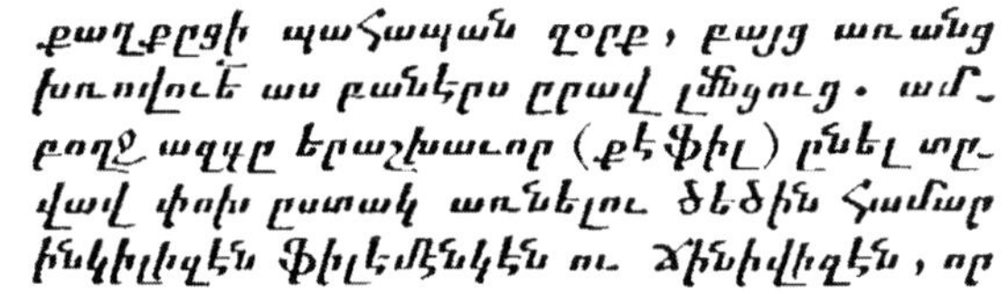
քաղքըցի պահապան զօրք, բայց առանց
խառնուելու աս բանէրս ըրավ լծնցուց. ամ-
բողջ ազգը երաշխաւոր (քէֆիլ) ընել տը-
վավ փոխ ըստակ առնելու ձեռքին համար
ինկիլիզէն Ֆիլէմէնկէն ու Ճինիվիզէն, որ

FIGURE 14.2 From a Book Published in Venice that Gives the Turkish for 'Guarantor' ('Kefil,' written in Armenian Letters) After the Armenian Word (Indjidjian, 1828: 3). Courtesy of Daniel Ohanian.

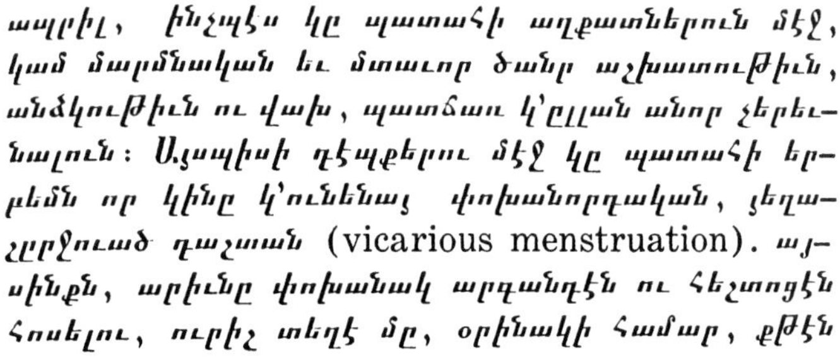
ապրիլ, ինչպէս կը պատահի աղքատներուն մէջ,
կամ մարմնական եւ մտաւոր ծանր աշխատութիւն,
անձկութիւն ու վախ, պատճառ կ'ըլլան անոր չերեւ-
նալուն: Այսպիսի դէպքերու մէջ կը պատահի եր-
բեմն որ կինը կ'ունենայ փոխանորդական, յեղա-
շրջուած դաշտան (vicarious menstruation). այ-
սինքն, արիւնը փոխանակ արգանդէն ու հեշտոցէն
հոսելու, ուրիշ տեղէ մը, օրինակի համար, քթէն

FIGURE 14.3 From a Book on Sexual Health Published in Boston that Invents Medical Terms in Western Armenian, Leaving the English for Reference (Torosian, 1916: 119).

Conclusion

In revitalizing endangered languages, there is a tendency to look to the past for sources of linguistic legitimacy (O'Rouke & Pujolar, 2013), cementing the assumption that the past is authentic and the present is adulterated. New speakers have the power to challenge this convention both by questioning what it means to have a single legitimate variety of a language (Costa, 2015) and by "challeng[ing] the belief in the automatic and complete competence of 'native speakers' in their 'native languages'" (Doerr, 2009: 36).

New speakers of Western Armenian have not yet entered Armenian cultural consciousness, nor have they been acknowledged any more than anecdotally in scholarship. But as native speakers continue to turn away from their ancestral language, seemingly invisible new speakers may find themselves at the helm of Western Armenian, bringing with them stamps of their multilingualism. In this scenario, the calque of my English 'I'm proud *of* you,' the nasalized *an* in a French Armenian's pronunciation of ֆրանսերէն [fr*an*seren] or an Egyptian Armenian's search for masculine and feminine forms of *you* may foretell a linguistically splintered future for Western Armenian and shifting forms of linguistic *legitimacies*. The overlaying of globalized languages onto Western Armenian can, then, be seen not as one of the language's last tremors of death, but rather as one of its vital signs.

Questions for Discussion

1. What are the defining characteristics of a new speaker?
2. What is linguistic legitimacy? Why is it important for new speakers?

Author Profile

Jennifer Manoukian is a translator of Western Armenian literature. She earned her MA in Middle Eastern, South Asian and African Studies from Columbia University and her BA in French Literature and Middle Eastern Studies from Rutgers University. Her interests lie in Western Armenian literature and issues of identity and cultural production in the Armenian diaspora. Her first book-length translation, *The Gardens of Silihdar* by Zabel Yessayan, was published by the Armenian International Women's Association Press in 2014 and her second, *The Candidate* by Zareh Vorpouni, was published by Syracuse University Press in 2016.

Notes

1 Research on new speakers is an emerging field and has been treated most substantially in a special issue of the *International Journal for the Sociology of Language* 2015 (231/1), entitled "New Speakers of Minority Languages: The Challenging Opportunity," in which new speakers of Basque, Breton, Catalan, Corsican, Galician, Gaelic, Manx and Occitan are studied.

2 It is important to note that many of those who identify as Armenian today are descendants of Turkish-speaking, and to a lesser extent, Kurdish-speaking and Arabic-speaking, families, whose ancestors did not speak standard Western Armenian or any of its dialects. In the Ottoman Empire, religion—not language—was the supreme marker of identity, meaning that, as long as Armenians identified as Christian, there was a place for them in Armenian communities.

3 In 2010, UNESCO estimated that the number of Western Armenian speakers worldwide was 200,000, but the competencies of these speakers were left undefined.

4 At the forefront of the development of Western Armenian in everyday life as well as in arts and technology is the Calouste Gulbenkian Foundation. Along with funding primary and secondary schools across the diaspora, the Foundation funds projects with an eye to preventing the loss of Western Armenian as a living language, such as support for online dictionaries and lexicons as well as language-learning apps and electronic publications that encourage the production of culture in the language (Panossian, 2014).

5 During the same period, a similar standardization process was taking place for Armenians in the Russian Empire, which resulted in an equally extensive Eastern Armenian linguistic tradition. Today, Eastern Armenian is the official language of the Republic of Armenia and is spoken in Iran, Russia and the post-Soviet diaspora (Panossian, 2006).

6 The term *new speaker* attempts to do away with the implicit hierarchy in terms such as *native-speaker and non-native speaker* (O'Rourke & Pujolar, 2013).

References

Bakalian, A. (1992). *Armenian Americans: From being to feeling Armenian*. New Brunswick: Transaction Publishers.

Bourdieu, P. (1977). The economics of linguistic exchanges. *Social Science Information, 16* (6), 645–668.

Bourdieu, P. (1991). *Language and symbolic power* [translated by G. Raymond & M. Adamson]. J. Thompson (ed.). Cambridge: Polity Press.

Chahinian, T. & Bakalian, A. (2016). Language in Armenian American communities: Western Armenian and efforts for preservation. *International Journal of the Sociology of Language, 237* (1), 37–57.

Costa, J. (2015). New speakers, new language: On being a legitimate speaker of a minority language in Provence. *International Journal of the Sociology of Language, 231* (1), 127–145.

Crystal, D. (2000). *Language death*. Cambridge: Cambridge University Press.

Doerr, N. (2009). Investigating native speaker effects: Toward a new model of analyzing native speaker ideologies. In N. Doerr (ed.), *The native speaker concept* (pp. 15–43). Berlin & New York: Mouton de Gruyter.

Donabédian, A. (2001). Tabou linguistique en arménien occidental : 'gor' progressif est-il 'turc'? In A. Donabédian (ed.), *Langues de diaspora, langues en contact, faits de langue* (pp. 201–210). Paris: Ophrys.

Garmiryan, A. (2015). *Tabula rasa: Rethinking the fundamentals. Innovation in education: Challenges in teaching Western Armenian in the 21st century* [Conference]. Paris, France. 21 Sept. 2015.

Hornsby, M. (2015). The "new" and "traditional" speaker dichotomy: Bridging the gap. *International Journal for the Sociology of Language, 231* (1), 107–125.

Indjidjian, G. (1828). *Դարապատում, որ է աշխարհամար կամ ընդհանուր պատմութիւն. Քաղաքական, եկեղեցական, ուսումնական, եւ արուեստական, դարուց 'ի դարս բաժանեալ*, հատ. 6, Դար ութուտասներորդ, 1789–1795. Վէնէտիկ: Վանս Սրբոյն Ղազարու.

Jaffe, A. (2015). Defining the new speaker: Theoretical perspectives and learner trajectories. *International Journal for the Sociology of Language, 231* (1), 21–44.

Jebejian, A. (2011). Patterns of language use among Armenians in Beirut in the last 95 years. *Haigazian Armenological Review, 31* (1), 453–469.

Moseley, C. (ed.) (2010). Atlas of the world's languages in danger. Paris, UNESCO Publishing. Retrieved 5 June, 2016 from: www.unesco.org/culture/en/endangeredlanguages/atlas

O'Rourke, B. & Pujolar, J. (2013). From native speakers to 'new speakers': Problematizing nativeness in language revitalization context. *Histoire Épistémologie Langage*, *35* (2), 47–67.

O'Rourke B., Pujolar, J. & Ramallo, F. (2015). New speakers of minority languages: The challenging opportunity. *International Journal for the Sociology of Language*, *231* (1), 1–20.

Panossian, R. (2006). *The Armenians: From kings and priests to merchants and commissars*. New York: Columbia University Press.

Panossian, R. (2014) *Programming plan: Armenian communities department* 2014–2018. Lisbon, Portugal: Calouste Gulbenkian Foundation.

Tashian, P. (1926). Արուեստը խորհրդային Ռուսիոյ մէջ. *Նաւասարդ*, *9* (1), 261–263.

Torosian, B. (1916). *Սեռային առողջապահութիւն*. Բոստոն: Հայրենիք Տպագրութիւն.

PART V
Epilogue

ODE TO MY MOTHER TONGUE

Marwa Adina[1]

This is an open letter to my mother tongue
Thank you for nurturing me when I was young
Gave me tongue, I'm a part of you
You kept feeding me Arabic
I produced your sounds through my vocal cords
But after moving to the West, seeking a better life from the rest
I'm still stressed due to Islamophobic protests
Praying under pressure to rid of my Arabian attributes
Because this land wants me to be free
So here I am
Translating phrases
From Arabic into English
Questioning my identity
Who am I
I'm an immigrant in either country
Even if I was born in Ivory Coast
Moroccan by nationality
I'm allowed to be American through mentality
Dear mother tongue
You are east of Eden
The Middle East is demon
You tell me nothing about
Holy, Mother[2]
Your smothered stutter too terrorized to speak for
English in America is

Becoming my tongue
They say I'm
Quenched for linguistic homicide
Following words of silencers
Censuring words of ancestors
This is farewell to
Occupying my language
I know what this nation means
I have to give you up for this American dream
Stop
Your
Worry
I speak English now

Author Profile

Marwa Adina is a first-generation Moroccan-American undergraduate college student at Rutgers University. Born into a Moroccan family in the Ivory Coast in 1997, she was only three years old when her family left the Ivory Coast to the United States of America, due to the Ivorian coup d'etat that took place in 1999. Soon after, Marwa and her family found refuge in the US, where she has encountered many challenges in maintaining her religious, socio-cultural and linguistic identity. Along with her academic career, Marwa is in pursuit to inspire lives and promote peace, love and unity through her poetry. In 2016, she was chosen by HerCampus as their 22 under-22 most inspiring women in college. From the Ivory Coast to the coast of New Jersey, this is her story.

Notes

1 This poem should be read twice: once, from top to bottom, and the other time, from bottom to top. The message of the poem will be clear, only if the poem is read in this way.
2 The term 'Mother' stands, here, for my mother tongue, i.e., Arabic. To the rest of the world, this language may sound 'evil' with nothing 'holy' or good in it. Yet, to me, as I tried to show in my poem (if it is read backward), there is nothing evil in this language. Nor is the Middle East a 'demon' of the East. These are all false representations of other peoples, languages and cultures.

SOME DIMENSIONS OF ENGLISH AND GLOBALIZATION

An Africanist Afterword

Alamin Mazrui

Language and Globalization: An Autoethnographic Approach provides an extremely rich tapestry of the linguistic manifestation of globalization on a comparative scale. The autoethnographic approach has been particularly effective in highlighting the dynamics and counter-dynamics of the myriads of linguistic journeys across borders and boundaries in a way that is very engaging if disconcerting at times. The collection leaves no room for doubt that ultimately the sociolinguistics of globalization is a nuanced dialectical process, one that brings continuities and ruptures into a constant cycle of negotiations.

The term 'Global English' that frames the essays in one section of the collection captures perfectly part of the essence of this dialectic—the tension between homogenization and diversification, on the one hand, and between hegemony and resistance, on the other, within the context of the classroom. Central to this tension has been the continuing debate about whether we must continue to regard English, advertently or inadvertently, as a tool of a grand imperial project, or as a malleable instrument that has now acquired multiple ownerships and has been sufficiently transmuted in diverse spaces to carry the weight and stamp of different cultures and, at times, even serve counter-hegemonic functions.

But what does it mean to 'own' a language—to claim that the language is now African or Asian, for example? One dynamic, of course, is demographic—the emergence of significantly large populations in individual nation-states that acquire English as a 'first' language in three senses of the term. English may be considered a first language in a functional sense. There is a growing number of Africans, for example, whose lives are virtually dominated by the English language in meeting their communicative needs. Many members of the African elite, critically placed in the destinies of their nations, have come to rely on English in public interaction as well as in their private lives.

English may also be a first language in a chronological sense. There is an increasing number of people in urban spaces who are growing up bilingual in English and their own respective ethnic language. But because the children are exposed to the ethnic language primarily in the home, while they get English at home, in school and among friends, English begins to gain an upper hand. Though bilingual, these children of the elite may end up regarding English as more of their first language than are their ethnic languages.

The third sense of English as a first language relates to its role as a lingua franca, as a medium of interethnic communication, again, especially among the members of the elite. Interethnic marriages among educated Africans in particular are on the increase. If they do not have a common African medium of communication, spouses in such marriages rely almost exclusively on English—or French in Francophone Africa and Portuguese in Lusophone Africa—as the language of the home. Children of such marriages, therefore, are likely to grow up speaking English as their first language.

Even if we accept this demographic sense of 'ownership,' however, we must address the reality of global imbalances of power and the different levels of inequality that are necessarily produced by them. While multiple Englishes have indeed emerged across the global landscape, the standards of propriety in the majority of cases, of what is considered 'correct' or 'standard' English, continue to be pegged to nations like Britain and the USA, which continue to exercise a controlling influence on the medium and the flows of technology, communication, information and knowledge mediated through it. Until such a time when the English linguistic norm itself becomes diversified, or reflects the effects of multiple centers of influence from around the world, ownership of the English language by Africans, Asians, and so forth will continue to be a contested claim.

No doubt, there are several examples the world over that support the conclusions of some of the essays in this volume that there is widespread acceptance of the increasing consolidation of English in various countries. Nonetheless, we should not forget that there are also instances in which the language is meeting resistance. Sometimes the resistance to English has been due to the influence of Islamist ideology, as in the case of Arabic in the Sudan. At other times, it has been inspired by nationalist sentiments—as in the case of Swahili in Tanzania or the new emphasis on Hindi in India since Narendra Modi became prime minister (Subramanian, 2014). Modi is an example of a politician who rose from the ranks of the poor—having worked as a *chaiwallah* in much of his childhood years, helping his father selling tea at a railway station—to the elite political status he now enjoys. Soon after he took over the reins of power, Modi is reported to have vowed:

> to restore a sense of pride to India's dejected millions, many of them battling unemployment and grinding poverty. One quick boost would be

> giving prominence to Hindi, the language of the masses [. . .]. So a day after the new government took office, India's home ministry ordered officials to switch to Hindi on social media. Modi also ordered officials to use Hindi in all official correspondence and to take notes in Hindi. Modi himself declared he would only speak Hindi with foreign leaders. (George, 2014)

Modi thus demonstrates a peculiar mix—a staunch advocate of capitalist economics and a committed Hindu nationalist—a combination of economic motives and a political agenda that is posing a new challenge to the exclusive primacy of English in India in some social domains.

Of course, English is in part one of the legacies of colonialism. And under the colonial dispensation, in as much as the colonizer creates the colonized (as Frantz Fanon had once suggested), the colonial subjects too come up with their own constructions of the colonizer—sometimes resulting in those disturbing Manichean images mentioned in Elizabeth Erling's contribution (Chapter 7, this volume). We see here the complexities of the process of constructing self and others in postcolonial discourses. With growing immigrant communities in the West, this observation has led Hornscheidt to encourage the adoption of a transdisciplinary critical postcolonial linguistics to understand that "not only are the colonized constructed as others in hegemonic colonial discourses" during and after colonialism, "but the colonizers are constructed in those discourses in their 'normalized' and universalized positions" (2011: 268).

The need for a critical and transdisciplinary intervention in the study of language and globalization brings us to the necessity of the shift that has been emerging in some of the recent research, a shift away from a focus on language as such to linguistic resources that are constantly galvanized by practices of heteroglossia, of the blending of different 'voices.' Blommaert urges that we must:

> accept that abandoning a structural notion of language (a linguists' construct, as we know) compels us to replace it by an ethnographic concept such as *voice*, which embodies the experiential and practice dimensions of language and which refers to the way in which people actually deploy their resources in communicative practice. Traditional notions related to multilingualism, such as code-switching, then become moments of voice in which people draw resources from a repertoire that contains materials conventionally associated with 'languages.' (2010: 180–81)

In a sense, heteroglossia, this recurrent mixing and merging of voices, is akin to the concept of 'languaging' that has been invoked by Ruhma Choudhury in Chapter 8. However, heteroglossia is not wholly dependent on individual multilingualism. It can also occur within a single language.

Naturally, the question of ownership of English also raises the problematic of the interplay between language and identity. If there is an increasing, politically significant population of Africans, Asians, Arabs, growing up with English as a first language—sometimes as the only language—could we be witnessing the emergence of new 'tribes' of Afro-Saxons, Asian-Saxons, Arabo-Saxons in different parts of the world? But sometimes the linguistic construction of identity can take place even when the language in question is not a first language functionally or chronologically. Take, for example, the case of Cameroon in West Africa. This is a country that has more than one imperial language, English and French, as official languages. This policy has essentially framed much of the linguistic debate in the Cameroons along the lines of English-speaking and French-speaking regions, relegating the role of local languages to a subsidiary position. In the process several "sociolinguistic problems have emerged between the Anglophones and the Francophones because each of them prioritizes their colonially-inherited identity and language even over the locally-based indigenous language identity" (Anchimbe, 2011: 8).

But, perhaps the most fascinating research emerging globally on the question of language and identity has to do with 'youth languages.' The multilayered and sometimes oppositional currents of the urban space in many parts of the world have given rise to a range of youth languages, from Flaaitaal in Johannesburg to Rinkebysvenska in Sweden, often as a direct product of the interplay between identity and resistance, sometimes spreading "from the ghettos of juvenile delinquency and street gangs into the better quarters of students at secondary schools and universities" (Wolff, 2016: 127). A clear manifestation of the linguistic construction of youth identities under conditions of cultural mobility, these 'new urban vernaculars' demonstrate not simply the large-scale cultural and political processes that shape the lives of the youth, but equally how youth identities emerge through fine-grained details of interactional work and local linguistic practice.

An interesting example involving English are Sheng and Engsh in Kenya. The pattern of urbanization and urban settlement in Kenya varied substantially from other Swahili-speaking areas of eastern Africa. As a European settler colony, Kenya experienced a quasi-apartheid system which, in urban areas like Nairobi, translated into some degree of residential zoning. In the process, the eastern side of Nairobi, or Eastlands, became the primary area where African migrant workers were permitted to settle, while different parts of the west (or Westlands) were populated by Europeans and Asians. With the end of colonialism, members of the African elite gradually moved into the hitherto exclusive European and Asian locations, while the postcolonial stream of African migrant labor continued to settle in Nairobi's Eastlands. In other words, racial zoning in the colonial period now translated into social-class zoning in the postcolonial period. While this residential division has become more complex in time, it is nonetheless true that sharp socioeconomic disparity is one of the most glaring factors of Nairobi's settlement and residential patterns.

The residential partition may have stimulated the emergence of two youth languages in Nairobi, Sheng and Engsh, which later spread to other urban areas of the country. So far there has been little agreement on the classification of Sheng (Mukhwana, 2014), though most observers hold that it is age-marked, most commonly associated with the youth, and that Nairobi's Eastlands is its initial center of formation and diffusion. In addition to its primary demographic constituency, there also seems to be significant agreement that Sheng is essentially a hybrid language operating with a Swahili grammatical base and a lexical supply drawn primarily from English, but also from a number of local languages (Kioko 2015), that is often subjected to phonological creativity that underscores its 'in-group' function. But its population of speakers has broadened immensely over the years, both geographically and demographically within Kenya—showing clear signs of interethnic, interregional youth solidarity (Kaviti, 2015).

Less studied and less widespread than Sheng is another youth code, Engsh, which is said to be prominent among children of the well-to-do in more affluent residential areas of Nairobi. As Abdulaziz and Osinde suggest, "Engsh developed in the richer suburbs in the Westlands of Nairobi and is based more on English structure and vocabulary, but with words from Swahili and other local languages" (1997: 43). In other words, just as the ghettos of the urban poor in Nairobi's Eastlands were the crucial formative stimulants of Sheng, the emergence of relatively exclusive, suburban neighborhoods of the African nouveau riche in Nairobi, where the primary language of the school, the playground, the church, the place of entertainment, and so forth, is English, was an essential social condition in the development of Engsh. The grammatical system of Engsh seems to be entirely based on English, while its lexicon is drawn heavily from Sheng words derived from Swahili or other local languages and Kenyan urban English slang.

What is yet to be determined is whether Sheng and Engsh are developing as primary languages for an increasing number of any sections of Nairobi's population. Sheng shows the greatest promise of continued growth and consolidation, as there is an increasing number of Nairobi residents who regard Sheng as their main language of social interaction and who are growing up speaking Sheng as their 'primary or only language,' even at home (Githiora, 2002: 160).

The examples of Sheng and Engsh bring us to another section of the book, on language death and language birth. Both of these youth languages are instances of new language formations towards possible consolidation. There is also the case of the Nigerian Pidgin (English), a member of a continuum of English-based pidgins in West Africa and beyond, which may be in the process of creolization. One of the most comprehensive descriptions of Nigerian Pidgin is the one provided by Nicholas Faraclas (1996). Importantly, Faraclas argues that while pidgins generally function in limited-contact situations of interethnic interaction, Nigerian Pidgin has a much wider span of usage and cuts across virtually every social class in the urban milieu. In the process, Faraclas argues, the language has become elaborated in structure and is poised to becoming a stable creole as an increasing number of Nigerians acquire it as a mother tongue (1996: 2).

The other side of this coin is, of course, language endangerment and language death. There has been interest on whether the spread of ex-colonial languages and local *linguae francae*, those languages that are considered politico-economically powerful, are endangering the survival of 'weaker' languages. Several researchers—including Mufwene (2003), among others—have come to the conclusion that the languages that pose the greatest danger to minority languages are not the imperial languages, but rather the major *linguae francae* in the different parts of the world. And, of course, there is evidence to support this position.

In Tanzania, for example, the aggressive policy push in favor of Swahili has now endangered the survival of some Tanzanian languages. Legere's study of the languages of small ethnic groups with speakers that number 20,000 or less provides evidence of severe interruption of intergenerational transmission of ethnic languages caused especially by the exclusive reliance on Swahili as a medium of instruction in schools and as the official language of the country. The maintenance of languages of these smaller ethnic groups is no longer guaranteed and, according to Legere, there is reason to believe that some of them will become extinct (Legere, 2006). Legere's thesis is supported to some extent by an earlier study by Batibo on the fate of ethnic languages in Tanzania resulting in part from the Swahili-only policy of the country (1992).

On the other hand, we must bear in mind that the huge imperial prestige enjoyed by English has distorted educational opportunities, diverted resources from indigenous cultures towards giving English continued preeminence, and has sometimes diluted the esteem in which local languages were held. In the process, many native peoples have not only come to accept that their own languages are fundamentally inferior to the languages inherited from European colonizers, they have also become convinced that it is not worth doing anything about it. It is this sense of linguistic fatalism, one of the manifestations of the postcolonial condition, that may also pose a danger to the survival of local languages in the long run.

In the final analysis, taken together, the essays in this volume show that while certain hegemonic forces have persisted in spite of the fact that colonialism came and went and the Cold War emerged and subsided, the struggle continues between the forcers of dependence and the tide of authenticity. And language is one of the grand arenas of that struggle on a global scale.

Questions for Discussion

1. Drawing upon your own experiences, discuss some of the ways in which globalization can foster new forms of identity marked by linguistic difference and linguistic formations.
2. How is the phenomenon of heteroglossia dependent upon such factors as in-group or out-group status of the intended audience, and the formality or informality of the interaction and topic of conversation?

Author Profile

Alamin Mazrui is professor in the Department of African, Middle Eastern and South Asian Languages and Literatures at Rutgers University, New Brunswick. He holds a PhD in linguistics from Stanford University with specialization in the political sociology of language. Over the years he has taught in universities in East Africa, West Africa and the United States. Mazrui has authored and edited several books over the years and written numerous articles in political sociology of language, education, literature and linguistics. In addition to his scholarly books and essays, Mazrui is a published Swahili poet and playwright. Mazrui also has a special interest in the study of human rights and civil liberties and has written policy reports on these subjects.

References

Abdulaziz, M. H. & Osinde, K. (1997). Sheng and Engsh: Development of mixed codes among urban youth in Kenya. *International Journal of the Sociology of Language, 125* (1), 43–63.

Anchimbe, E. A. (2011). Postcolonial linguistic voices: Stitching together identity choices and their representations. In E. A. Anchimbe & S. A. Mforteh (eds.), *Postcolonial linguistic voices: Identity choices and representations* (pp. 3–21). Berlin: Mouton De Gruyter.

Batibo, H. (1992). The fate of ethnic languages in Tanzania. In M. Brenzinger (ed.), *Language death: Factual and theoretical explorations with special reference to East Africa* (pp. 85–98). Berlin: Mouton De Gruyter.

Blommaert, J. (2010). *The sociolinguistics of globalization*. Cambridge: Cambridge University Press.

Faraclas, N. G. (1996). *Nigerian pidgin*. London: Routledge.

George, N. (2014). Indian bureaucrats scramble for Hindi dictionaries. Associated Press, June 19, 2014. Retrieved October 4, 2016 from: http://news.yahoo.com/indian-bureaucrats-scramble-hindi-dictionaries-073115866.html.

Githiora, C. (2002). Sheng: Peer language, Swahili dialect, or emerging Creole? *Journal of African Cultural Studies, 15* (2), 159–81.

Hornscheidt, A. L. (2011). Postcolonial continuities in Danish monolingual dictionaries. In E. A. Anchimbe & S. A. Mforteh (eds.), *Postcolonial linguistic voices: Identity choices and representations* (pp. 265–98). Berlin: Mouton De Gruyter.

Kaviti, L. (2015). From stigma to status: Sheng and Engsh in Kenya's linguistic and literary space. Retrieved October 4, 2016 from: www.researchgate.net/publication/286945582

Kioko, E. M. (2015). Regional varieties and ethnic registers of Sheng. In N. Nassnstein & A. Hollington (eds.), *Youth language practices in Africa and beyond* (pp. 119–48). Berlin: Mouton De Gruyter.

Legere, K. (2006). Language endangerment in Tanzania: Identifying and maintaining endangered languages. *South African Journal of African Languages, 22* (3), 99–112.

Mufwene, S.S. (2003). Language endangerment: What have pride and prestige got to do with it? In B. Joseph (ed.), *When languages collide* (pp. 324–46). Columbus, OH: Ohio State University Press.

Mukhwana, A. (2014). Je, Sheng ni Lahaja ya Kiswahili? Nadharia ya Utambulisho wa Maana. In S. I. Chacha & M. Osore (eds.), *Miaka Hamsini ya Kiswahili Nchini Kenya*. Twaweza Communications, Nairobi.

Subramanian, S. (2014). India after English? *New York Review of Books*, June 9, 2014. Retrieved October 4, 2016 from: www.nybooks.com/blogs/nyrblogas/2014/jun/09/india-newspapers-after english/

Wolff, E. (2016). Language in Africa between the local and the global: How political are 'dialects'? In R. M. Beck & K. Kresse (eds.), *Abdilatif Abdalla: Poet in Politics* (pp. 123–31). Dar es Salaam: Mkuki na Nyota.

INDEX